MILESTONES

Markers on the Journey Toward Becoming a House of Prayer

P. Douglas Small

MILESTONES
Markers on the Journey Toward Becoming a House of Prayer

©Copyright 2018 by P. Douglas Small

Published by Alive Publications
a division of
Alive Ministries: PROJECT PRAY
PO Box 1245
Kannapolis, NC 28082

www.alivepublications.org
www.projectpray.org

Purchase the companion Power Point
and additional resources for your prayer team at:
www.alivepublications.org.

Cover Image: © www.123rf.com/profile_iakov

CONTENTS

Foreword

Dear Pastor,

This book, at first glance, if you are a typical pastor, will be regarded as insane!

You are willing to add a bit of prayer – but this book calls for a radical new prayer paradigm. It assumes that the reformation is still on. Sadly, the church remains less than a house of prayer. Five hundred years after the clarion call for the priesthood of all believers, the church, as a 'kingdom of priests' has not emerged.

After 25 years in the prayer ministry and almost 50 in ministry, I am convinced that we have narrowed the church! That we see it far too often just as a building in which we gather for a weekly praise and preaching exercise – at least that is view of our people.

What I am suggesting in this book will seem over the top – too much. You will say that such change, such intentional prayer structures and plans are unnecessary. You believe, quite sincerely, but erroneously, that prayer will find its own course, and that course will be noble and right, since prayer is so natural. You may believe it to be always naturally pure, needing neither instruction nor direction nor stewarding. In truth, without teaching and training, prayer becomes far too self-interested, worship-less and void of concern for the lost. There are few things that need more cultivation than the prayer lives of both your people and your congregation. We can no longer take prayer for granted!

I often meet with pastoral fears about prayer. One pastor expressed concern that 'prayer not take over his church.' The comment is telling! How can there be too much prayer? He felt that prayer was a nice thing, in its place. Another pastor confided, he had never found prayer an important practice in his own life. He had been successful without praying – and therefore, he had never taught his people to pray. Have we, out of our own sufficiency, developed models for ministry success that eliminate reliance on God or the Holy Spirit? Are we, perhaps unwittingly, teaching our people to rely on us, our preaching, rather than living out of a direct relationship with God over an open Bible? Yet another pastor complained that prayer was inaction. It was not *doing* – he wanted his people to '*do ministry*' and too much time in prayer diminished time for ministry. His pragmatism is common. In our culture *doing* trumps *being, activity* is exalted over *relationship.* This pastor was wrong. He was a victim of his own diminished theology of prayer. Biblical prayer moves us to mission! Jesus made it clear, that witness before a watching world would rise out of 'waiting in prayer for the promise of the Father, the Holy Spirit' (Acts 1:8).

Nothing will move your congregation into transformation and mission more quickly than to see your people engaged in making your church a house of prayer for the nations.

I am convinced – that with praying people, everything changes for the better. And that prayer, transformational prayer, prayer over an open Bible, prayer that is both worshipful and missional, re-centers the church. Sadly, that is not the model of prayer in which our people engage. Prayerful worship results in a constant recalibration of our values toward a Christ-center. Missional prayer causes us to see the lost around us and become instruments in evangelism, Christ in us and through us. Worshipful prayer produces Christ-centered lives lived with Biblical values; and that empowers a credible witness – both noun and verb – to a watching world.

I think we need
a _prayer_ reformation in the church!

Not one that displaces praise and preaching, but one that makes prayer – direct communion with God by our people – the priority. Increasingly, worship is passive. 'Worshippers' listen to praise teams sing about God and a preacher talk about God, but they do not engage God themselves.

This book is a roadmap toward making your church *a house of prayer.* It is a call for a pastor to be first, a man of prayer, a holy man of God, and only then a preacher. It is a call for him to *watch* the flock which he feeds in prayer. It is a call for the church to be a missional community, as concerned for the lost as they are for their own nurturing. It is a call to bring prayerful creativity and deep dependence on God to the heart of all the church does – not merely making prayer a prop for congregational activities we plan. Everything begins in prayer and is sustained in prayer – a praying people constitute a praying church; and a praying church is a church revived and awakened.

We have prayer problem!

It is not the culture, not the Evil One, not the times, not a deficit in training, not a lack of funds or manpower. We have a deficit in prayer.

Whether you follow this guide fastidiously or casually, you and your prayer team will be stretched in their thinking, advised, admonished, counseled about the practical aspects of change as your congregation re-centers itself in Christocentric, transformational prayer with a missional interface.

Blessings on your journey!
P. Douglas Small

Introduction

Milestones – Markers on the Journey
Toward Becoming a House of Prayer

This is a strategic prayer leaders guide. Your pastor, and perhaps associate, your director of prayer, and key prayer leaders should be exposed to this material. It is not recommended for wide exposure, except in pieces that might be instructive for learning and leading teams as your process moves forward.

This collection of prayer ministry milestones is designed to augment and clarify the process for congregations on a mission, not to *add* prayer to existing ministries, but to change the culture of the congregation into a house of prayer for the nations.

This is supplemental material, and while it has stand-alone value, you will be greatly helped if you have these resources from Project Pray available through Alive Publications:

The Praying Church Made Simple

Excellent material for the first three milestones in your process. Recommended for the pastor and lay prayer leader(s). Your learning team will benefit from the exercises in the book, as well as relevant material from the *Perspectives* volume.

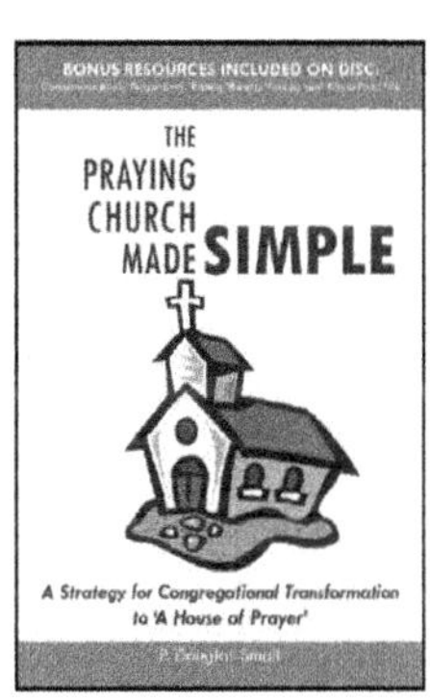

Transforming Your Church
into a House of Prayer – Revised Edition

This redesigned material is recommended to all those interested and involved in your prayer process. Much of the material is designed for us in a planning retreat for leaders. This book provides an overview of the Seven Markers and the Four Dimensions of prayer, as well as, the Milestone process.

Praying Leader Continuing Education

You will be greatly helped, if you launch a prayer training quarterly process. Get a leader certified. Use the curriculum to keep your prayer leaders learning and involved.

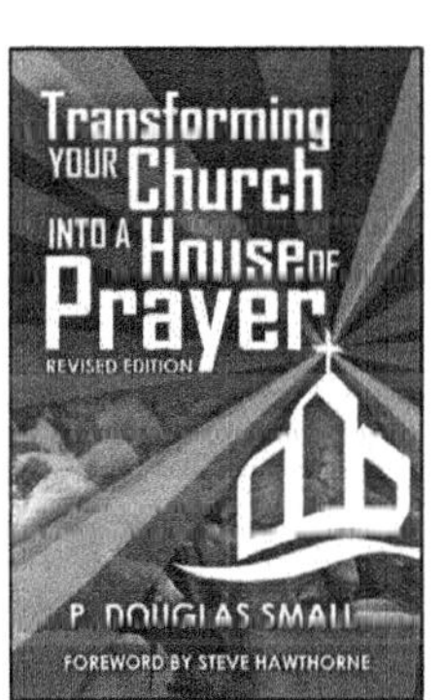

Seven Markers of a Praying Church

1. A praying pastor and prayer leaders
2. At-home, daily, Jesus-be-Jesus-in-me praying
3. Pervasive prayer at church – out of a prayer meeting
4. Identified, trained, directed, debriefed intercessors
5. An external, missional focus – prayer evangelism
6. On-going training
7. Physical prayer space – room, center, wall

The Praying Church Resource Guide

A 700-page notebook packed with practical prayer resources.

In addition, you might consider becoming a certified Prayer Trainer with Project Pray, and leading or participating in our Prayer Leaders Continuing Education training process in your area – a quarterly gathering of pastors and prayer leaders from congregations who want to bring prayer to the heart of all they do. Get certified and start a learning group in your area. You may also choose to be certified to present Project Pray Schools of Prayer.

Resources are available at www.alivepublications.org or by contacting Alive Ministries: PROJECT PRAY, 855-842-5483 (www.projectpray.org).

Seven Markers of a Praying Church

1. Led by **a praying pastor, aided by a prayer leadership team**, we commit to bring prayer to the heart of all we do!

2. We will encourage **at-home, daily, Jesus-be-Jesus-in-me praying.** We will reestablish our personal and family altars.

3. We will call our congregation to **regular prayer,** with the goal of establishing a regular weekly prayer meeting for the entire church.

4. We will honor those who carry a special calling to pray – **intercessors.** We will identify intercessors, encourage them, train them, team them, deploy them, and debrief them.

5. We will **engage in prayer evangelism, turning prayer outward** onto the neighborhood, the city, state and nation, and we will adopt a mission field for prayer, one near and one far.

6. We will **offer regular training in the area of prayer** – for our people, leaders, intercessors, prayer evangelism, our youth and children, our families.

7. We will **work toward the creation of a prayer room or center,** a physical space dedicated to prayer at our church, and we will encourage the use of such a space by members and prayer groups.

Ten Prayer Values

What we believe and how we behave:

- **We value prayer;** *therefore, we will feature prayer in our worship and make prayer a central element of all ministry.* We value prayer as repentance and integrity before God; as brokenness and humility; as the central place, over an open Bible, where we are transformed.

- **We are a praying people;** *therefore, we will nurture at-home daily prayer,* family prayer, husband-wife, parent-child prayer connections, providing resources, training and nudging new and old Christians to deepen their prayer lives.

- **We believe that we are a kingdom of priests** and that prayer and worship is our highest calling, and that as priests, we are not only recipients of blessing, but the conveyors of blessing; *therefore, in prayer, we commit to pray for the favor and blessing of God upon others;* for protective care, upon our pastor, the church staff, the church family, our city, and our nation. *We bless,* we do not curse. We ask God not for what we deserve, but for blessing – for continued grace and mercy!

- **We value holiness and righteousness** as the mark of God upon a people, and we recognize that the church desperately needs revival and our nation needs a great awakening; *therefore, we regularly and consistently cry out to God for revival in the church and a great awakening* for our nation.

- **We believe in the power of petition,** that God answers when people pray rightly; *therefore, we faithfully take the needs of the church, one another, the city and the world before the throne of God and ask for grace!* We provide a means whereby requests for prayer are taken seriously and held up in prayer persistently, beseeching God expectantly for an answer.

- **We believe in the power of God through intercession;** *therefore, we identify, train, team, and mobilize intercessors* for the under-girding of the ministries of the Church, and for the support of the various mission endeavors of the congregation.

- **We believe that prayer is essential to the success of every endeavor,** that without Him we can do nothing, and whatever we do in His behalf without dependence upon Him is less than it might have been, given dependence in prayer; *therefore, our rule is no one works unless someone prays!*

- **We believe that the reception of the gospel unto salvation is a spiritual issue;** *therefore, we pray for the harvest,* that blind eyes will be open to the gospel, ears will be enabled to hear and receive the truth of Christ: hearts may be receptive to the good news that goes forth in power out of prayer.

- **We believe that there is a definitive connection between prayer and the harvest;** *therefore, we insist that prayer must have a missional dimension,* that we must pray for lost loved ones, for the unreached in our city and the world.

- **We believe, "God governs the world by the prayers of His people;"** *therefore, we pray for our city, state, and national leaders.* We pray about world conditions and various global crises. We invite God's intervening reign. We pray, *"Thy Kingdom come, thy will be done."*

OVERVIEW

The Milestone Process

This document was designed for use in the Prayer Leadership Continuing Education (PLCE) effort, a grassroots prayer training model planned as a 43-month process and based on the Seven Markers of a Praying Church, impossible without (Marker #1) a pastor who prays and desires his congregation to be a people of prayer, and empowers leaders to spearhead a movement of congregational prayer. This movement occurs in four spheres or dimensions – (Marker #2) a praying people; (#3) a praying congregation; (#4) mobilized intercessors; (#5) all with a definitive external prayer evangelism interface.

The model demands (Marker #6) on-going teaching and training in the area of prayer, an expanding prayer leadership team (#1), and (#7) a physical-visual connection point for recruitment and engagement (a prayer room/center or even a prayer wall).

The first three markers are your starting points – (Marker #1) pastor and a developing prayer leadership team, (#2) personal daily prayer, and (#3) a congregational prayer meeting – and they are the essence of the *Praying Church Made Simple* book and model. Preoccupy yourself with these during the first year. Here is the process:

- ✓ As a pastor, look for teachable people who can be trained in the area of prayer and who might develop as members of a prayer leadership team.

- ✓ Pray, personally, daily, at home, and encourage these leaders to do the same.

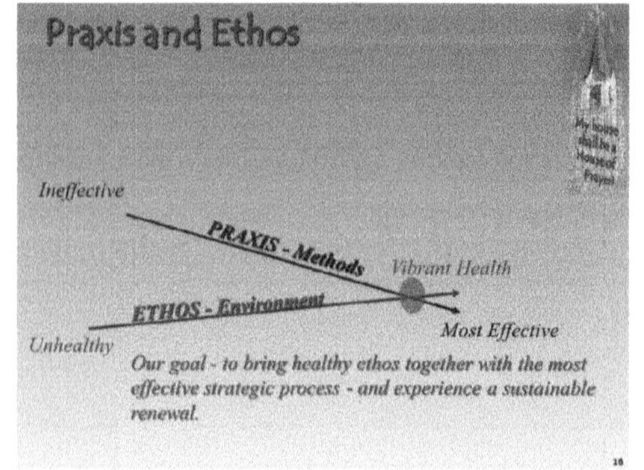

✓ Start a prayer meeting *to pray* – don't worry about the numbers. You are learning to pray, together, as a church; and that fuels daily prayer; and from that pool, you will recruit prayer learner-leaders.

The first three milestones are these simple, first-year steps. The material in this book could possibly stand alone, but it was written as a supplement to the book, *The Praying Church Made Simple*, and the book, *Transforming Your Church into a House of Prayer – Revised Edition* and their corollary materials. For those familiar with the *Praying Church Resource Guide*, these milestones will be very helpful in knowing the order in which to integrate and use that material along with other resources produced by P. Douglas Small and Alive Publications for The Praying Church Movement.

It is critical that the reader understand – This is not a collage of prayer programs. It is, rather, the description of a systematic and, yes, somewhat complex developmental prayer process aimed at changing the *culture* of the congregation from passive to participatory, from horizontal faith nurture to living out of a vertical relationship with God, and then from 'church' as enriching one another to ministering to a lost world. Any significant transformational process in which you engage, out of which you experience progress, will have programmatic elements – but the goal is not the introduction of prayer programs, per se. It is the recalibration of congregational values and the introduction of a strategic process to affect every aspect of church life. The process demands the embrace of the *discipline* of prayer, both by the congregation in a regular gathering for corporate prayer; and, daily at-home, personal prayer; and the discipline, indeed, a *culture of learning among leaders*. Discipline proceeds to delight. Structure produces the stability that allows the freedom to grow and explore.

A healthy *ethos* is the environment in which effective and productive *praxis* is employed for its greatest impact. Praxis involves the *practical,* both strategic and tactical, programmatic elements that move you from being ineffective to most effective. Ethos represents the degree to which the organization is unhealthy, healthy or vibrantly healthy. Sadly, we are in a season of spiritual decline and apostasy, and the church itself is not healthy – it lacks unity and humility, it lacks holiness and the boldness to differentiate itself from the world. It is self-sufficient and prayerless – and the list goes on.

The most effective praxis will fail in an unhealthy culture – not characterized by humility and deep dependence on God. Likewise, healthy culture (being) must employ sound praxis (doing). It must understand and appreciate the role of tools and exercises, without glorifying them and abandoning their relational essence.

What is being presented here is not a program; it is a transformational journey. It has *praxis* elements. However, this is a relational process, with vertical and horizontal aspects, aimed at engaging increasing numbers in the congregation, in regular, disciplined, delightful, and transforming prayer encounters with God.

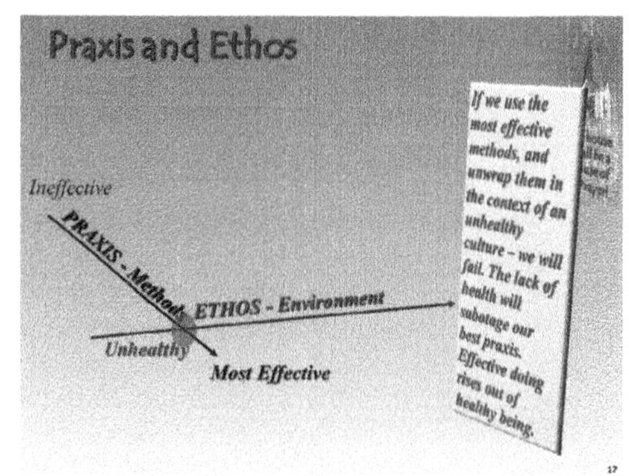

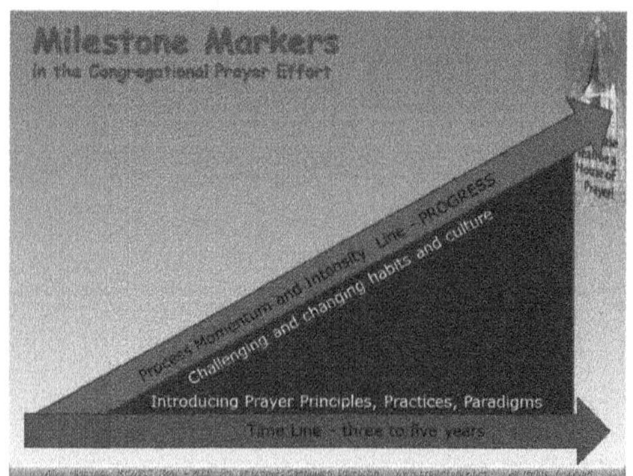

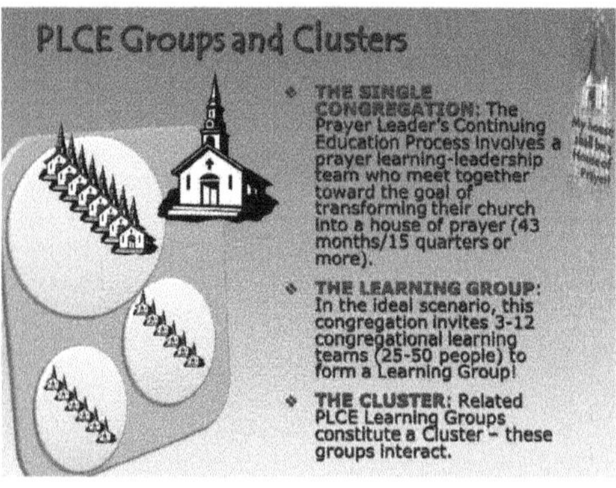

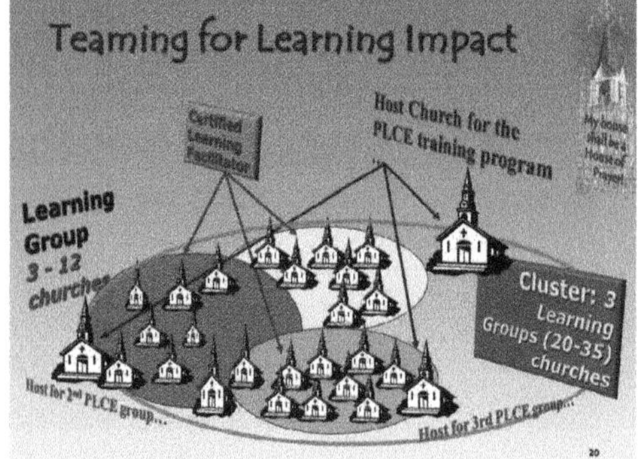

A Word about Prayer Leader Continuing Education (PLCE)

It is not necessary to establish or participate in a PLCE group or process to make use of the milestone material or process. However, it could be helpful. In either case, the milestone process was created to measure the movement toward becoming a house of prayer – to churches in the process and those on the journey independently.

The PLCE process consists of three-to-twelve congregations, meeting four times annually, to create a PLCE group. A congregation can use the curriculum independently, however, an optimum learning group involves multiple congregations for peer learning, each with teams of three-to-twelve individuals. The entire learning group should not exceed forty-to-fifty participants, on average. It is also recommended that each congregation's prayer leadership-learning team meet monthly in the alternate months, between the quarterly PLCE multi-congregational meetings, with a focus on the development of prayer in that particular local church. This is the best of both worlds – a potential prayer leadership team in a congregation meeting, growing and developing, learning and praying together, but also connecting with other similar teams from nearby congregations, drawing strength and ideas one from another.

In addition, if two or more PLCE groups (each composed of three-to-twelve congregations) are near one another, at times, the learning facilitator(s) of these groups may choose to conduct a joint meeting – two or more learning teams together. These are called *clusters*. In fact, a learning facilitator or team may serve multiple groups and from time to time, bring them together, usually no more than once a year except for extracurricular activities.

The teaming (clusters) allows a facilitator to serve multiple PLCE groups, and to find ways to connect them for additional training. The facilitator increases the pool of early successes in the multiple groups, and that allows peer leadership. When a handful of congregations experience resolve and breakthrough, it encourages all in the learning group and the cluster. With the PLCE groups meeting once quarterly, it is possible for a facilitator/trainer to serve more than one location. These may be different denominational streams or congregations in different cities altogether.

Each congregation will set forth a *prayer leadership-<u>learning team</u>* for the process. Each PLCE Learning Group will be anchored at a *campus church*. On request, monthly conference calls to inspire and inform participants are available from Project Pray in connection with the PLCE local leadership team. In addition, for the certified Learning Facilitators who lead the PLCE quarterly sessions, a <u>*quarterly resources update*</u> serves to move the process forward, keeping the learning facilitators abreast of new resources and answering the challenges they face. The goal of the PLCE endeavor is each congregation working independently - together.

Again, participation in the PLCE process is optimal. PROJECT PRAY offers facilitator certification for the PLCE process as well as curriculum.

Milestones represent the markers of progress on the PLCE journey, therefore, throughout this document, the PLCE process will be cited.

A Quick Overview of the Milestones

The first step in learning to be a house of prayer is – *prayer*. The *congregation* needs to gather to pray together. This is not merely people praying in the same room. It is people, the church, praying as one, from the office of the church; and in addition, embracing the discipline of daily, *personal prayer*.

Simultaneously, a small group of *leaders* will meet quietly and learn about prayer ministry together. They will 'do' prayer and explore models of prayer for the congregation. At first, their learning will be conceptual. Then, practical – exploring other models of congregational prayer. They will complete *research* on the history of prayer in the congregation and collect data to determine the current level of congregational prayer. They will assess prayer needs in the community, the mission field of the congregation. From such facts, they will develop *an informed plan* to *engage the congregation* in a serious pursuit of God's presence and a spiritual awakening. They will *envision the congregation* – calling the people to prayer engagement. They will recruit *additional leaders* to a stable prayer leadership team. The enlarged team will *expand the prayer effort*, growing all four dimensions of the praying church - the congregational prayer meeting, encouraging the family altar, identifying and mobilizing intercessors, commissioning prayer teams and groups, turning prayer outward onto the community – prayer evangelism. Then, they will work to strengthen the congregation as a house of prayer for the nations.

The depth of the process is found in the fifteen milestones. These, however, are not a dominant feature of the quarterly meetings. Each congregational prayer leadership team is charged with the responsibility of integrating prayer ministry change at their own pace. They must also determine the order in which they will approach the milestones – though we recommend an order. Further, they alone may choose to add a component not included or emphasized, or skip a recommendation. The milestones, however, are not random. They are built on the concept of the Seven Markers of a Praying Church, the

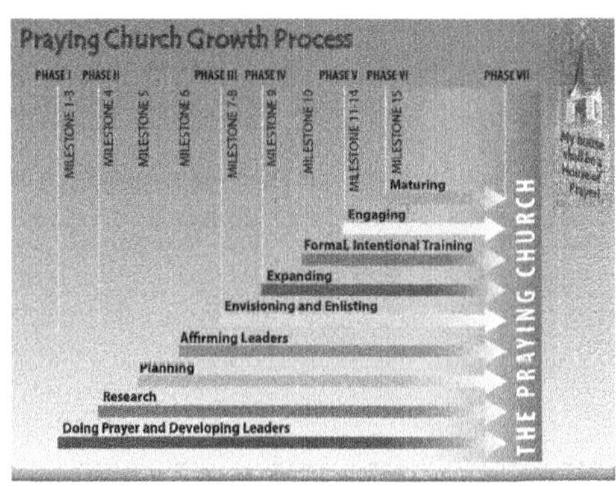

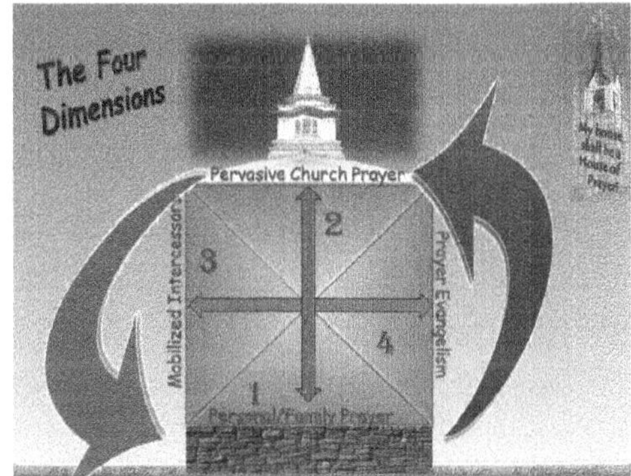

four dimensions and two cogs that drive the entire process. And they represent a comprehensive vision of how to integrate these principles into the life of a congregation.

The 43-month PLCE process, more or less, is measured by congregational change. The 15 quarterly meetings do not mark the end of the process, only the end of the program. The process goes on until Jesus comes. Indeed, our mission is forever prayerful worship, evangelism, and discipleship. The PLCE training process lays the conceptual foundation and sets the trajectory for participating congregations. Its design allows new congregations to enter the training process at any point and exit when they have achieved their goals. That means that the process can be ongoing. Some congregations may decide to stay in the learning loop as long as necessary to complete their 15 milestones.

The one unique session that entering congregations need to complete in order to join the process is *Orientation* to the PLCE training process. It provides an overview. During the 43-month process, participants, prayer leaders, will have met together for 15 sessions. But learning is not the end goal – the goal is the transformation of the congregation into a praying people.

It's Simple

PHASE I – Learning About and Doing Prayer – The Launch (3 Simple Processes)

Milestone One: Launch a Church-Wide Prayer Meeting. To *be* a house of prayer, you must *do* prayer. It becomes a *delight*, but it begins as a corporate *discipline*.

Milestone Two: Develop a Prayer Leadership-Learning Team. Look for humble, teachable, learning-leaders. Start meeting with them to establish a culture of prayer throughout the homes of people and in every ministry endeavor of the congregation. You need a training plan for this group.

Milestone Three: The Personal Prayer Life Challenge. Encourage your learning-leaders to embrace the

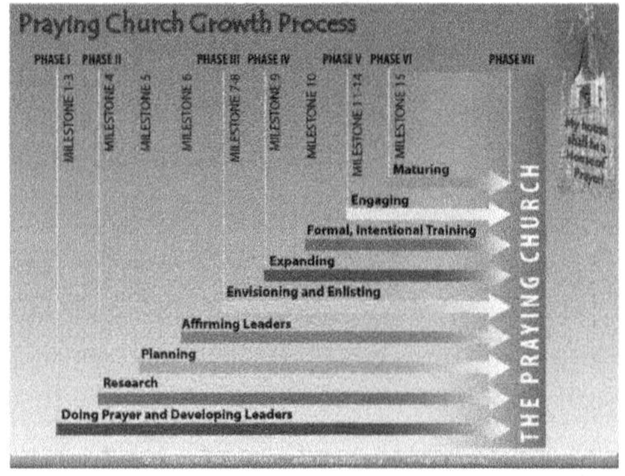

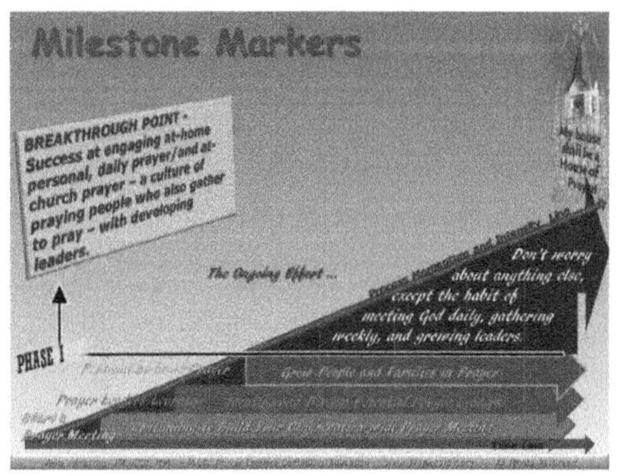

habit of grace-based daily prayer. Gently urge this standard on your entire congregation.

In an attempt to make the complex simple, it is not my desire to over illustrate. Nevertheless, for drill, let us make the point that these three milestones, while they are simultaneous, they also build one on another. They create synergy. With corporate prayer, personal prayer intensifies, and with positive corporate prayer experiences, personal prayer is enriched. All the while, the learning-leaders are motivated to meet, learn, and pray, and consider how to infect the entire congregation in a spirit of prayer.

Your breakthrough comes when the corporate prayer experience is gaining traction, and you have discovered a model that is both corporately transformational and transactional (time to both pray for personal needs and engage in missional prayer).

Without some level of maturity in the embrace of corporate and personal prayer, at least among the leaders, don't try to advance.

Throughout this presentation, again, perhaps over illustrating, I will use the analogy of the prayer ministry effort as building a 3-legged stool. The three legs are the first three milestones – congregational prayer, personal prayer, with family engagement, and developing leaders. Later, we will talk about the rungs of the stool, and the prayer room/center, that is the crown of the congregational prayer effort, where everything converges and from which your various efforts flow. For now, think of your prayer effort as a 3-legged stool (Whatever analogy works for you!).

 **YOU ARE NOW AT A CHECK POINT!**

Don't press any further _until_ you sense that your prayer meeting is catching heaven's wind and fire; and, you have a small team of developing leaders who are learning and growing together with the promise of leading the congregation through significant prayer reformation; and they evidence a hunger for God as they meet with God daily, personally. Without leaders, and a growing number of

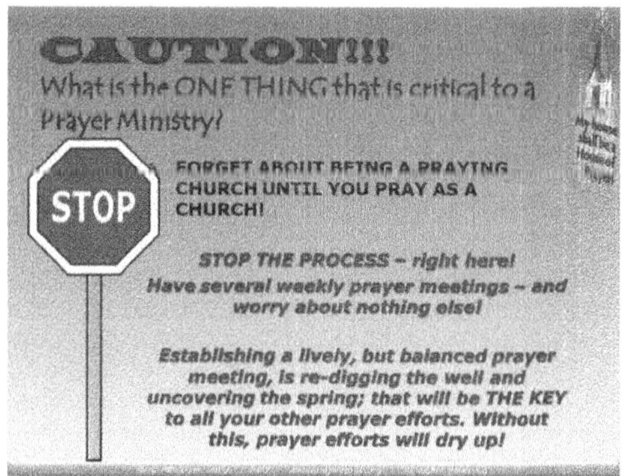

people attending your prayer meeting, whose daily prayer habits evidence new vitality – you can't move forward.

Information and activities have been the goals of church-life in this era of major spiritual decline. Your goal is not *information* about prayer, but *formation* in the presence of God in prayer, not merely the *activity* of prayer – but a *transforming relationship* with God, personally and congregationally. If this is happening – move forward; if not, something is awry in your recipe.

These three – a healthy congregational prayer meeting; humble, praying, learning leaders, and the promise of recovering the family altar out of a daily personal at-home prayer time – are critical foundation pieces.

PHASE II – Discovery (Three Milestones)

Milestone Four: Research and Discovery. Here you will need to lay assumptions aside.

- ✓ You are going to look INSIDE and discover how engaged the congregation is in prayer. Are they praying? How much? About what?

- ✓ You are going to look BACK. Was there a time when the tide of prayer was higher in your congregation than now? When? What did that look like? How long ago? Are there people who can tell the stories of your church as a praying congregation?

- ✓ You must look AROUND to discover other congregations that are taking prayer seriously, and learn from them.

- ✓ You must look OUT – about who and what should you be praying? See the harvest around you, the neighborhood and city needs. Prayer must not be inwardly focused – it must have a missional, prayer-evangelism dimension. You must define your harvest field, your mission field in the city-county. The first step, after awareness, is prayer mobilization for the needs of lost people who are your neighbors.

- ✓ You must look UP to God for His help. In truth, you are joining Him in His mission.

To accomplish this research, you will need to add members to your learning team without diluting the culture of your learning team.

Milestone Five: Planning – Articulating Vision, Mission, Strategy and Tactics. Now you will begin, using the research, to **set forth an informed plan**. You want to raise the level of prayer in your congregation, in all four dimensions. This will rekindle revival fires. You want to implement best prayer practices discovered from other congregations. You want to engage the congregation to not only pray for internal needs, but also to focus on the harvest and see the church as a community transformational force – all without losing prayer's heart, the fixed personal and congregational exposure to God's loving and holy Presence. For this milestone, a leadership planning retreat is recommended. Use the *Transforming Your Church into a House of Prayer* as a guide. Your learning-leaders, your discovery team members who helped you with research, and, key congregational leaders (staff, elders, deacons, department/ministry leaders, etc.) need to be at this retreat.

Milestone Six: Affirming Leaders (Leadership Structuring and Affirmation). With an informed plan, you now need more than learning-leaders. Restructure your leaders, affirm and empower them to move forward. They have prayed together, learned together, explored and planned together – now, they must boldly, but humbly lead. Name a strategic prayer leadership team – a core of key leaders. Do this without dismissing your other leaders.

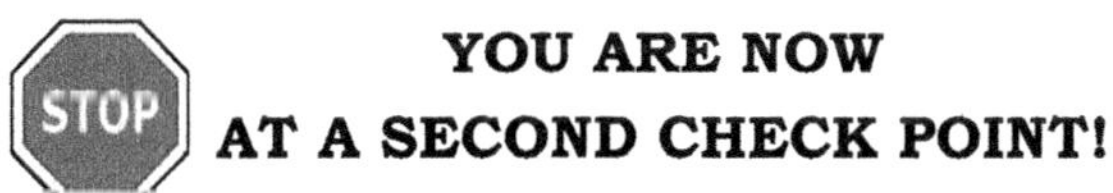

YOU ARE NOW AT A SECOND CHECK POINT!

Don't go forward, if you have not set forth an 'informed plan' out of significant research. Accurate information is fuel for intercession. You need the jolting awareness of what you are facing, the challenge of the harvest. The congregation must 'see the harvest' in order to 'pray to the Lord of the harvest' with greater passion. It must sense its own prayerlessness and acknowledge the depth of tearless praying and the lack of appropriate concern for God's missional agenda. Only with 'informed leaders' and a compelling plan out of sound data should you move forward.

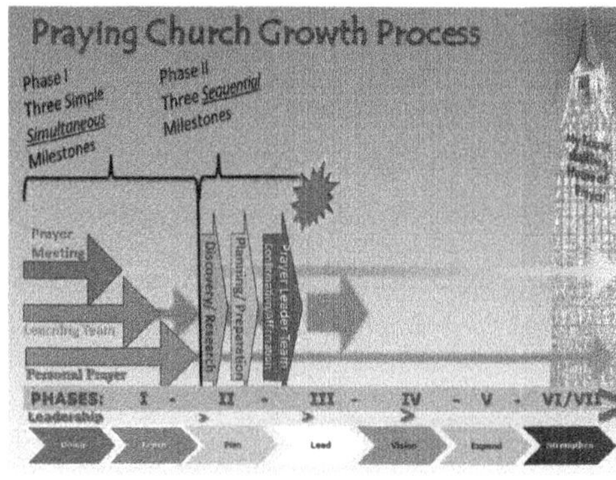

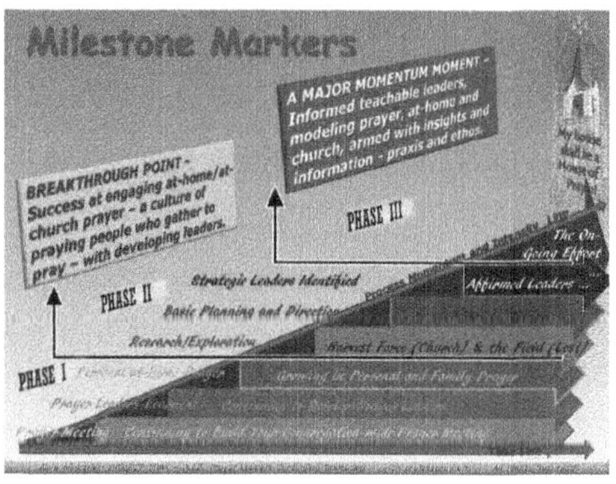

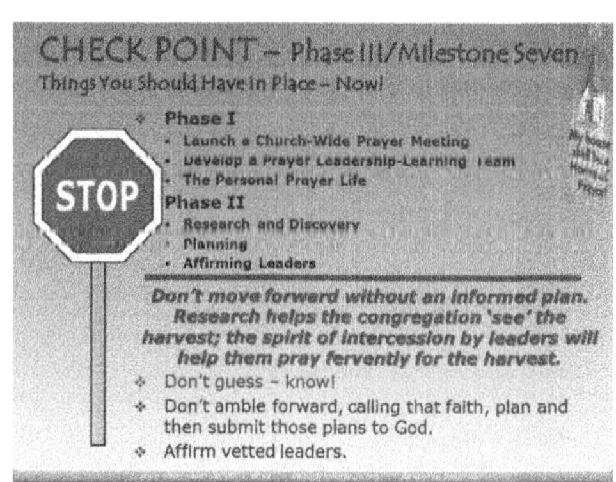

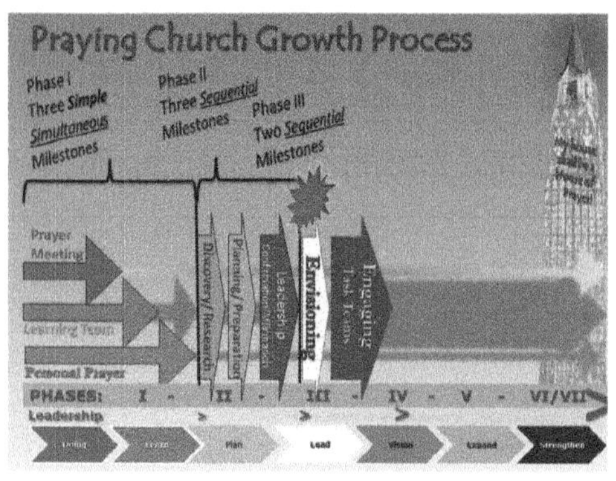

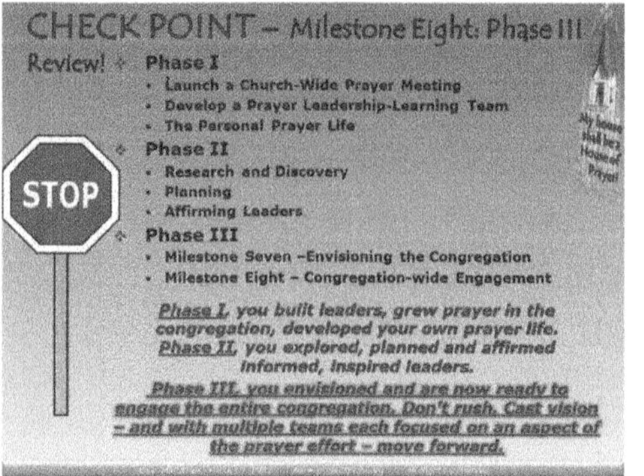

PHASE III – Going Public: Feeding the Prayer Fire and Finding Leaders (Two Milestones)

Milestone Seven: Envisioning the Congregation. You are now ready to *envision the congregation* to become a house of prayer for the nations. You have quietly envisioned learning-leaders. You have touched on vision, certainly, in your prayer meeting and preaching-teaching. In the discovery process, from your research, your vision enlarged along with all those involved in the research endeavor. With an informed plan for moving forward, and committed, grounded strategic leaders – it is time to call the congregation to own the vision of becoming a house of prayer. You have invited them consistently to a congregational prayer meeting. Most, perhaps, have never come. You have been vetting and testing leaders, attempting to go more deeply than wide – now, you are ready to go wide.

Milestone Eight: Church-Wide Enlistment. Gently and persistently, you want to engage the congregation to embrace the practice of prayer. Around your SLT, draw from the pool of learners-explorers-planners and those who expressed interest at your vision gathering. Create implementation task teams to plan prayer events and experiences over a 6-12 month period. For the next year, offer a variety of prayer challenges beyond your weekly prayer meeting – personal prayer, couples and family prayer, intercessory prayer and evangelism, prayer for the church, the nation and the world. Use the many resources that exist and introduce them into the calendar of the church. If you have been hovering at the 10-20 percent level in terms of your participation in the weekly congregational prayer meeting, then your goal now is to engage 25-35 percent of the congregation, over the course of a year, in alternative prayer activities. Keep raising the bar. You are deepening the level of prayer, and simultaneously, developing additional prayer leaders.

YOU ARE NOW AT A THIRD CHECK POINT!

Do not rush. Take another year or longer to cast vision and engage the congregation in a variety of prayer experiences. Offer multiple opportunities to pray as a congregation. Point out resources. You will have a chance now, to measure the appetite of your members for prayer. You will see their readiness and their reluctance. You will probably experience push back. You are no longer *talking* about prayer; you are calling the people to *actually pray* – and do so daily, at-home, with their spouses, and about the lost-ness of people around them – to pray beyond their own narrow slice of pain and self-interest. You have declared war against the devil and the flesh. The flash points of resistance are a gift – don't miss them. They may reveal a fear of prayer, a lack faith and understanding of the importance of prayer. They will show the congregation's perception of the theology of prayer and its place in God's scheme, and perhaps, a deficiency in compassion for the lost. These are your teaching and training cues. You must graciously teach and train into the learning gaps. As you teach and train, you build confidence and faith. As learning gaps persist, as some close, others will be revealed, you continue to teach and train into the learning gaps.

PHASE IV – Expanding Leadership Teams and Long-Term Planning (The Big Leap: Two Milestones)

NOTE: The first three milestones in Phase I were simultaneous. In Phase II, the research and discovery, the planning and then the affirmation of leaders was sequential. In Phase III, you envisioned and then enlisted the congregation, first one and then another. Moreover, you have functioned with one core leadership team. Now, you are at an intersection that will send you in four planning and leadership directions simultaneously. You know the baseline of prayer in your congregation. You established this in your research and discovery process. And, in the following year, you offered prayer engagement opportunities. You have measured the response to family prayer, intercession, prayer evangelism, prayer for the city, etc. You have vetted more leaders by their participation as members of task teams, and that is now critical for your leadership expansion.

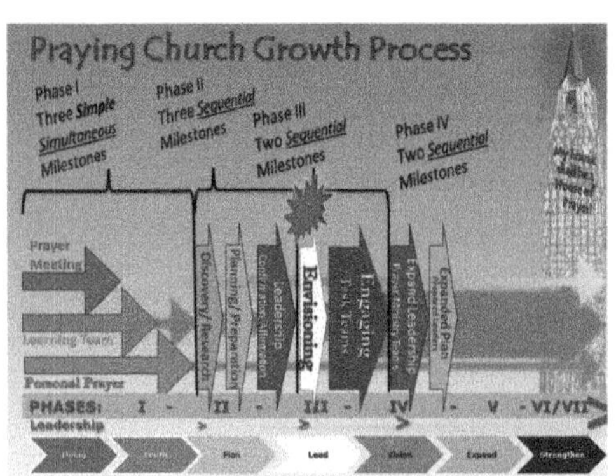

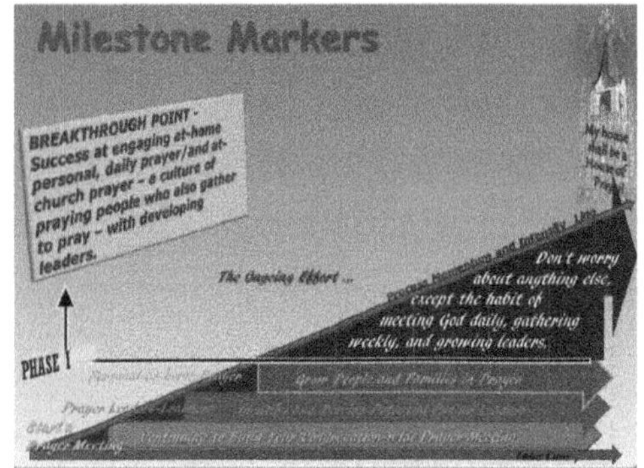

Milestone Nine: Multiple Leadership Teams. You have had one leadership team to this point. You should have created 'task teams' to implement various prayer exercises and activities during the last year – that was after planning and envisioning. These teams operated out of and around your SLT. They may have been led by members of the SLT. That gave you an opportunity to test their leadership. Now you want to transition the 'task team' into leading some component of the prayer ministry itself, beyond mere exercises and prayer activities. They will now plan some aspect of your prayer effort, train and envision, recruit and work to see the prayer effort mature in that facet of church life – personal and family ministries, prayer groups and the church-wide prayer gatherings, intercessory prayer and evangelism. The 'task teams', now vetted, now transition to provide permanent leadership over the various dimensions of your prayer effort. In a small congregation, this may be the members of your 'core' prayer leadership team each taking a leadership role in some aspect of your prayer effort. In a slightly larger congregation, each leader of your core prayer leadership team (SLT) will recruit two-to-three others to help them with, for example, mobilizing the intercessors; or, the systematic prayer evangelism effort; or, the resourcing of the various ministries of the church for prayer engagement and enrichment.

Milestone Ten: Diversified Training. The SLT will continue to direct the macro prayer effort. The micro-teams will focus on specific aspects, pieces of the prayer effort. The macro-teams should now revisit the research-discovery data and information related to other areas of focus. They will recall the levels of response during the year of congregational prayer engagement in which various prayer opportunities were presented. And they will set forth a plan to teach and train, to engage in the various dimensions of prayer. Each team will lay out a multi-year plan for teaching, training and prayer engagement, moving forward – at least over the next three years, in a specific focus area personal/family/intercession/congregational prayer engagement/prayer evangelism/youth and children engagement, etc.). That plan needs to be reviewed, approved, and calendared, by the 'core' prayer leadership team – they are the keepers of the vision. They guard the mission and purpose along with the overarching values. From these 'Strategic Task Teams' permanent prayer ministry teams will emerge. (I have used a variety of terms to describe the Strategic Task Teams (STT) – implementers, task-teams, micro-teams, etc. The term STT seems most appropriate, contrasted with the SLT.)

In the past, you have offered prayer training and various prayer experiences. You have emphasized the importance of personal and family prayer. You have hinted at the profile of a healthy intercessor. You may have prayer-walked or conducted a 'pray for your lost friends' campaign. In each instance, you were testing the openness of your congregation to embrace the prayer reformation. Change comes slowly. Like Israel in the wilderness, you probably experienced push back at multiple junctions. You started with a group of hopeful leaders. Some are still with you; others are not. As you moved forward, it became clear that some could embrace change, others had hardened wineskins. As you introduced the congregation to a new prayer paradigm, you were also growing strategic task teams to lead the process in various areas.

Now you are ready to move in several directions simultaneously. You need multiple vetted STTs, each with a leader who has passion for a specific area of prayer. Of course, these teams need to collaborate with each other through their representation on the SLT. Previously, you may have emphasized the family altar, then the church prayer meeting, then intercession, then prayer evangelism – and the experiences you offered the congregation serially might have been overwhelming. Then, you were seeding the various dimensions of your planned prayer effort. Now, your tested leaders have surfaced, and you are ready to engage multiple STT and prayer targets simultaneously.

Each STT will plan, teach, and train in their specific area. They will revisit the data of earlier planning, the vision and mission objectives, and they will develop a plan for their specific area.

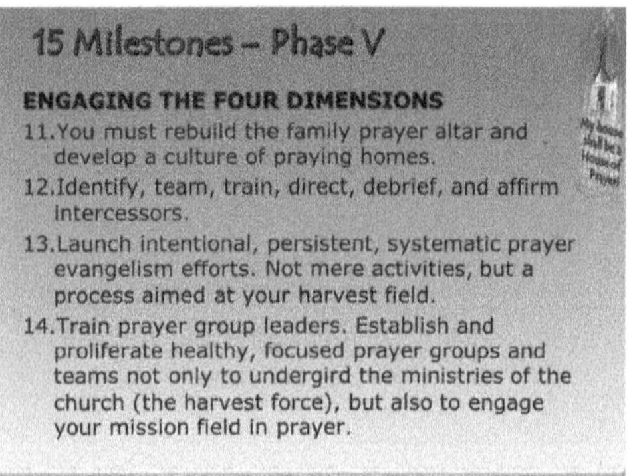

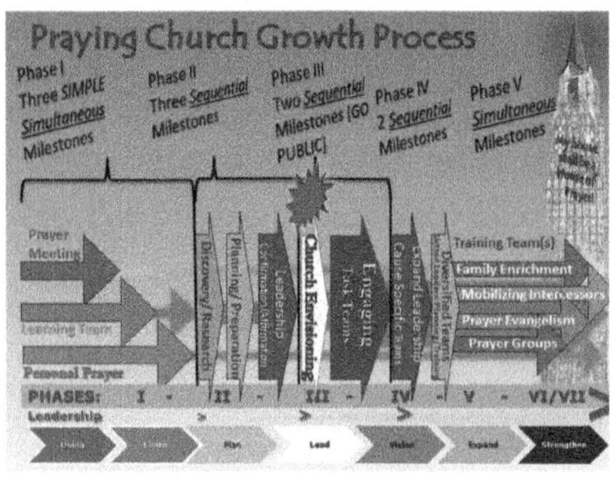

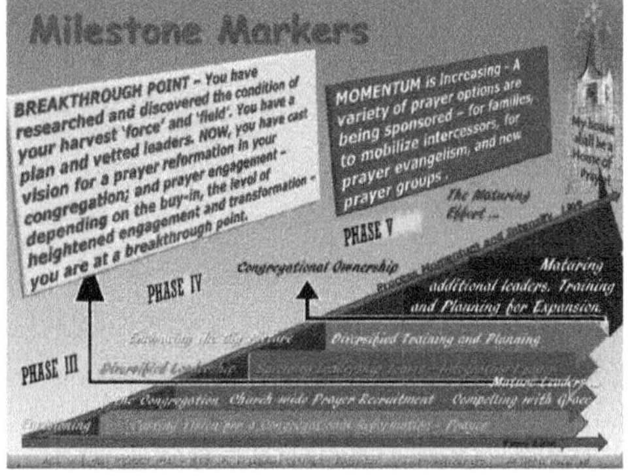

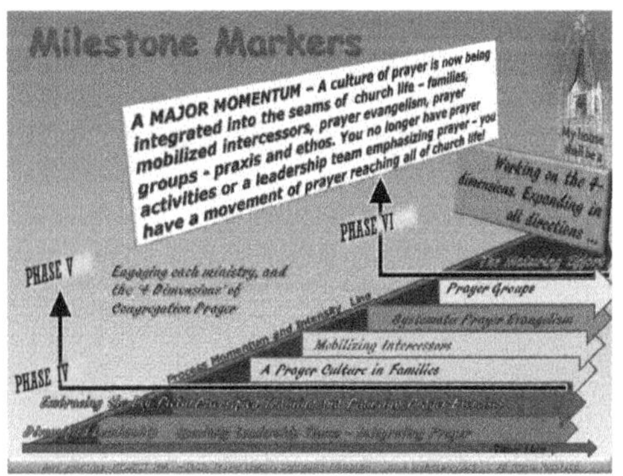

Using the Seven Markers of a Praying Church and the Four Dimensions as a guide, you will now move forward toward permeating congregational life with prayer.

PHASE V – Engaging the Four Dimensions (Five Simultaneous Milestones)

Milestone Eleven: The Family Altar. Work to see families engaged in prayer together. Rebuild family altars. Work toward a culture of prayer in the homes of the people.

Milestone Twelve: Intercession. Identify, train, team, direct, debrief, and affirm the intercessors of the congregation, with the goal, of creating an intercessory community of the congregation itself.

Milestone Thirteen: Prayer Evangelism. Develop a systemic plan for prayer evangelism in the congregation, the neighborhood, the city-county, and the nations that God has assigned the congregation. This includes regular, systematic prayer for the lost, for community leaders, for bars and schools, the pain and promise of the city or a definitive sector, members praying for their neighbors.

Milestone Fourteen: Prayer Groups. You started with one prayer group in your congregation – the church gathered to pray with the pastor leading in prayer. Now, you want to proliferate prayer opportunities around that one, church-wide prayer gathering. These small prayer groups, never larger than a dozen, are where people often learn to pray, especially, as intercessors, not only for the needs of other believers, but for the lost. For every 100 adult attenders, set a goal of seven prayer groups of 3-to-12 participants.

Note: You now have multiple prayer leadership teams caring about the four dimensions – and that assures balance and breadth in your prayer journey.

Phase VI – Maturing the Prayer Church (One Milestone)

Milestone Fifteen: Establishing the Prayer Room/ Center. You may have had a room that you have used for a prayer meeting. Now, you want to multiply the resources located there for prayer. Some congregations use their sanctuary. They use banners as prayer stations. They create a prayer corner or a wall and make resources available for prayer engagement. If you create a prayer room, add prayer displays. Allow each of the prayer team leaders to have a display – on personal and family prayer, on intercession, prayer evangelism, prayer needs, etc. Encourage the prayer groups to use the prayer room. Open it daily, if possible. Encourage intercessors to come to the church and spend an hour, once a week, in prayer. To pray, not only in the prayer room, but in the sanctuary as well. Bathe the building in prayer.

Phase VII – Forever

You never stop your prayer effort. You continually re-visit the 'Seven Markers of a Praying Church.' You continue to develop leaders and challenge new converts and members to be a people of prayer. You continue to move into mission out of prayerful dependence on God.

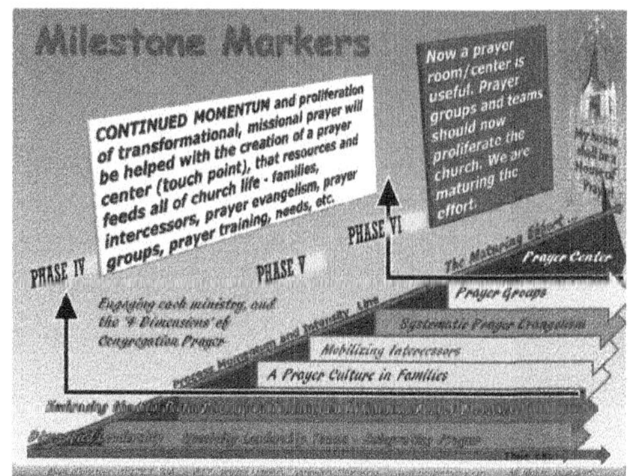

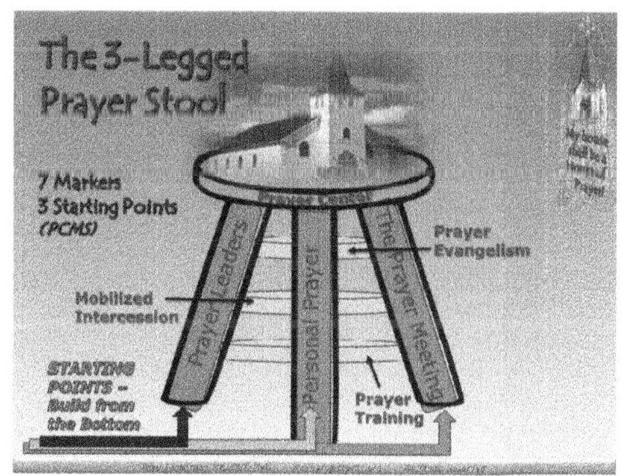

Learning About and Doing Prayer – The Launch

Phase I

Congregation: A relentless grace-based call to prayer.

Leaders: Identify potential prayer leaders. Engage them in learning, praying together, loving one another. Test their resolve and growth capacity.

People: Your goal is the embrace of the practice of daily, personal, private prayer, not out of duty, but delight. Grow your people by getting them to go deeper in God alone, by establishing the habit of the 'prayer closet' and living out of God's Presence.

First, start the Prayer Meeting!

- You are not praying as a church unless you are meeting to pray.

- You must pray from the office of the Church; personal prayer cannot take the place of corporate prayer.

- Every church needs a worship-word service, a training-education-discipleship meeting, AND A PRAYER MEETING.

Second, look for teachable, potential prayer leaders.

- Don't appoint prayer leaders, call together prayer learners!

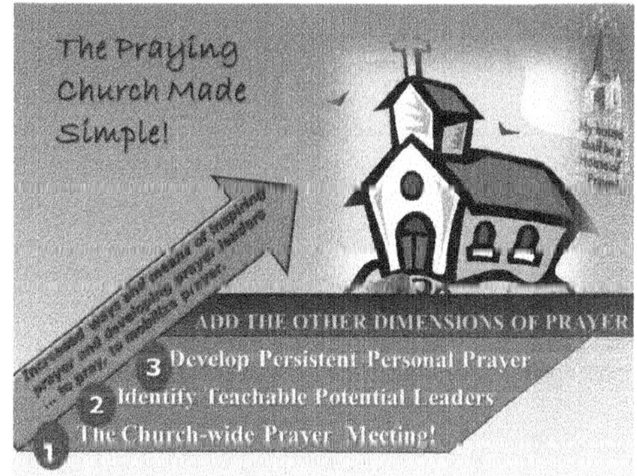

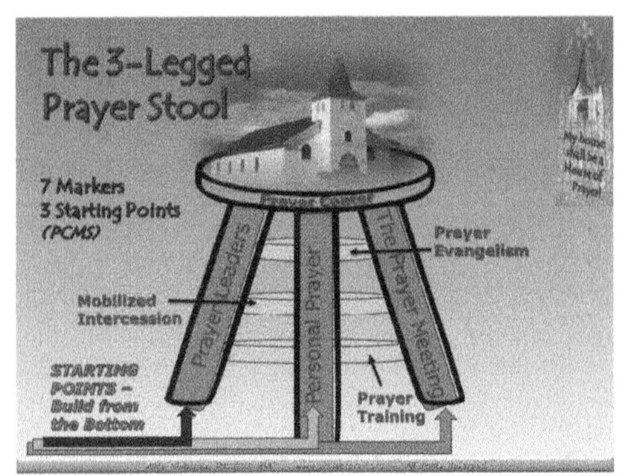

- If prayer leaders are not humble enough to learn, if they are stuck in styles of prayer that confine them in a prayer culture that is narrow and self-interested – your effort will be stymied at best or perhaps completely fail.

- Cultivate an openness to prayer styles, a more holistic understanding of prayer and a healthy prayer leadership team dynamic.

Third, pray!

- <u>Cultivate the habit of daily time with God!</u>

- Emphasize its importance, but make it grace-based, not guilt driven.

- <u>Prayer-less leaders can't lead a prayer effort</u>. It is more than taught; it is caught!

- As your prayer leaders pray – God will inspire and speak, direct and unify them. They, by the habit of prayer, will invite God into the leadership team, his blessing on the church-wide prayer gathering, his inspiration on the direction of the team.

- Pray!

MILESTONE ONE
Launch a Church-Wide Prayer Meeting

Proposition

Every congregation needs <u>a regular corporate prayer meeting</u>. Here, the church gathers, not to hear the scripture *preached*, but to *pray* the scripture. And, to pray one for another as well as the lost; to discern the will of God and corporately cultivate sensitivity to the ways of God. Here, humility and brokenness before God are nurtured. Here, the church demonstrates dependence on God for direction, provision and protection. Here, the church waits on God.

The Homogeneous *Prayer Celebration!*

The Prayer Celebration is the <u>whole Church</u> seeking the face of God together <u>in one place, at a fixed time,</u> for an extended period or season, as an expression of dependence on God, of unity and love, for the sake of the spiritual transformation of their lives and <u>the whole Church</u> – every age-

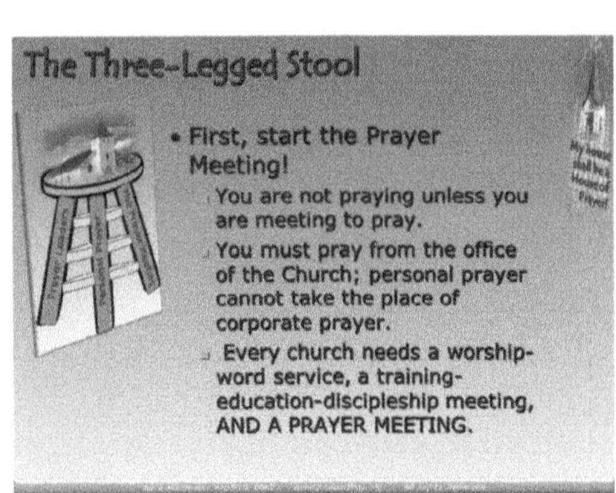

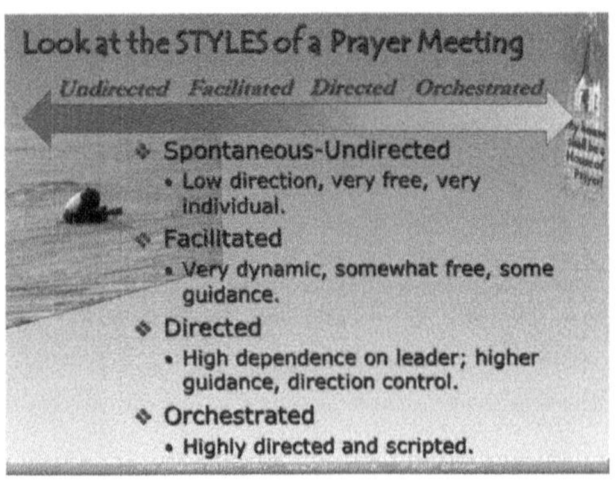

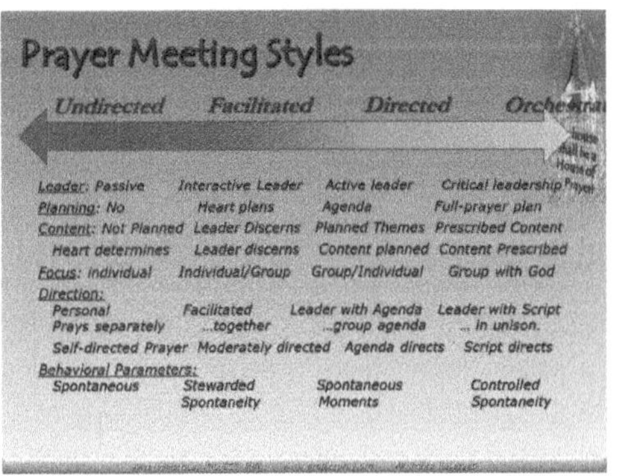

group, department, ethnic representation, gender, status, rank and position; and then to participate in the mission of God.

Timing

This prayer gathering should take place <u>weekly, if possible</u>, and not less than monthly. This is not the weekly worship-preaching event, or the weekly Christian Education/Family night event – this is the regular, persistent prayer meeting of the congregation before God – waiting worshipfully, petitioning, interceding, listening, hearing.

Duration

<u>A sixty-to-ninety-minute prayer experience is optimal</u>. You may build pre and post prayer meeting activities, but keep the prayer meeting itself within whatever time perimeters are stated, unless God changes the beginning and ending times of the meeting. If you do add pre or post activities (prayer for the sick, teaching or training, etc.), keep the 'main thing' – the prayer meeting - the 'main thing.' Don't subordinate prayer to something else, though that something else may be noble.

Style

This is an important consideration. We are blind victims of our wineskins and methods. <u>There are models for prayer gatherings</u> that are different from those to which you are accustomed. <u>If you are struggling with success in your prayer meeting, have you considered the problem may be found in the model you are using?</u>

The styles range from <u>undirected to orchestrated prayer</u>. If you lead an orchestrated prayer gathering, you need a full plan with prescribed content, something often alien to Evangelical-Pentecostal prayer meetings. Will you use a pulpit-directed, leader-centered gathering? This is typical, especially with larger groups, but with a small group, it is harder to maintain.

Another alternative <u>is a relational prayer gathering</u>. This is a facilitated gathering often in a room without pews, the chairs arranged in a circle or a layered circle, depending on the size of the room and the number of participants. Prayer participation, energy and involvement, drives this gathering. It is more intimate. You typically need twenty or more participants in terms of an effective group dynamic for this experience. With a group larger than one hundred it loses its intimacy and is much more difficult to manage.

You may call for a prayer meeting that is completely undirected, just folks gathering to pray in the same room, without leadership or direction. This is the least effective model for a corporate experience.

Focus

The premier focus of the corporate prayer gathering should be 'congregational communion' with God and their corporate transformation into a worshipping, missional community. It is Christ, the head of his Church, encountering his church. Make the prayer gatherings about him and his need, his agenda. Use the Bible as a prayer guide. Keep the focus first vertical, and then move to the missional horizontal. Subordinate personal needs and prayer requests.

Involvement Goals

Obviously, you want your entire church involved and present for prayer. However, in the early stages, given the current apostate spiritual climate of the Western church, this is usually not realistic. Set an initial *threshold* goal of 20 percent of your Sunday morning attendance in a prayer gathering on a regular basis. When that occurs, you will begin to feel the impact of the regular prayer meeting, assuming it is healthy. Health means, among other things, that you are praying scripture and focused on transformation, not only of the individual but also of the corporate congregation. You have also distinguished adequately between corporate prayer and individuals praying for themselves or one another in the same room. You have included, but subordinated personal prayer requests to worshipful, scripture-based, transformational prayer. Your center is worshipful, transformational

In 1866, Spurgeon instituted daily prayer meetings at the Tabernacle. They were held twice daily, at 7 a.m. and 7:30 p.m. The one main prayer meeting took place on Monday evenings and was attended by some 3,000 parishioners. Spurgeon was a great preacher. That fact is well-known. Lesser known is his commitment not only to personal prayer, but to congregational prayer.

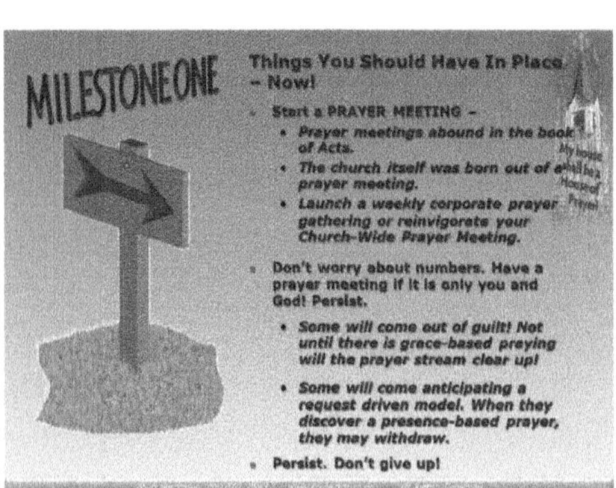

prayer; your edge is missional, and the church as an intercessory missional community. There is a high level of engagement. There is a faithful group of regular participants. There is a sense of God's presence in the prayer gathering. There is regular repentance and respect for His holiness, without celebrating sin. God is speaking and in some manner, there is a clear congregational sense of His voice. You are now moving toward a healthy prayer meeting. Keep praying and pushing toward the fifty-percent involvement threshold for complete breakthrough.

In addition to your weekly prayer meeting, plan a handful of congregational prayer events during the year. This mainstreams prayer, bringing it front and center, in an obvious, but gentle manner.

The Congregational Prayer Meeting: Common Mistakes

<u>Everyone brings expectations</u>, based on assumptions and past experiences, <u>to a prayer meeting</u>, and <u>those expectations often give birth to common mistakes</u>:

- <u>Making the prayer meeting about prayer requests</u>.

- <u>An intercessory prayer meeting</u> – not one focused first on corporate transformation and communion with God. The identification of intercessors and the launch of an intercessory prayer effort is not the same as a congregational prayer ministry – intercession alone is too narrow to describe the whole, and yet it is a vital part of any prayer ministry effort.

- <u>Prayer as wishing</u>. Prayers detached from scriptural principles and promises. Not doing consistent Bible-based praying.

- <u>Individuating</u> (a symptom of our culture), and not keeping the corporate in mind. Keep reminding the group: "We are not here merely as individuals, seeking after an answer to prayer; we are here as one, as a body, as the church, after the will of God for our mission together." This constitutes a declaration of war against pragmatic individualism, but a war that is worth fighting if you are to have a healthy *corporate* prayer meeting and not just a prayer gathering of differentiated individuals praying for their own needs and agenda in the same room.

- <u>Making one prayer style too important</u> – quiet and reflective prayer, powerful declarative prayer, spiritual warfare prayer, conversational prayer, concert prayer (everyone praying aloud at the same time; or no one who is courageous enough to pray aloud apart from a concert of voices).

- <u>Developing a prayer style rut</u> – failing to experience variety in prayer (the psalms involve both reflection and then militant prayer language; repentance, then jubilation, etc.). On the other hand, you will err by making the prayer experience exotic, dancing at the edges of prayer experimentation, failing to make the prayer gathering predictable at one level, and open to the Spirit's leadership at another.

Keep the Seven Critical Components of a Corporate Prayer Gathering in view:

1. *Invocation* – *the formal recognition of God's Presence,* and the surrender of the time and contour of the meeting to His leadership. The request for blessing and favor, the refusal to take for granted His Presence. The submission to do as He commanded, namely, to humbly, but boldly ask in faith, giving glory to Him!

2. *The Table* – the blood and the bread. Whether or not you have the elements of communion present or you conduct a communion event, *the church gathered in prayer is always gathered around the table-altar.* Moreover, around the invisible blood and bread. Prayer then must engage the blood – repentance, forgiveness, reconciliation, peace receiving and giving; and the broken bread – nourishment, prayer and scripture, praying scripture, etc., indeed, a call for our brokenness. There should be a confessional dimension to our praying – with a simultaneous acknowledgment of our sins and of God's dynamic grace; grace that not only forgives, but also liberates. Such grace deals with both the guilt and grip of sin. It both forgives of sin and fuels freedom from sin. It is at the table where we experience fellowship with Christ, the sense of his Spirit, where he ministers to us the cup and the bread, both an affirmation of our relationship and an expression of his

abiding presence. He is still at the table, nourishing his children. At the table, our prayer is made one. We pray as the bride partner of Christ, his body, and as the missional people of God. Here collective prayers are forged as one voice – the prayer of the church.

3. _Missional Praying_ – Praying the prayer Jesus taught us to pray and seeing its worshipful, missional content.

Jesus gave us a model for corporate prayer. We commonly call it, 'The Lord's Prayer.' In fact, it is 'our prayer.' Never once in the prayer do you find 'me,' 'my' or 'I.' The prayer begins with God and His kingdom and it ends with His "kingdom, power and glory." Our prayers are far too self-interested.

Notice the first few words, *"Our Father...who art...in heaven...holy."* In this preamble to prayer, we have both intimacy ("Our Father") and transcendence ("in heaven – holy"). Notice the divergent language of both warmth and wonder. The God to whom Jesus instructed us to pray is not impersonal, even if He is transcendent. He is revealed relationally, as the Father we all share.

"Our Father _who art_..." dwells outside of *time*, in eternity. He is *"in heaven"* – not only beyond the bounds of time, but also of *space*, in another dimension. Further, He is to be *'hallowed...'* – that is, He is holy, *utterly other*, transcendent, infinitely pure, morally and spiritually, ethically and pragmatically, beyond comprehension or comparison, immutable.

Here intimacy and transcendence all move toward mission. The earthly concerns we bring to prayer are not the primary concerns of true prayer, nor the biblical focus of prayer. They are secondary, subordinate to a more critical alignment. First, we must grasp God's fatherhood and that in the light of His glorious transcendent grandeur. Not one without the other. We pray in this tension – between intimacy and awe; the God that can be known and the God we can never fully know; our approachable Father, and the awful (awe-full), holy utterly other One. This is the backdrop of all prayer; the context in which it occurs.

The mission is that we might hallow His *name* (*"Hallowed be thy name"*), advance His kingdom (*"Thy kingdom come..."),* and do His will (*"Thy will be done..."*). Everything else that follows in the so-called 'Lord's Prayer' is subordinate. There are, in prayer, felt needs and for us, such pulsating needs often drive us to God in prayer. However, in the instruction of Jesus, they are not to be primary. The manner in which we carry His *name*, our passion for advancing His *kingdom*, our willingness to surrender by binding our will to His *will* are the filters through which our petitions must pass. Provision (daily bread), pardon (guilt-free relationships), and protection (from evil and the Evil One) are important, but subordinate requests. The provision, the inner peace and the protection are benefits offered to those who do His *will*, for the purpose of advancing His *kingdom* rule, and glorifying His *name*, and that out of an exalted, transcendent view of the nature of 'Our Father.'

Always remember, *prayer is at its heart worship; and at its edge mission*, and in between, God meets our needs. Move your congregation to worshipful prayer, then to missional praying. Consistently pray that each member lives in a way that honors the name of God; that corporately, as the bride-partner of Christ, we carry his name with dignity and integrity; that we live as representatives of His Kingdom – seeking to advance His rule in the earth, beginning in our own heart. That means binding our will to His will. Pray regularly to be a people of mission. A missional congregation. Adopt nations for prayer, as well as unreached people groups. Adopt the neighborhood around the church as a mission field.

4. *Petition/Needs* – the corporate prayer time should *focus first on God's agenda*, not on personal needs. Yet, personal needs should not be omitted. Have folks pray for one another's prayer requests in small groups, as a regular feature in the prayer gathering. Mention before the entire group only the more critical needs. If prayer requests begin to take over your meeting, narcissism and self-interested praying will kill it. At that point, consider

making prayer for personal needs an afterglow with elders or leaders, and retain the integrity of the prayer gathering as transformational and missional. All petitions and supplications must be wrapped with thanksgiving. No legitimate request is acceptable without the reflection on God's past grace. Gratitude is the partner to petition. It is faith's support, and prayer without faith is futile.

5. <u>*Anointing*</u> – first, *there is an anointing to pray as surely as there is an anointing to preach.* You want to move to a point in corporate prayer where God is anointing the prayers and the participants. Here, the church is edified – praying around the table altar, over the bread (word), in and by the enabling of the Spirit. Of course, you may want to offer anointing to those present – for upcoming missions, for sickness, for the fullness of the Spirit, needs (direction, provision, protection, etc.). The hand of the shepherd/elder on the sheep in tender care is a comfort.

6. <u>*Pastoral Blessing*</u> – this is the expression horizontally of what has been requested vertically. *It is the bestowal, out of the pastoral office, of God's promised blessing.* You may use the Biblical language, *"The Lord bless you and keep you; The Lord make His face shine upon you, and be gracious to you; The Lord lift up His countenance upon you, and give you peace."* Numbers 6:24-26. You may use the language of a psalm.

7. <u>*Benediction*</u> – by definition, is <u>the utterance or bestowing of a blessing, especially at the end of a religious service</u>. It is a devout or formal invocation of blessedness. The word *bless* in Hebrew, is *barak*, meaning knee. To go to one's knee, thus, to pray, is to position oneself for a blessing from God. The purpose of the blessing is that we might be fruitful (evidencing inner life and growth), that we might multiply (evangelism), that we might live in an empowered state, not as victims, that we would see the world as our parish, and spiritual authority in our tool-kit, that we would worship and serve, evangelize and make disciples of the nations.

Bless those who come to a prayer meeting. Build in them a confidence in God's watchful love and care.

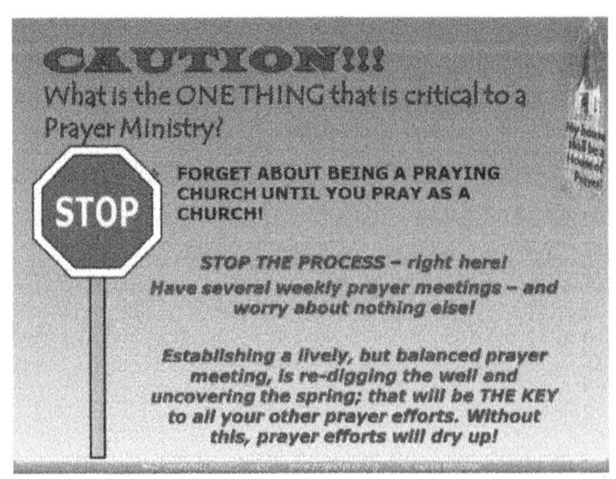

Start a prayer meeting. Don't worry about the numbers. Forget about being a praying church until you have a prayer meeting – meeting to pray as a congregation.

 **YOU ARE NOW AT A CHECK POINT!**

Establishing a lively, but balanced prayer meeting, is re-digging the well and uncovering the spring; that will be THE KEY to all your other prayer efforts.

Without this, all your other prayer efforts will dry up! Here, the congregation, or at least a core, enough to make a difference in the direction of the church and its purpose and mission, will hear God together. They will experience His Presence, together. They will learn prayer models – even if that is not the primary purpose of the gathering. Find a style that fits your congregational personality – that is biblical and principled. Pray!

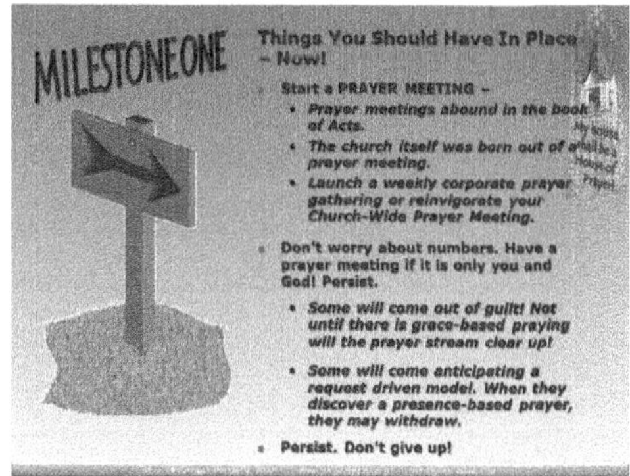

A simple model for your congregational prayer gathering.

- 10 minutes – the preparation of the heart in thanksgiving, <u>praise and worship</u>.

- 15-20 minutes – <u>Praying from the Bible</u>. Don't preach – pray! Use a Bible passage as a model for prayer. Read and pray. You are both engaging scripture and being engaged by it – and not in a passive manner. We are changed over open Bibles in prayer.

- 15-20 minutes – <u>Mission Prayer – Intercession</u>. Praying for others. This is not 'prayer requests' in the typical sense, it is missional praying. Pray for a nation, an unreached people group, for the lost friends and family, for members to be missionaries where they live and work.

- 15-20 minutes – <u>Petitions – Pray for one another and personal needs</u>. Offer prayer for the sick and for special needs. It is not a healthy balance to either ignore personal needs or to make them, and thus 'us', the first agenda item in prayer. There are people among us who are hurting.

- 5-10 minutes – Spend time in <u>worship and thanksgiving</u>. Leave on a positive note. Leave with a focus turned away from needs, back toward God.

- For those who not in a hurry, offer a season to tarry before the Lord.

Notice the movement: Thanksgiving and Worship; Transformational Bible-based Prayer; Intercessory Missional Prayer; Personal Needs; Praise and Worship; Waiting before the Lord. Listening.

MILESTONE TWO
Develop a Prayer Leadership-Learning Team

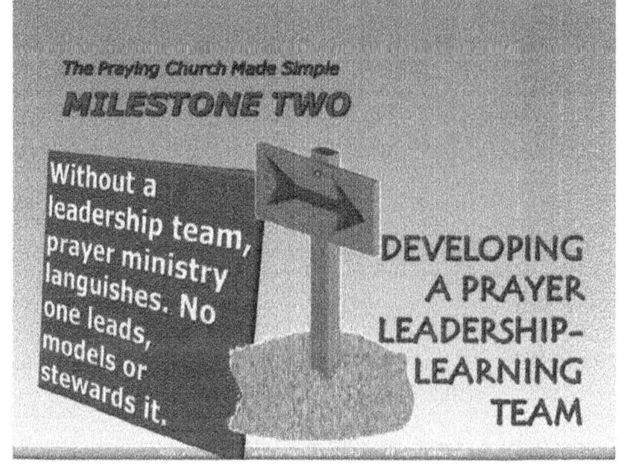

Proposition

Every congregation needs a group of people stewarding and championing prayer – personal prayer, couple's prayer, the family altar, parents blessing their children, corporate prayer, prayer groups, intercessory prayer, prayer support for every ministry in the church, prayer evangelism, praying walking, prayer missions, community-focused prayer, praying for those in authority, crisis prayer – and more. To be a congregation, not merely with a prayer *ministry*, but to be a praying church, means prayer must permeate the life of the congregation and reach into the community and around the world – and that requires intentionality. It is more than prayer as an

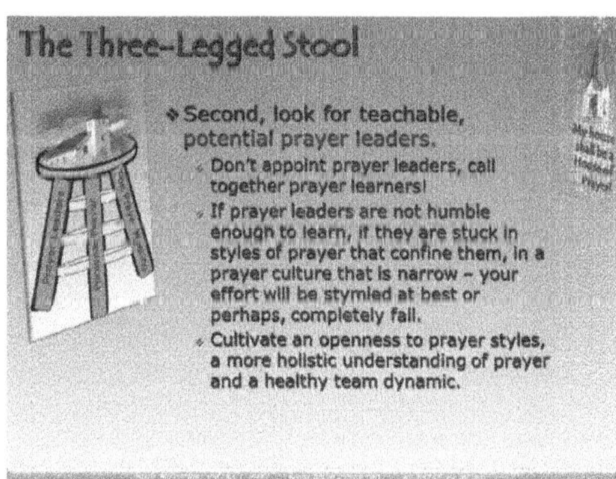

activity – it is the creation and preservation of a culture of prayer.

Timing

Plan to <u>take as long as a year to identify potential prayer leaders</u>, meet together, train and team them. If you are using the quarterly Prayer Leader Continuing Education (PLCE)[1] materials or participating in a learning group, plan to meet in the intervening months for prayer and learning.

Resources

If you are using <u>the PLCE materials</u>, then you probably have a PROJECT PRAY certified trainer resident on your developing prayer leadership-learning team. That's a major plus. In your congregational learning team, you will always want to consider reviewing the materials covered during any recent quarterly meeting (videos, handouts, Power Point, new resources, etc.), especially those in the trainer's guide that may not have been covered adequately or may need reinforcing. Your certified resident trainer will have a copy of the PLCE Trainer's Manual with those resources.

Another helpful curriculum resource are the six lessons called *Learning Team* materials (found in the *Praying Church Resource Guide*). That guide may be the most comprehensive collection of resource materials for a prayer leadership team available anywhere. It is a 700-page compendium of practical prayer materials. It is available at www.alivepublications.org.

You may also choose to use the book, *Transforming Your Church into a House of Prayer - the Revised Edition*; or, *The Praying Church Made Simple* by P. Douglas Small.

To prevent a narrow focus, you need a curriculum for your prayer leadership training. This is *internal* learning

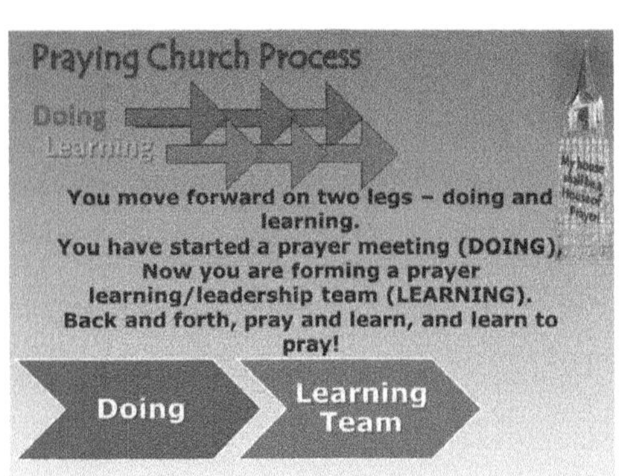

---

1   If your community does not have a PLCE training effort – start one. Get your leaders certified. Contact Project Pray (www.projectpray.org) and ask for information on the Praying Church Movement and PLCE.

As you meet with your small group of potential prayer leaders, remember the following:

- The most important element is **relational.**

- The second is a learned **appreciation for the value of prayer** – and at the heart of that value is a celebration of God's love and a developing passion for Him. Short and simple. Create a group who will 'catch' your passion for the Lord!

- The third element is the invisible glue of grace that flows in the room. It is a **cultivated respect – the ethos** that we have spoken of, the kind of atmosphere and relational health that you would like to characterize the entire church. This intangible will hardly be recognized by most. It is like the wallpaper, like the air we breathe – it is mostly noticeable in its toxic absence. "'Lot of tension in the room tonight, honey, wasn't there?'... 'I don't think they like one another very much!'...'Wonder what she was so stressed about?'...'Can you believe what he did/what they said?'" Pride and conflict appear like flashing lights and screaming sirens; humility and unity are more like a quiet, comforting stream, sadly, hardly noticed. As much as you want to get to *content,* you must give priority to cultivating culture – a prayer culture. You are redefining Christianity from a performance (doing; works) and content (knowing) basis to that of humility and dependence (being) on God, yet not without bold confidence and solid faith.

- The fourth element is **content.** Stretch the group's theology of prayer. Expand their prayer experiences. So, of course, a part of your time together is teaching/training. As you teach, look for those who are most teachable. You will discover several different types of folks in the room. Superficial learners and profound learners – the latter group will take learning seriously and apply it to their lives. You will discover those who learn with their head and others who learn with their hearts. You will discover those who are ready learners, some because they have no prior learning about prayer or prayer models, theology or philosophy. Others will be 'resistant learners.' They may be struggling with prior learning about prayer; stretched, by new ideas. They behave like someone trying to find a place to rest an object that is both heavy and fragile. They don't have a ready mental slot for the idea; they need more even though you are using outside resources. Two dynamics will occur. Objective learning will occur. Equally important is the subjective learning that is occurring.

The small core of prayer leader-learners is developing a collective mindset about prayer and their prayer effort using these resources – and their chemistry and spiritual unity is as critical to success as the objective ideas they collectively own. Subsequently, they will, as a group, explore living prayer models. When they do explore prayer rooms and centers, the prayer ministries of other congregations, you will find both their exposure to objective principles and the chemistry they have developed, including trust and value congruence extremely valuable. It will be the grid they use for evaluation. It will help them stay centered, processing the information as a group, not merely as individuals, discovering best practices from fads. Be selective about the ideas you import.

Duration

<u>Meet together at least ninety minutes, once monthly</u>, for one year or more as a learning team. You may, at times, focus, for example, on prayer evangelism, perhaps, with one or two members of the group; prayer ministry team development with a key leader; men or women's prayer efforts, etc. CAUTION: Don't allow sidebar meetings to take over your primary training.

Style

<u>Keep the style of the meeting informal</u> enough to encourage personality blending – teaming is a key element here. Your goal is not merely downloading *information*, rather, it is life *formation*. Balance praying together as a potential leadership team and learning together – and observe how the team relates, both to one another and to the conceptual material.

Focus

<u>The focus is on the development of a prayer leadership team</u>. In this year of prayer leader development, you are

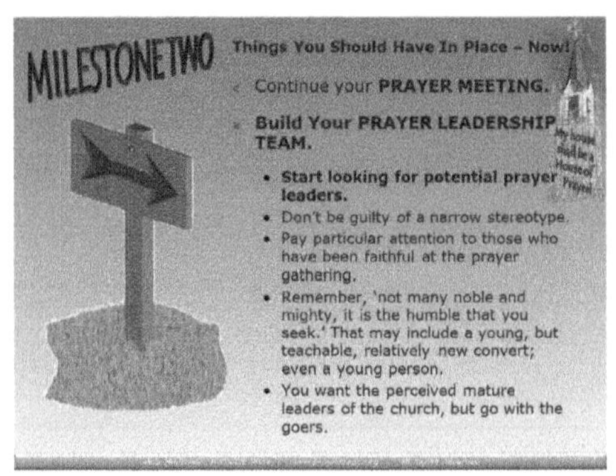

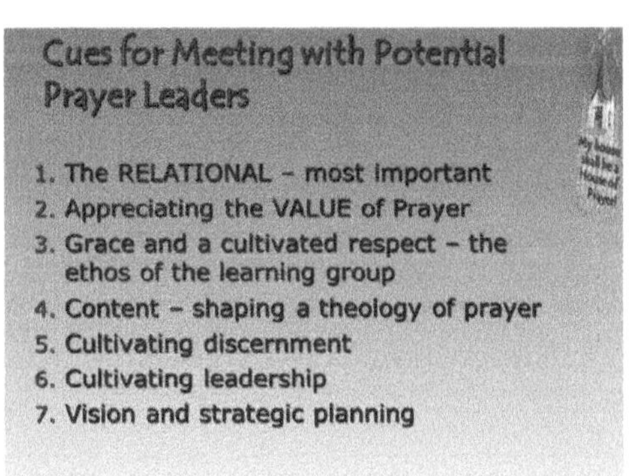

time to process. Keep investing in the heart learners who struggle to think through the material (Learning Team Materials, Coaching, etc.).

- The fifth element is **the cultivation of discernment**. Do you have a group that, first of all, discerns truth? They will begin to have 'aha' moments as you proceed to unwrap the theology of prayer and proceed with 'learning team' content? They will also make connections to pieces of truth they already possess. You can see them taking their prayer puzzle apart and putting it back together with new pieces. They develop an ability to disagree agreeably. They state principles of truth in love. They hold to certain convictions but in a complimentary, not contradictory, way. They see the value of teaming. They discern one another's gifts; they add value to one another. A teaming culture develops.

- The sixth element is **leadership** and cultivating prayer leaders. Who in your group can teach the material to others? Who can lead or organize? Who will make a great partner to a leader/organizer? Who leads with grace? Who are the finishers? Finishers are folks who understand the principles but are not stage folks. They pick up the stragglers, move along the edge of the crowd and settle those who misunderstood or need a bit more personal attention. They are like shepherd leaders who bring up the rear. They keep people from falling through the cracks. They are great glue in a social group. They love everyone.

- The seventh element is **vision and strategic planning**. Once a 'big picture' of prayer (vision) emerges, and you see the exploding possibilities of prayer ministry and how it relates to all the other aspects of ministry, you need a 'big picture plan' (strategy) that conceptualizes how the parts fit together and how they are unwrapped tactically. For example, do you start with prayer walking or with the mobilization of intercessors? Do you train in prayer basics or spiritual warfare? Values clarify vision. Vision (the big *picture)* needs strategy (a big picture *plan)*, and strategy is unwrapped piece by piece (tactics). Each tactical component and its leader should know how the prayer cause they lead relates to others. For example, if we fail in getting men to pray, it is unlikely that we will succeed with the family altar! If we fail in training healthy intercessors and mobilizing them, our efforts in prayer evangelism will face great challenges.

exploring and testing the growth capacity of your learning team. Who is capable of change – embracing new paradigms, new ideas and ways to pray? Who is capable of leadership – of the entire prayer effort? Of one particular aspect - training, championing men or women's prayer, family prayer, prayer evangelism, youth or children's prayer? Who among your group leads? Who, in the group, do all respect? Who is teachable? Who could lead the entire effort, stewarding prayer for the church, with deference for pastoral leadership? Don't rush – people grow and change slowly.

Involvement Goals

Begin your recruitment effort for your prayer leadership-learning team from those who show up at your prayer meeting. Leaders who are not motivated enough to attend the prayer meeting will not lead the church into prayer. They can't. We lead by example – especially in the area of prayer. As you look at those in attendance, you may find veteran intercessors next to new converts, week after week. Ask the Lord to direct you, regarding who should be involved in the prayer leadership effort. Based on the number in your congregation, use these ratios:

Congregational Size:

- 0-50   Team of 3/5 (with the pastor)
- 50-100   Team of 4-7
- 100-200   Team of 5-8
- 200-500   Team of 7-12
- 500 plus   Team of 12 or more

Constituency

- Leaders and intercessors;
- Prayer-evangelists;
- Those with a positive devotional life;
- Those who might be capable of resourcing/teaching;
- Those who might lead youth/children in prayer;
- Those who might engage men/women/and families in prayer;

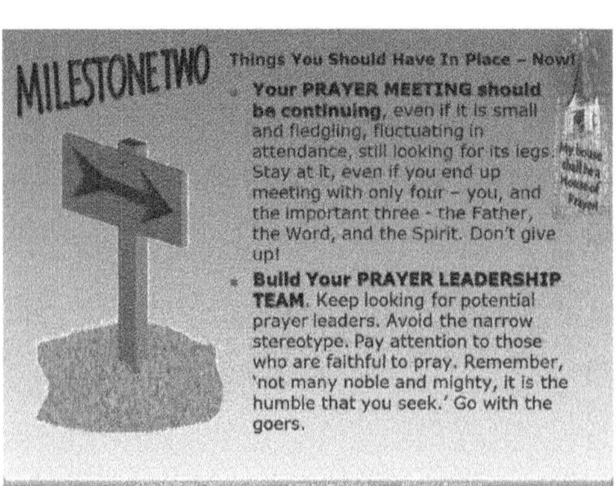

- Someone who might help you establish a prayer room/center.

Keep these hunches about prayer leaders between you and the Lord. Watch and pray. These ratios are only a suggestion. You may begin with a larger number – it is very common to see people begin with an interest in prayer and prayer leadership, but drop out. They may be sprinters; you are looking for a marathon team. And it is not uncommon to see a group of potential prayer leaders suddenly experience an assortment of highly consuming and distracting life events – the fingerprints on such uncanny happenings are often from the Evil One. From the beginning, your prayer effort, particularly, your leadership team will be fraught with spiritual warfare. The typical prayer leadership-learning team will fall apart about three times before it solidifies.

Allow your leadership learning team to expand and contract, allow some to come and go, and then perhaps, come again. This is God's work. You may have a 'no-show' night or two. Pray. Don't fret. Only God can raise a church from the dead. What an opportunity!

Transition

<u>Your prayer leadership-*learning* team should evolve into a prayer research and *planning* team</u> – plotting the growth of your effort for the next 3-5 years. That planning team should evolve into the prayer *leadership* team. See the *Praying Church Resource Guide* and *Transforming Your Church into a House of Prayer – Revised Edition,* for more details about this transition.

Perhaps, more importantly, your prayer learning team must grow.

- First, you want them to experience 'personal revival' out of daily prayer. You want them to evidence loving God with all their heart, and that means quality time with God.

- You also want them to experience a 'relational revival' whereby they love one another more fervently. We are called to 'love our neighbor as ourselves,' but Jesus raises the bar, telling us that we are to 'love our enemies.'

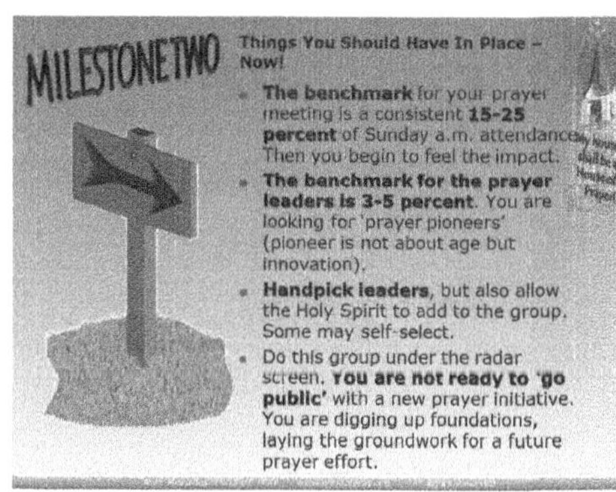

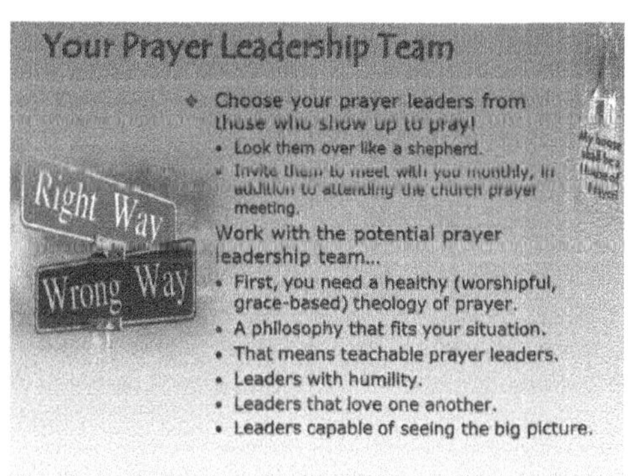

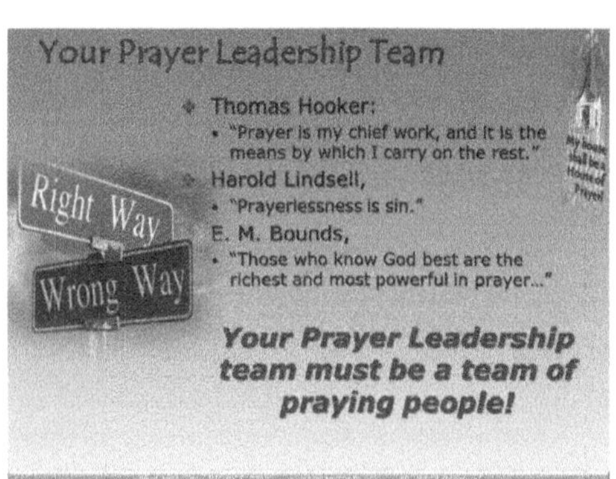

- You also want them to experience a 'missional revival' in which they see folks around them as lost, as needing God's love.

Truly saved people sing better – even if they can't sing. There is a song of love and joy exuding from them. They also fellowship better, and more deeply. They not only sing; they harmonize. They make music together. And they are contagious. The music of saved people proliferates.

This is cultural renewal. It is awakening. It is life – from the inside out, infectious, communicable, transmittable prayer. It is a formula (personal, relational, missional) for your congregational prayer meeting and a developmental grid for your leaders – the person and God; the congregation in fellowship and God; the world and God through the church.

You also need *structural* renewal – <u>but that is secondary</u>. There is little need to work on structural renewal before you sense revival. You will never infect a congregation with God's Presence by making structural changes to your prayer ministry - merely appointing new leaders, calling for more prayer activities, reorganizing your prayer effort. You must affect the culture and then the new wine will demand a new wineskin. Pray. Keep praying. Pray until you feel the difference in prayer – in your own prayer, in the prayers of your learning leaders, and the prayers in the budding congregational prayer meeting.

The typical church begins with structural renewal. It assumes, wrongly, that all is well with the soul of the church. It does not have the patience to persist in the cultivation of a fresh, heavenly culture of prayer; nor the discernment to recognize the need for profound change in their own hearts as leaders.

Common Mistakes

- <u>The most common mistake is not praying about who to invite to a prayer leadership-learning team.</u>

- The second most common mistake is being too casual – too indiscriminate. <u>Don't invite everyone</u>. Be intentional. Select the potential leaders one-by-one. Keep the meetings and the training off the public radar screen, but not necessarily secret.

That is probably impossible in a small congregation. Do involve some key leaders – staff as appropriate, elders/deacons/church council, others. While you do not want to invite everyone *carte blanche,* don't exclude that off-the-radar screen person that wants to be involved.

- Third, make it clear – "I am not asking you to *lead* this...just to meet with me to discuss our need to be more intentional about our prayer process." If you plan to participate in the PLCE effort, add, "We will also be attending a quarterly gathering with other churches who are also exploring the same transformational goals." We want to keep asking, "Is our congregation praying? Are we a house of prayer? If this is a Biblical mandate, will we do this or ignore it?'"

- <u>Make it clear that this is a *learning* team</u>. Self-declare "I too, am a student." If you start your process with prayer *experts*, you will fail. "<u>Our times demand new prayer protocols. Everyone must come with a servant-student heart.</u>"

- In your leadership learning effort, work on component parts of prayer ministry, but <u>keep the big-picture in mind</u>. Some on the team will gravitate to some prayer ministry piece – that might be their calling, their burden. That's good news – you need a team, each member with a passion for their slice of the prayer effort. Keep looking for those who value the pieces, but <u>keep the whole vision in view</u>.

- Don't allow your prayer leadership effort to shrink to a devotional prayer effort, an intercessory prayer effort, a prayer-requests exchange, a prayer partner ministry. The temptation is to climb the lesser mountain. Be daring. <u>Set the goal as the transformation of the church into a house of prayer</u> – a praying congregation made up of praying homes.

- Information is an important goal – cognitive learning, new prayer insights and approaches, but equally important is the quality of relationships that the team develops. <u>You want a non-competitive, collaborative team</u> that values one another, and one another's contribution to the whole.

- <u>Don't learn – and not pray</u>. Praying together, in the formative season of your prayer leadership effort, is

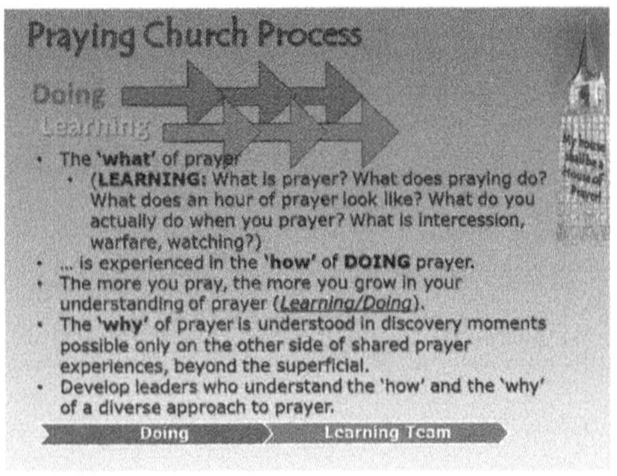

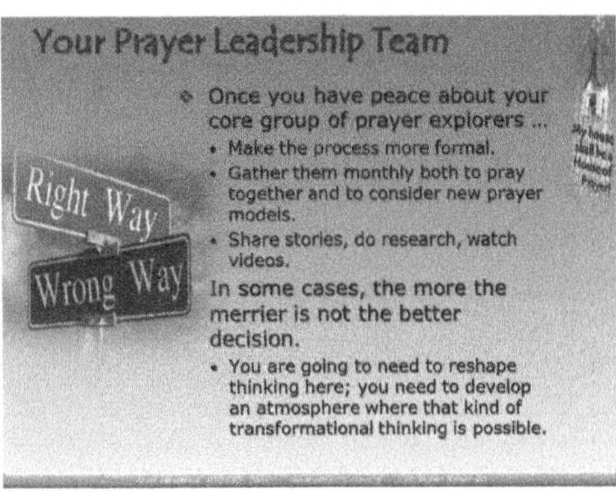

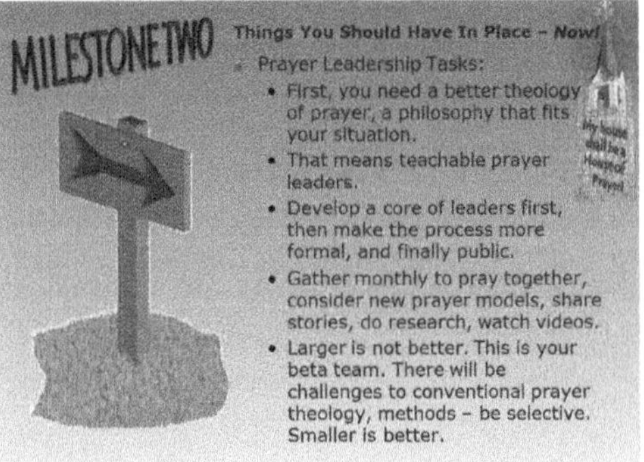

as important as the learning effort. Do and learn, and then learn and do.

- <u>Learn deliberately, systematically</u>. Use the *Praying Church Resource Guide* or the book, *Transforming Your Church into a House of Prayer – Revised Edition,* or, the *Praying Church Made Simple.*

- Learn the 'what' of prayer; the 'how' of prayer, and most importantly, the 'why' of prayer.

You should now have a group of developing, learning leaders in place. Each month as you meet with them you are helping them examine their prayer practices, all to the end that they develop a healthy theology of prayer. To lead they must be teachable. And to be a team, they must be humble toward one another. Pray with them. Envision them. Teach them. Go deep before you go public.

You move forward on two legs – doing prayer and learning about prayer and prayer ministry leadership. Do personal and corporate prayer. When you meet with your leadership team – learn together. Grow in your understanding of prayer and allow this group to make that journey with you. Of course, doing prayer is by far the more important. You catch prayer. You learn to pray by praying. Some things are not taught, they are caught.

There is little doubt the western church, and probably your congregation and the leaders you will begin with, need a better theology of prayer. You will need to develop a philosophy of prayer ministry that fits your situation. That will require teachable prayer leaders. Develop this core of leaders first. Then make the process of moving to the congregation more formal. Gather with this learning team monthly to pray together, consider new prayer models, share stories, do research and watch training-teaching videos.

The more the merrier is not the better decision. You are going to need to reshape thinking here. You need an atmosphere where transformational thinking is possible.

MILESTONE THREE
The Personal Prayer Life Challenge

Proposition

Congregational prayer must have a partner in personal prayer, indeed, in family prayer. <u>Public prayer without private roots is a house without a foundation</u> (Mt. 7:24-27). This hidden part of our lives, our depth in Christ, allows us to be an able vessel through which Christ works. A church can never be a house of prayer without praying people and praying homes; and a church will never be prayerless if it has praying people and praying homes. The missing ingredient in most prayer ministry plans is the absence of an adequate emphasis on personal prayer space (prayer closet), the power of a couple praying together, the family altar and family worship. This is the most challenging aspect of the prayer effort, the most difficult stake to drive. Simultaneously, it is the wellspring,

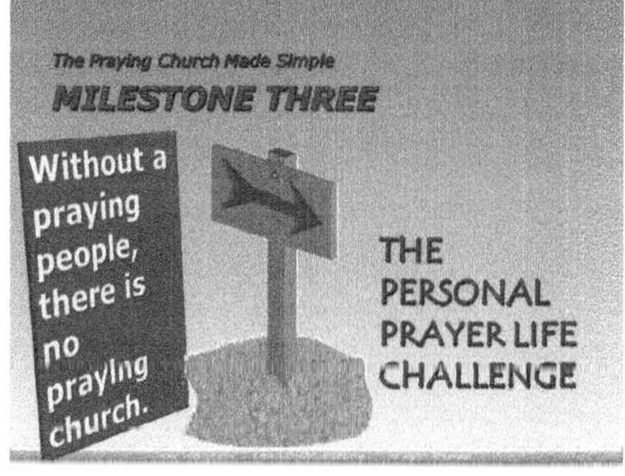

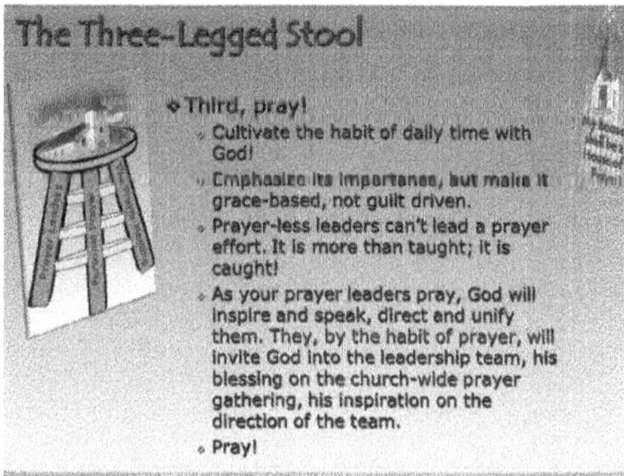

which will provide the most water. <u>Prayerless people can never lead a prayer ministry effort.</u> You may be able to survive on Sunday-to-Sunday Bible and prayer engagement, but you can never thrive at such a minimal level. Eventually, the souls of the people will dry up and the church itself will die – or morph into something less than vital New Testament Christianity.

Timing

You started your prayer ministry effort with a prayer meeting! A grace-based prayer gathering open to the entire congregation. You searched the attendees – and identified a prayer leader-learning team and you still may be recruiting to that team. Now, in both the church-wide praying gathering and the leader-learning team meetings, <u>emphasize the importance of a disciplined, daily time with God in prayer.</u>

Keep coming back to this, gently, but relentlessly, "To lead prayer, we must be people of prayer. How are we doing with our daily devotional time with God?" It cannot be a matter of legalism, a 'have to.' It must be a 'want to.' You cannot have a praying church without praying homes. Sadly, we avoid this, due to our own dismal record at daily prayer. This cannot be avoided. If you attempt to build a public prayer effort without a hidden life of prayer, it will fail. Personal prayer is the hidden foundation for the house of prayer, the private and personal precede the public. In private, before God daily, we *demonstrate* dependence on Him. We invite Him into the daily routine our lives, refusing to take Him for granted. We declare our love for Him, prayerfully. A personal love relationship with the Lord is spelled T-I-M-E. The corporate is the personal writ large. The church is not an entity apart from its members. If its members are praying people, it is a praying church; and if they are not meeting with God, it is not a praying church. These feed each other – the personal and the corporate; the private and the public; demonstrated dependence on God. We cannot

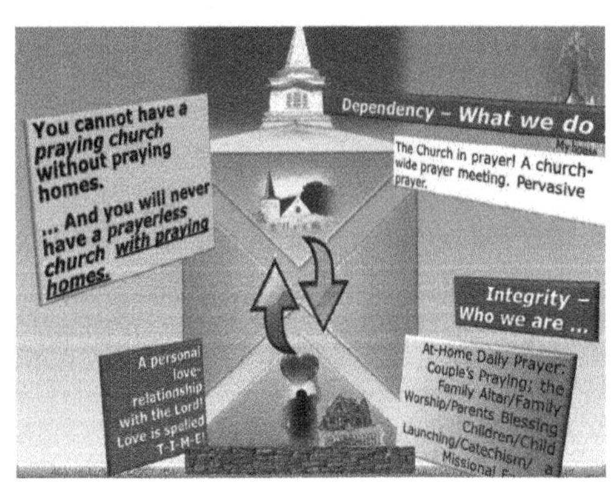

claim, with integrity, to be the people of God if we spend no quality time with God.

Your weekly prayer gathering should also encourage daily personal prayer time – and the daily prayer times of the people will feed the fervor of the church-wide prayer gathering. Your leadership team should encourage each other onward in daily personal prayer. As you move forward, you will want to consistently invite the entire congregation to join the weekly, church-wide prayer gathering, and to spend time with God daily. Every gracious mention of these prayer emphases sets the bar higher and feeds the message – "We intend, by God's grace, to be a praying church."

Resources

<u>Choose resources</u> to promote the practice of daily personal prayer time with God and the creation of a prayer space. Consider simple materials, such as *Our Daily Bread* (odb.org). This classic resource is available online and as an app on Twitter. Consider *Seek God for the City*, an evangelism prayer guide produced annually in the season of Lent (waymakers.org). A great couple's prayer resource, though dated, is *Moments Together for Couples*, by Dennis and Barbara Rainey. They have other devotional materials for family life as well. Simply using an annual Bible reading guide is a starting place. Encourage men to read a Proverb a day for a month. Three psalms a week is another threshold recipe. The Navigators have many helpful personal prayer resources (www.navigators. org/Tools/Prayer%20Resources). Prayercast is a web source of videos to pray for the nations of the world (www. prayercast.com). Find a great personal prayer guide from Pastor Chris Hodges (open.life.church/items/120348-personal-prayer-guide-pdf). Another great location for such resources is the North American Mission Board (www.namb.net/prayer/resources). Also consider the Global Prayer Resources website (www.globalprn.com/ prayer-resources) as well as the World Network website (www.worldnetworkofprayer.com/personal-prayer).

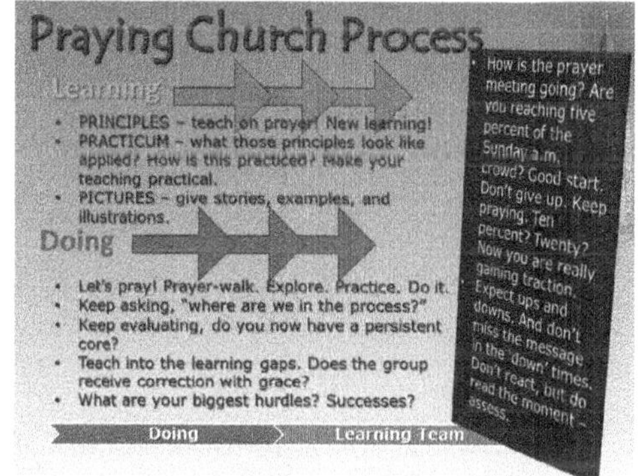

A number of resources from Alive Publications might be helpful. The book *The Prayer Closet* is a guide for creating a personal prayer room and understanding its importance. *Transforming Your Personal Prayer Life* is a guide to developing a healthy, balanced personal prayer practice, loaded not only with practical and Biblical concepts, but also with prayer exercises. Both these books have study guides and support materials for group studies. The latter also has a video component. One other book, *Entertaining God and Influencing Cities*, is designed to see prayer as hosting God's Presence. It rises out of the principles found in Genesis 18. It can be used as a basis for Bible study.

Duration

<u>Once a year, do a gentle church-wide personal and family prayer emphasis</u>. Invite, indeed, challenge folks to spend time with God daily and urge couples to pray together. If men will lead a family time, wives and children most often participate willingly.

1. Call the men together and introduce the simple idea of daily prayer. (Men's Prayer Group resources: www.maninthemirror.org/a-look-in-the-mirror/220-how-to-lead-a-weekly-mens-small-group). Gateway Church offers a number of prayer resources for men, including a 'Field Manual for Your Home' (gatewaypeople.com/ministries/men/mens-resources).

2. Consider the '<u>40-day Prayer Covenant</u>' (theprayercovenant.org) materials – a simple but powerful prayer partner plan. Do this first – man-to-man, perhaps in quads. Then, introduce this to couples. In doing so, in the space of three months you will experience covenant-partner praying, man-to-man, perhaps also woman-to-woman, teen-to-teen; and then, use the same materials to introduce simple covenant praying between couples and then family members.

3. Do a couple's prayer evening to introduce the idea – and then reconvene at the end of the 40 days. Here is a great resource (www.coupleprayer.com/series). Here some additional adaptable materials (www.

umesupport.com/and-when-you-pray). Here is a LifeWay resource to start the process (www.lifeway.com/Article/marriage-prayer-how-to-pray-together).

4. Encourage members of your prayer leadership learning team to do a personal prayer retreat during the first year. You will find resources for this in the *Praying Church Resource Guide,* Personal and Family section. Here is a simple resource from Christianity Today (www.christianitytoday.com/pastors/2016/april-web-exclusives/how-do-i-take-prayer-retreat.html). Here is an extensive layout of materials and suggestions, including a schedule (www.christianitytoday.com/pastors/2016/april-web-exclusives/how-do-i-take-prayer-retreat.html).

5. Host a family prayer meeting in which all the members of each participating family sit together, take time to pray together, perhaps discuss the ideas of praying together, of faith as a family, the legacy of the family's faith. Find an article on family prayer at Focus on the Family (family.custhelp.com/app/answers/detail/a_id/26005/~/praying-together-as-a-family). Another discussion starter for praying together can be found at www.beliefnet.com/love-family/galleries/6-benefits-of-praying-together-as-a-family.aspx.

All of these ideas are introductory. Don't attempt at this point to launch an intercessory ministry or yet, a family prayer ministry, prayer evangelism or a prayer group ministry – that will come later. At this point, you are tasting samples! It is premature to attempt to organize these into subsets of your prayer ministry effort. The water is not warm enough!

Watch the response as you engage your member families in these various prayer experiences. At this point, many don't even understand the importance of prayer covenants, of couple's praying together, of prayer evangelism. You are looking for clues of receptivity and resistance, and your response must be that of grace. The meaning of their embrace or avoidance of prayer ideas will not be clear this early in the process – for some it may simply be nostalgia, but without a willingness to learn;

John Wooden, the great coach at UCLA, a believer, said, "When you improve a little each day, eventually big things occur...Don't look for quick, big improvement. Seek the small improvement one day at a time. That's the only way it happens — and when it happens, it lasts." The power is in 'small visible goals' that build momentum.

—   Chip Heath and Dan Heath, *Switch: How to Change Things When Change is Hard* (New York: Broadway, 2010), 144.

for others, it may be a lack of experience with prayer, a fear of the unknown.

Focus

Keep the focus on the development of a daily transformational prayer life by the members of your congregation, and eventually, the resurrection, in many cases, of the family altar. This is a process. It will take more than a few weeks to re-center the family in vital daily faith. Don't give up.

Think in terms of concentric circles. First, begin to emphasize daily, personal prayer with your emerging prayer leadership-learning team. Be patient. Not all of them will adopt the habit of daily prayer, at least, not quickly. Remember, it takes 66 days, on average, for a person to own a new habit.

Begin with these leader-learners. Then, challenge the congregational prayer meeting attendees. Finally, engage the Sunday morning congregation in the idea of daily personal prayer. Monitoring the disposition of staff and lay leaders to you calls for personal, at-home prayer.

Two groups are critical to congregational change, and that means they must take seriously their daily prayer times. Those groups are your church staff and your lay leaders (board, council, elders, deacons, etc.). The church cannot go where leaders are not leading. Take this slowly. Ultimatums do not work here. Give the Holy Spirit time and room to convict hearts. Lead by your own habit.

You are working to enlarge the circle of people who are engaging in daily time with God as a holy and happy habit. You are also vision casting with your leaders. Your goal is a multi-layered family prayer culture in your congregation.

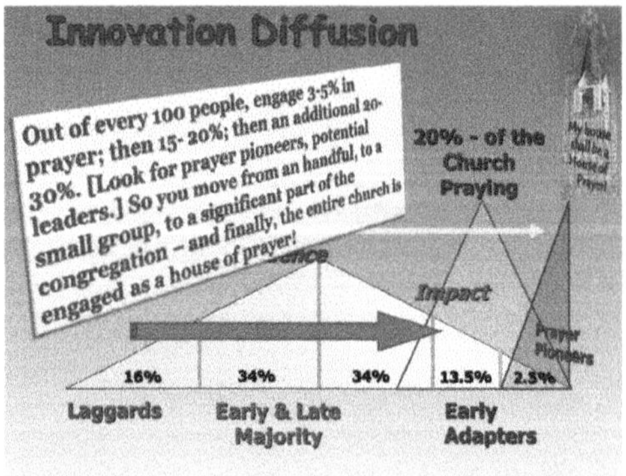

Involvement Goals

Begin your personal-family prayer effort, as before, with your prayer leadership-learning team, and encourage those who show up at your prayer meeting to meet God daily. You are moving each person and family, over a period of months and years, from personal daily prayer to establishing a family altar and becoming praying,

<u>missional families</u>. This is upward growth, into transformation. Simultaneously, you are engaging the entire congregation in this process, incrementally.

When you reach the 20 percent threshold – you will begin to feel change. And that will be true at each level and with each outlying concentric circle (diagram above).

Transition

Never abandon the cultivation of the personal prayer life of leaders or members – never. Do <u>transition through a building emphasis on the seven levels of family prayer and faith engagement</u>; and outward, from prayer leaders modeling personal and family prayer, to other congregational leaders and to the congregation, and finally, to how the faith of family and congregational life impacts the community.

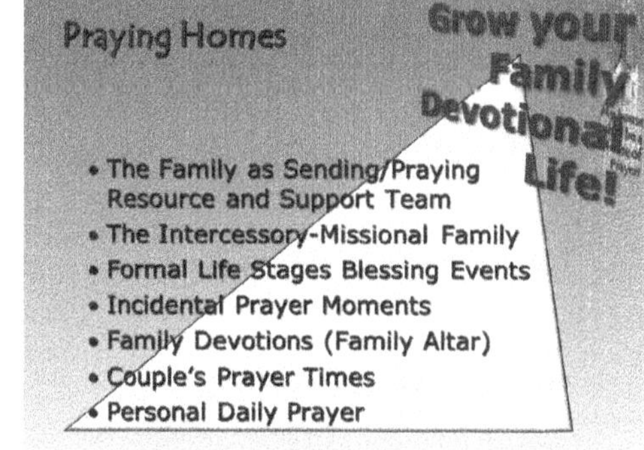

Common Misconceptions:

- <u>The most common mistake is thinking, "No one knows that I do not practice, regular, personal, daily prayer</u>." Or, "I can make it without daily prayer: I can fake it." Such pride and self-sufficiency is deadly. God knows that you speak for him, represent him, but never talk to him. You may talk at him, bark commands heavenward, submit work orders – but you do not evidence a longing to meet with him privately, for no reason other than to love Him. You are about public ministry, not the hidden life of prayer. One day, that catches up with all of us.

- <u>Another mistake is all or nothing</u>. Perfectionism, another way pride manifests, is to say, "I must have some kind of advanced personal prayer life or I will not set myself forward as a prayer leader." It is in the context of learning about prayer and prayer leadership that we grow in prayer. No one will ever have a 'perfect' prayer life – such an emphasis is on performance, and prayer is not about performance, it is a relationship. It is not something we 'master' as we master algebra or chemistry or some subject. God is the subject of prayer – and He is past finding out. Start the prayer journey – humbly, as a learner.

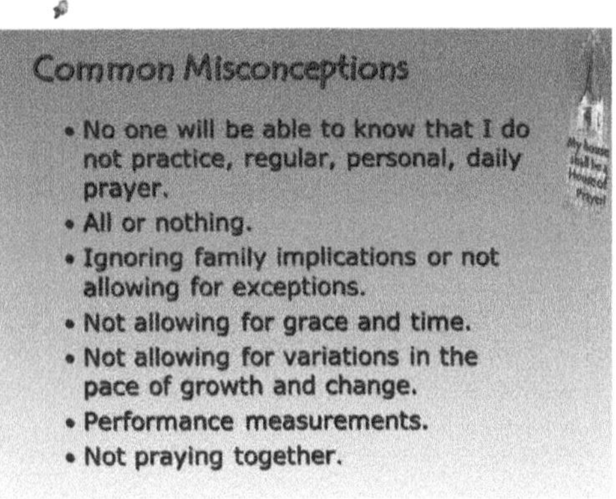

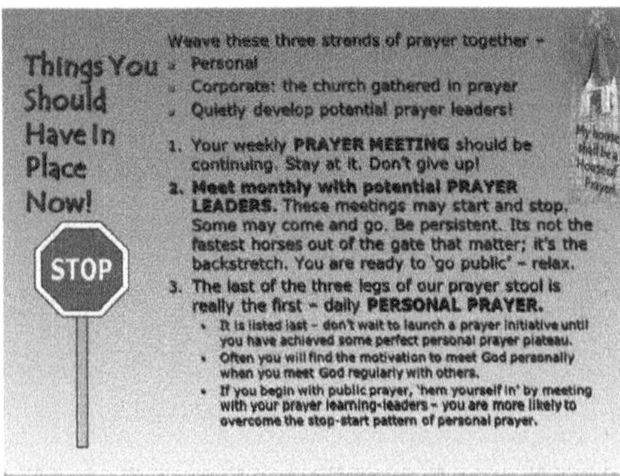

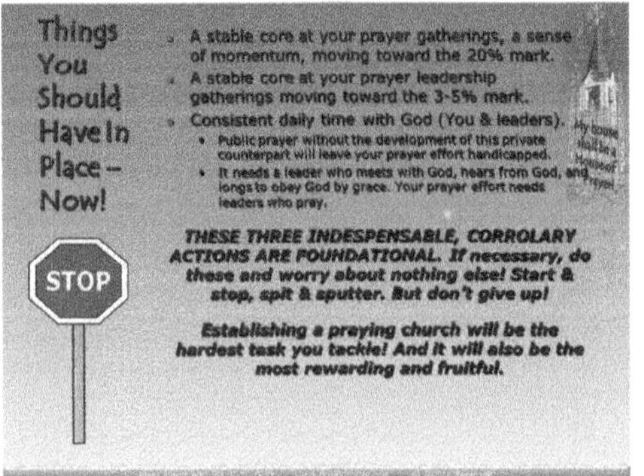

- <u>Yet another mistake is either ignoring the family implications or making them all-important</u>. You may have a potential prayer leader who is single or whose spouse is not a practicing Christian. They may be immediately challenged by the difficulty of a family altar in their situation. We certainly need prayer leaders who can develop father-mother, faith-family models; but the reality of our current culture is brokenness. Do not make the ideal model an inflexible rule – you also need single parents who are models of prayer; and believers who find ways, despite the unbelief of a spouse, to integrate prayer into their homes and engage their kids as well. <u>Allow for exceptions to the ideal, but don't make exceptions the rule</u> – or you will lose the Biblical ideal; and don't make the rule a legalistic yardstick, make it a flexible principle.

- <u>Allow for grace – and time</u>. As you begin to establish personal prayer closets, altars, engage spouses and families in prayer, share your success stories and your setbacks. Become one another's support teams. Remember, less than ten percent of American Christians have anything resembling a family altar today. A few centuries ago, mainline churches might refuse to serve communion or baptize family members if you did not certify that you practiced your faith at home. Then, the absence of prayer and faith practices in the daily lives and homes of members was interpreted as the absence of any meaningful faith. How far we have fallen. Begin the journey back to the historic and Biblical norm by the practice of daily faith encounters with God, first, among your developing prayer leadership group. This is an important narrative for your entire congregation. You will learn by trial and error how to lead the congregation into daily encounters with God.

- <u>Let everyone on the team grow at their own pace</u>. Some may seem to speed ahead, others may lag behind, then burst forward. Keep loving and supporting one another to pursue God.

- Don't allow anyone to measure themselves by their performance – <u>our relationship with God is grace-based</u>. God loves us. That's the good news that invites us to meet with him daily.

- <u>You want meaningful prayer encounters with God rising out of personal prayer</u> – spiritual invigoration, prayer insights, strength and faith, reports of the whispers of God. As you experience such moments, you <u>want to cultivate a team spirit in your prayer group over these personal prayer moments</u>.

- Don't forget to continue to pray together – and for one another's families. Each may be experiencing additional 'uncanny' interferences since they joined the prayer leadership team. Hold each other up in prayer.

NOTE: The above constitutes the first three of 'Seven Markers of a Praying Church,' and the heart of the Praying Church Made Simple model. What follows are milestones that aim at the integration of all the marks of a praying church, at changing the culture of the congregation and the habits of the people.

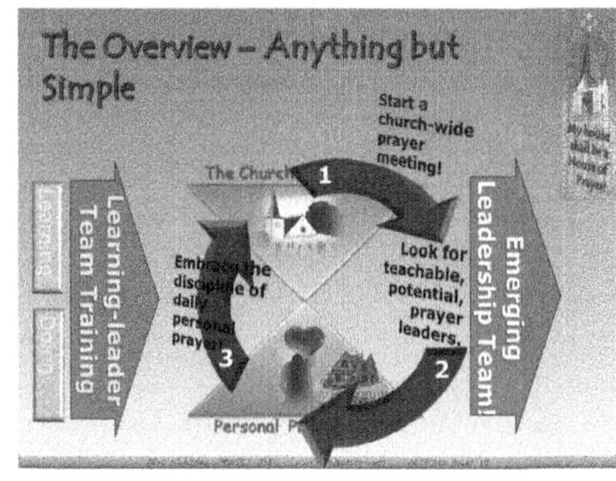

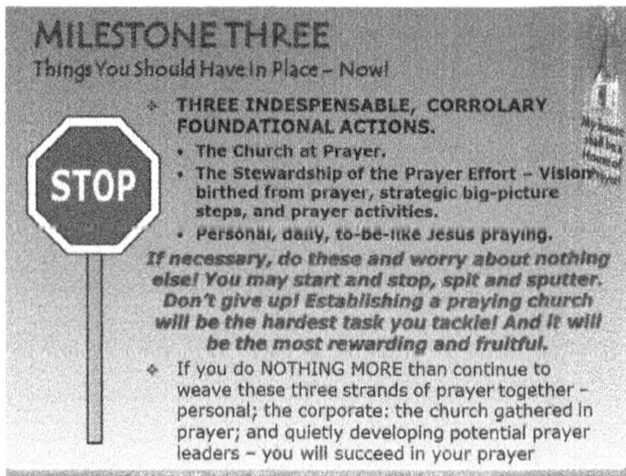

Phase II

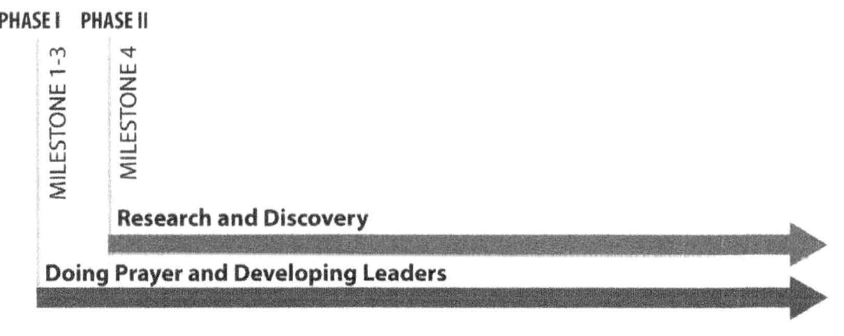

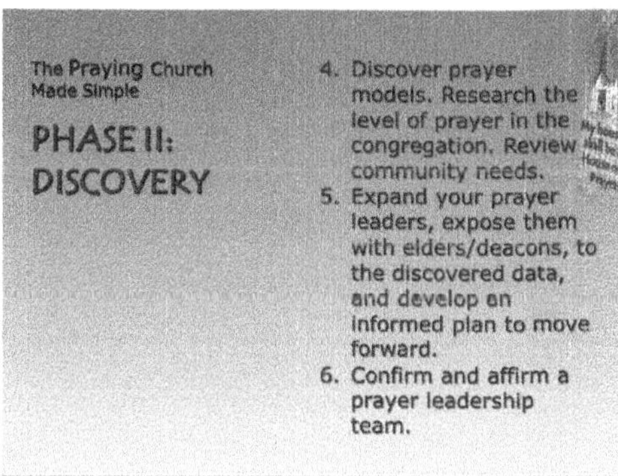

Your leadership team to this point has been a 'learning' team. You *have been learning* as you prayed together corporately and met God personally. Much of your learning in your team meetings has been content driven, conceptual and internal. Now, in order to move to planning, you need to 'know' the level of prayer among your members, their theology of prayer and their openness to learn. You also want to explore and learn from other congregations. You may have done some of this already, in conjunction with your participation in the PLCE process. Now, you want to take field trips together, look at prayer rooms/centers, and talk to prayer teams from other congregations. This is external learning.

To help measure the actual degree of prayer inside the congregation, a number of survey instruments have been developed for your use. It is important that your plan be an informed plan – by your learning and by your exposure to outside models; also by your awareness of the current level of congregational prayer engagement. <u>Don't press beyond this level if you sense *too little prayer* engagement. Prayer must drive the prayer reformation of the church.</u>

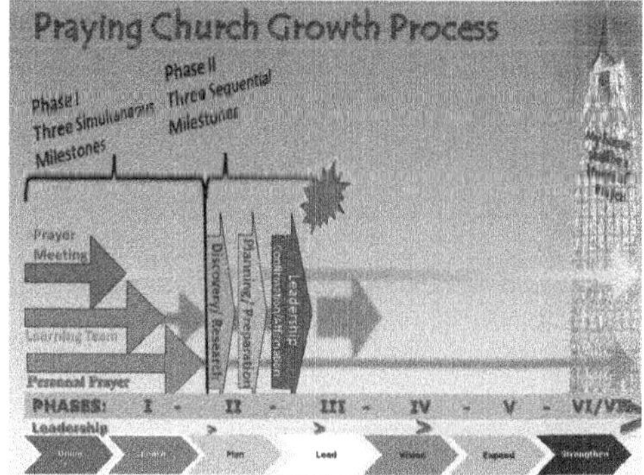

Information will not do it; this is a movement of *formation,* by the Spirit. Prayer is the most important aspect – and that cannot be intercessory prayer, prayer requests, or a flurry of heartless prayer meetings. Activity is not what you are seeking; it is the development of hungry hearts bent toward God, daily. That is your goal.

Congregation

In this phase, <u>the congregation will be increasingly aware of the prayer effort</u>. In addition to continuing to invite them to the congregational prayer meeting and your occasional efforts at Sunday prayer engagement as a part of your worship experience, you now want to increase the circle of leaders.

You will also survey the congregation early in this phase to quantify the level of prayer in the congregation, its leaders, members and families.

Survey instruments are found in the *Praying Church Resource Guide.* More are found in the *Praying Church Made Simple* publication.

Leaders

<u>Your 'learning team' will now explore models of prayer</u> in nearby churches and ministries. You will review the data from the congregational prayer surveys and create a report on the 'state of prayer in the church.'[1]

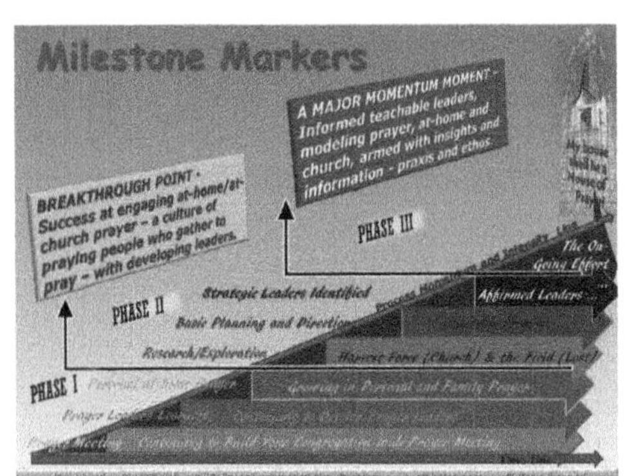

---

1   A note about surveys. A sampling of 20 percent of your congregation's personal and family prayer habits will give you, within a 10 percent margin of area, 95 percent accuracy. To state it differently, suppose you have a congregation of 100. Survey 20 members. You can then assert, based on the survey, with a +/- 10% margin of error, your survey results. National polls are based on average on about 800 people. However, to get usable data, the contact rate in the late '90s, was 2000-2500 people, out of which 800 participated in the survey – 32-40%. Today, with increased coolness and the desire for privacy heightened, pollsters report having to contact 8,000 people to get 800 usable respondents. Some folks in your congregation might not want to be surveyed. Be kind.

Consider developing several short surveys that involve the different types of information you want to collect from your congregation. Don't ask everyone the same questions. For example, get a sampling, adequate to measure the data of each set of propositions. Place these in your bulletin – make them anonymous. Tell your congregation what the data will be used for – to help them and the church become a house of prayer. Ask them, over several weeks, to complete the short surveys, probably no more than a half sheet, front and back, short enough to be completed in 2-3 minutes. They can be placed in the offering plate or a basket as people exit.

Use the rating sheets found in the companion material of *The Praying Church Made Simple* as a guide.

You will also want to collect information on every prayer effort in the congregation. Do you have prayer partners? Is there a men's prayer group? A women's prayer group? Do they pray? How much of their meetings are given to prayer? Is there organized prayer for missions? For unreached people groups? For the city? For the lost? For the ministries of the church? The families of the church? As you collect this data, place it in one notebook. That will result in a kind of 'ragged notebook' of your existing prayer endeavors. It will be priceless for the future. (More information on this in Milestone Four.)

That collage of prayer activities, including your history of congregational prayer, which you might gather from senior members, plus the results of the survey and your 'current state of prayer' in the church report, as well as your learning together as a team, will be the basis of your planning.

People

<u>You must discover the actual level of prayer</u> not only 'at church' during your gatherings, but by the people during the week. To do that, you will use anonymous surveys to reveal the actual state of prayer among the people. Keep encouraging grace-based personal and family prayer. Use the data to emphasize the call to prayer and to enlarge the leadership circle.

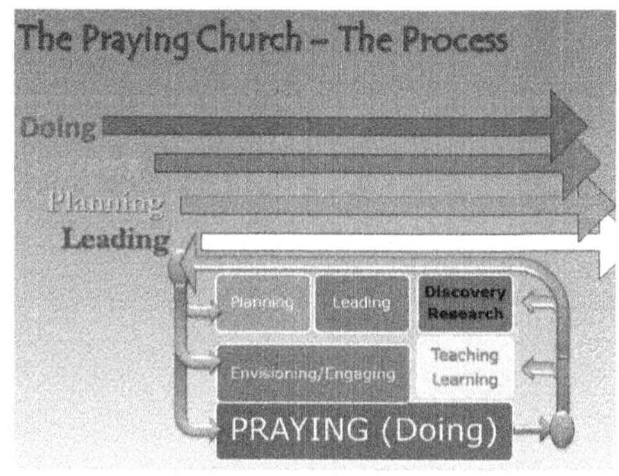

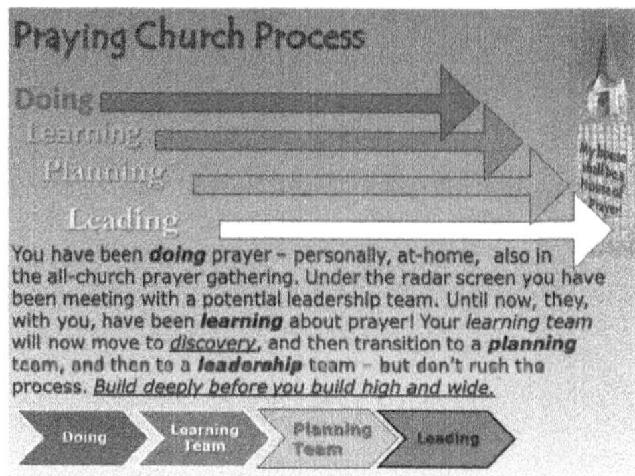

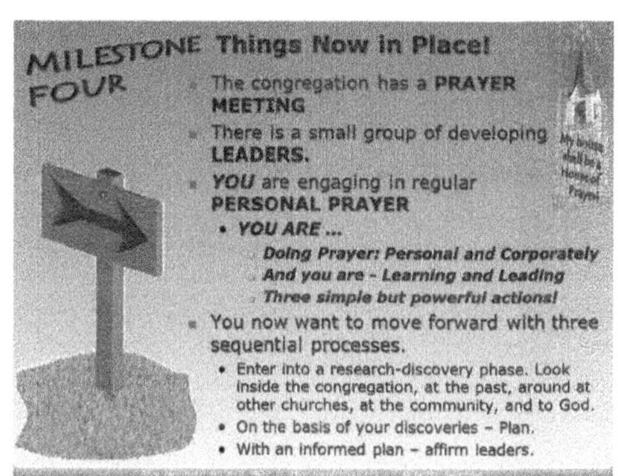

MILESTONE FOUR
Research and Discovery

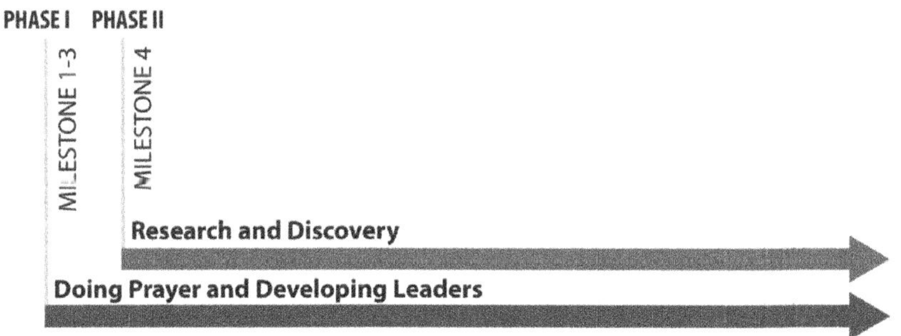

Proposition

There is a veritable reformation of the church taking place across the nation and around the world. The 500-year-old Protestant reformation, it turns out, is still on! And a critical component at hand now is the restoration of the church, to a house of prayer. At this point, the movement is still on the fringes, but it promises to become a mainstream movement – since it is the heart of God, that His people pray.

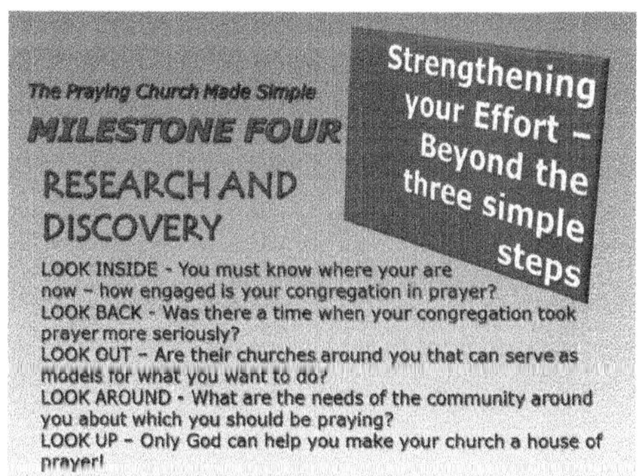

The Praying Church Made Simple
MILESTONE FOUR
RESEARCH AND DISCOVERY

Strengthening your Effort – Beyond the three simple steps

LOOK INSIDE - You must know where your are now – how engaged is your congregation in prayer?
LOOK BACK - Was there a time when your congregation took prayer more seriously?
LOOK OUT – Are their churches around you that can serve as models for what you want to do?
LOOK AROUND - What are the needs of the community around you about which you should be praying?
LOOK UP – Only God can help you make your church a house of prayer!

There are models emerging, congregations that have established viable prayer ministries, prayer rooms, even prayer centers. A growing number of congregations see the importance of a minister of prayer, a prayer pastor or a prayer coordinator. Pastors are now seeing the vital link between congregational health, the vibrancy of members, and prayer and evangelism-mission. Increasingly, congregations are establishing vibrant prayer meetings and encouraging personal and family prayer.

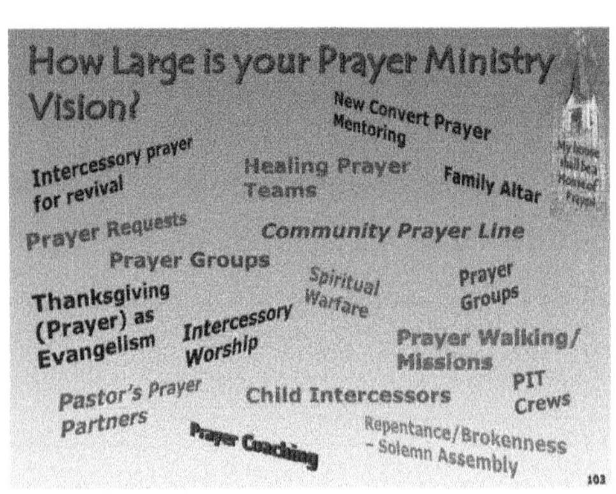

RESEARCH AND DISCOVERY

1. LOOK INSIDE - How engaged is your congregation in prayer?
2. LOOK BACK - Was there a time when your congregation took prayer more seriously? Was more engaged in prayer?
3. LOOK OUT – Find churches around you that model what you want to do?
4. LOOK AROUND - What are the needs of the community about which you should be praying?
5. LOOK UP – Only God can help you make your church a house of prayer!

Discover churches around you that have launched a prayer effort from whom you can learn. Now you will move from internal, conceptual learning, to external, exploratory learning. The conceptual learning is foundational. Without it, you will not be able to discern between faddish prayer practices and those that are sound. Your learning will help you interpret what you see as you explore. Not everything will be worthy of integration into your process. Without internal, conceptual learning, your exploration is likely to degenerate into a collection of disconnected, eccentric prayer practices that you attempt to implement. Be careful.

You are on a journey – that demands a map. You are building a house of prayer, and that demands an architectural plan. But you have a problem. You have heard the voice of God calling you, but you don't have a clear sense either of the exact next steps to take or how you will know that you have completed your journey. What will your house of prayer look like when it is built? Is it merely an addition, a room added on to the house of praise and preaching you now have? You need to explore. Interview others on the same journey. Learn from their failures and successes.

Research should inform your plan.

- First, ***look inside*** the congregation. Survey the state of prayer in your own congregation. What is the level of interest among those who are members of your church?

- Second, ***look back*** – what is the history of prayer in the congregation? This may be a simple matter of summary statements from oral interviews of senior members with a history in the congregation. If these are recorded – video or audio – they would be priceless as reflections on the prayer-life of the congregation in the past.

- Then, ***look out*** – find models of prayer in other congregations. Call them. Visit them.

- Fourth, ***look around***, this time for prayer needs – not in the congregation – but in the community, in the neighborhood around the church, among the friends and family of the members of church. What should the congregation be praying about? Don't look for the typical 'prayer requests,' look at the city. What are the compelling needs in the harvest field nearest you?

- Finally, don't forget to **_look up_** to God – <u>What is He saying</u> to your group about your prayer effort?

Timing

<u>You should now be well into your church-wide prayer effort. Your potential leadership team should be increasingly stable</u> – although, it may still expand and contract. <u>The team should have established a healthy habit of meeting with God daily</u> with the result of a growing level of satisfaction in their prayer life.

By now, you should have a list of questions about prayer ministry. You are searching for answers, and that signals readiness to begin to explore prayer ministry models. It is time to add members to your small core group of developing learner-leaders.

Resources

<u>Use the congregational prayer ministry surveys</u> found in the *Praying Church Resource Guide*. Explore the number of formally organized and informal prayer groups that meet in your congregation. Use the surveys in the *Launching Community Prayer Movements,* for research on the harvest field, the needs of the community around you.

Don't develop your prayer ministry in a vacuum. You may be thinking about starting prayer groups – but there may already be prayer groups in your congregation, meeting informally. Are you going to compete? Can you collaborate with them? Is it possible to synergize the power of existing small groups with the efforts of the new prayer ministry? In some cases, the answer will be 'yes.' On the other hand, the hardened wineskins you may find in some existing prayer groups must not inhibit your efforts. And yet, don't allow those who have quietly and without fanfare been praying for some time to feel displaced and overlooked by all the new interest in prayer.

A modified excerpt from the *Praying Church Resource Guide* that might be helpful in your discovery process:

<u>*Create a prayer ministries notebook*</u> detailing all the prayer ministries and activities that already exist (noted earlier). The manual would list each "prayer ministry" and the person designated as leader. Note the objective of each prayer ministry - its focus, its target participants, the frequency and duration of its meetings, the length of time in existence, a vitality rating, a projection for its future including ministry expansion plans and maximum number of participants anticipated.

This resource manual will be a "ragged" notebook. All the various activities, the initiatives of and out of prayer, are gathered and compiled in one volume. This notebook is NOT FOR PUBLIC consumption. It is a for-your-eyes-only compilation of existing prayer activities.

<u>You are cataloging 'the state of prayer' in your congregation</u>, among your people.

CAUTION: This cannot be a judgmental exercise. But, you cannot afford to assume that people are in fact praying and praying effectively. You cannot be blind to the spiritual practices of those you want to help. Make sure you also engage in a humble, gracious, self-examination. You need cooperation and transparency to get good data – don't judge. Dispassionately collect the data and categorize it:

1. LOOK INSIDE

Conduct your survey of prayer ministry interest in the congregation.[2] Determine the prayer materials and resources currently available to the congregation.

<u>*Discover the existing prayer ministry efforts:*</u>

- Is there a regular church-wide prayer meeting?
- Is the congregation allowed to pray or do the professionals do all the praying?
- What prayer ministries are doing well? Not so well?

---

2   See Resource Section of the *Praying Church Resource Guide* for a basic model survey.

- What prayer ministries do you have that you can build on? How can they be improved? How can they become more effective?

- Are the leaders of these prayer ministries teachable? Is it *"their ministry?"*

- What is the status of personal prayer (including family and couple's prayer levels)?

- What is being done to encourage prayer – by individuals, families, intercessors, for evangelism?

- Begin to discover those who are praying daily, who have a hidden life of prayer – and perhaps, a prayer closet.

- Determine the degree to which the children and youth are being exposed to prayer in the current ministries of the church – in youth meetings, discipleship, children's church, etc.

- Is there organized congregational prayer support for the lead pastor? A pastor's prayer partner program?

- Have the intercessors been identified, trained and teamed. Are they regularly directed, debriefed, and encouraged? (Mobilizing intercessors does not constitute the organization of a whole, balanced, prayer ministry; but no prayer ministry is whole without this specialization.)

- Do the elders/deacons/council members pray when they meet together – other than an opening prayer? Do they get on their knees and pray earnestly for the congregation and its ministries?

- To what degree is prayer embedded in the various ministries of the congregation?

Discover the state of the "prayer communication system."

- What do you do with the prayer requests that come forth Sunday after Sunday?

- Is there a "prayer list?" A prayer newsletter? A section on the website for prayer?

- Are prayer requests recorded, managed and taken seriously?

- Do you have or keep a record of answered prayers?

- How does the church communicate prayer needs and opportunities to the congregation?

- Is there a system to mobilize intercessors for emergency prayer?

- What about answers to prayer and praise reports – how are they collected and distributed?

Discover the prayer teams and groups already in place:

- The church and prayer – How many participate in prayer meetings? How many attend the church-wide prayer meeting?

- What is the degree of congregational awareness of your church-wide prayer meeting and of prayer groups?

- How many active prayer groups are there in the congregation?

- Have the intercessors been identified?

- Are prayer meetings focused – prayer for missionaries, unreached people groups, community concerns, unsaved family members?

- Are these open prayer groups? How do they recruit new people? Are they closed, without knowing it?

- Are the wineskins of these groups already hardened?

- What new groups need to be started?

- Do the men pray when they gather? The women? Youth? Children?

- Does the staff pray together?

- Are there prayer support teams for your ministers and ministries? Are they considered vital?

Discover the level of prayer training and teaching.

- What prayer training is now taking place?

- Is there regular preaching or teaching on prayer?

- Are their discipleship classes on prayer?

- What resources are available? What is needed?

- Do your couples understand the power of praying together?

- Does the congregation understand the importance of the family altar?

- What is the theology of prayer in your congregation? Among your leaders? Families? Your teens? Your millennials?

How much prayer is focused outside the congregation?

- Explore the breadth of the prayer effort in and beyond the congregation. Is prayer primarily an inward exercise, something practiced at church, for the problems of the members of the church? If so, it is fundamentally unhealthy – it is far too self-interested. It has no missional component. James reminds us that in such a prayer paradigm answers dry up (James 4:1-5).

- Do you have a prayer room, center or even a wall in your sanctuary or foyer to inform and inspire prayer? This is the place where prayer requests might be posted, maps which detail the location of missionaries and nations for which you are praying, UPGs, etc., even a map of your city and concerns about that city – your harvest field, a 15-20 minute drive around your facility. This room is a window on your city and the world.

- Where are you in taking the prayer commitment challenge of the apostle Paul seriously? (1 Tim. 2:1-8) For example do you pray for "kings and those in authority," as the scripture commands? For the mayor and city-county-state-national leaders?

- Is there, in the congregation, any regular, systematic stewarding of prayer for the community, the state and nation, and the world? Or, is it random?

- Are there any city-wide prayer efforts? When they occur, does your congregation participate?

- Do you have a definitive prayer mission focus, with identified mission fields, one near and one far?

- Are there mission and prayer-evangelism activities? Systematic prayer-walking? Prayer missions into the city? Prayer treks and journeys to far away places? Prayer for the lost loved ones of the church? Prayer for significant lost leaders in the community? Prayer for police and fire personnel? Prayer for peace in the city?

- Is prayer evangelism an organized focus of regular prayer?

- Is there a group praying for lost friends and family?

- Is there prayer for mission endeavors?

- Is there prayer for your missionaries?

- Has the congregation adopted an unreached people group for prayer?

- What is the status of teaching and training on prayer? (For example: Is there a Sunday School class devoted to teaching on prayer? Do you have a teaching plan to regularly offer prayer classes? How do people learn about prayer, prayer in all its varieties, its various functions and inferences. How do you expand their theology of prayer, from pragmatism and self-centered praying?).

  (Obviously, you have a group of learner-leaders you have been discipling in prayer and prayer leadership. Has teaching and training on prayer reached beyond them?)

Remember, you are measuring your prayer effort in the categories of the '7 Marks of a Praying Church.' Your ragged notebook tells you where you are now; and, by using the categories of the *Praying Church Movement* you are forecasting the direction in which you want to move.

2. LOOK BACK

This could be very exciting. Visit the older members of the congregation and ask them about <u>the state of prayer in the congregation in years past</u>. Take an audio or video recorder. At least transcribe their testimony. It belongs in the archives of the church. Glean stories of the 'way it used to be'. In this case, such reminiscences may be windows, not only on the past, but old wells that need to be re-dug. Collect stories of answers to prayer in the life of the congregation that older members still recall, stories that are largely unknown. <u>You are writing the prayer history of the congregation</u>. The journey may take you to folks who have moved, previous pastors, folks now attending another congregation – be brave. Cross the lines.

Of course, you may have to filter some of the responses. In the end, <u>you are looking for the prayer treasures of the church</u>, the yes-but-not-yet promises of God, the spiritual heritage.

3. LOOK OUT

The learning here will be informal – <u>the discovery of churches around you that pray</u>. This is no easy task. Ask other vibrant Christians if they attend a praying church.

One lead will uncover another. Call denominational offices and ask them if they can identify churches in their movement that have vibrant prayer ministry, an active prayer room or center in your city-county. Look for 24-7 prayer centers. Visit the nearest IHOP effort. These tend to be youth oriented and youth led, but they often embrace unique models and approaches to prayer.

You are exploring. Be daring.

In addition to living models, the book *Transforming Your Church into a House of Prayer – the Revised Edition* and the *Praying Church Resource Guide*, both by P. Douglas Small will be helpful as guides for a 'new normal' for your congregation. Another helpful resource is Cheryl Sacks' book, *The Prayer Saturated Church*; and Alvin Vandergriend's book, *The Praying Church Sourcebook.* Also, *The Praying Church Idea Book: Practical Ways Your Church Can Pray* by Douglas A. Kamstra is an extraordinary resource.

4. LOOK AROUND

Don't forget to look around – <u>what are the needs in the church neighborhood</u>?

- How could the church be a better neighbor? Often, the church is the absentee neighbor on the street with the fewest neighborhood friends. The church is only a building that *outsiders* to the neighborhood use – without the church's physical neighbors knowing anyone in the church or attending themselves.

- What are the needs in the neighborhood?

- What are the needs in the larger community, the city and county?

- If prayer is a watchman ministry, a means of spiritual policing – we have been absent. We do not have 'watchmen' on the walls of our cities, at least, in a regular, systematic and networked fashion. Is our absence on the wall of prayer contributing to the current condition of unrestrained evil? What should your church be watching prayerfully? Crime? The drug scene? A nearby school or hospital? Police or fire safety personnel? The local bar scene? The unsupervised youth and children's population? The teaming mass of people without God?

- Don't merely monitor the darkness – also look for evidence of God's work in your community – now and in the past. Watch for God signs.

- Know your neighborhood and your city – the state of the family, youth challenges, the drug issue, violence, gang activity, white-collar crime, the needs of children, the level of hunger and poverty, the absence of fathers and the resultant impact, the struggle of working, single mothers – how can you pray? What can you do?

- Are there Unreached People Groups in your county? You may feel ill equipped to evangelize them, but you can pray!

- Do you know the actual number of people in church each Sunday in your city/county? The data is usually available. What is the size of the functionally unchurched within 15 minutes of your facility?

- How many schools are near you? How can you pray? How can you help?

5. LOOK UP

Finally, look up. <u>Ask God</u>, as a team, in view of what you now know about the state of prayer inside your congregation, around you in other congregations, the needs in the city, and the promises of God over the city – <u>what do you do next</u>? How do you proceed? Keep your eyes on Him. You have been called to an impossible task. Only God can help you accomplish your mission (Isaiah 40).

Duration

<u>Plan to take three-to-six months in the research-discovery phase</u> of learning about prayer ministry models.

Focus

The focus is research - <u>discovery</u>. You are gathering information, <u>doing research</u>, <u>in order to plan more effectively</u>. By those activities, you are <u>developing your prayer ministry leader-learner team</u>. Are they ready for the next step? With a stable core of leader-learners, <u>add others</u> from your elders/deacons/council and even from your membership <u>to various 'prayer ministry exploration' teams</u>.

1. Have one team <u>explore the degree to which</u> your church and its <u>member families are now praying</u>. Use the resources (surveys, etc.) in the *Praying Church Resource Guide.*

2. Have another team <u>explore prayer ministry models</u> in other congregations. Don't forget to ask them about how they nurture and encourage at-home prayer, about the integration of prayer into children and youth ministries, about their intercessors and prayer evangelism efforts.

3. Appoint a third team to <u>explore 24-7 models</u>. Make sure you have young people on this team.

4. Ask the computer savvy among you to <u>research prayer ministry models</u> and <u>resources available on the web</u>.

5. Another team needs to launch a "Know Our *Church Neighbors*" campaign to explore <u>what needs in the community around the church</u> are most acute. Also, take a look at crime and violence concerns, safety for seniors and the poor, the needs of single-parent homes and latch-key kids, the state of housing. You may not have money, but you have prayer collateral in heaven – invest it. Give the gift of prayer.

6. You also want to <u>explore history</u> – ask the old-timers about revivals that might have come to the church in the past, promises yet to be fulfilled. Has there ever been a great revival in your city? Where is God at work in your community now? How can you join him? What does he want, not just for your church, but for the city?

7. You may want to consider having a small group fly to New York to observe the prayer meeting at either the Times Square Church or at Brooklyn Tabernacle and speak with their staff members about their prayer efforts.

KISS – Keep It Simple Saints!

If you are a smaller church, and most churches are small, (the average church in the USA has 75 in attendance on Sunday) – <u>don't be overwhelmed</u>, saying, "This is too much. We can't or we won't do this!" You may have a very small prayer-leader-learning team, even after you have expanded for this exploration phase. Flying to New York to attend a prayer meeting at Brooklyn Tabernacle or Times Square Church may be out of the question. So <u>simplify the process</u>. In pairs or triplets, tackle the items above, one at a time and start learning. Take a deep breath, lengthen your timeline. Do each of these steps serially, one at a time, as a team. <u>Make the process work for you</u>.

<u>CAUTION: If you don't do some discovery, the prayer model you choose will only be the same model that has failed in the past. Because it is then only a cut out of the old cloth</u> – it won't hold the new wine of the fermenting prayer movement around the world. Break out of the current paradigm – be courageous. Take the more difficult route.

Compile all your data. Plan for some extensive meetings for mutual debriefing. Be patient. Prayer is the most important thing you have ever attempted to revitalize in your congregation.

Involvement Goals

<u>There should now be a *core* of committed prayer learner-leaders. Around that core, add others to these research-discovery teams</u>. Ideally, each team should be composed of 3-5 individuals. In smaller churches, individuals may serve on multiple teams and teams might do double duty, covering more than one area. In some settings, one team will explore each area serially, one after another. Generally, at this point, the exploration phase should cause you to double, perhaps triple the number engaged in the process.

Transition

Of course, beyond this time, and throughout your process, <u>you will continue to learn and explore other models</u>.

The goal of this initial exploration effort should, however, stretch you and envision you – hopefully inspire you onward.

Once you have completed your discovery process, you have adequate data to begin to move from *learning* and exploring to *planning*.

Common Mistakes:

- It is sadly common, but tragic <u>to think that prayer is optional</u>, <u>that it is an additive, making little discernible difference</u> in our lives, our demeanor or our effectiveness. The common miscalculation is thinking that with sincere works and conscientious endeavors we can compensate for prayer.

- You will make a mistake if you <u>rely on anecdotal data</u>.

- Christians <u>too often assume</u>. They rely on hunches, not hard facts, as if hunches were spiritual. <u>Get the facts</u> – then pray for spiritual insight.

- <u>Do you</u>, for example, <u>know</u> that we are only retaining three percent of our kids once they graduate from high school and enter college? Do you know your post-teen congregational retention rate? That determines the future of your congregation.

- Do you know the median age of your congregation? Most Christian congregations in the USA are much older than the national median age of 37.8. <u>What is your plan for survival?</u>

- Do you know the number of people in your city/county? Do you know the number who are in church in your city/town on any given Sunday, or, over an eight-week period? <u>Have you ever noticed the neighbors around the church</u>, regarding their church attendance habits?

- Did you know that 70 years ago about 50 percent of Americans went to church each Sunday, and now that number is about 17 percent? That in 1900, we had 27 churches for every 10,000 people, and now our ratio is less than 10 to 10,000, a 60 percent difference? Would you say, from those statistics, that we are losing the culture? <u>What is the response of your congregation?</u>

COMMON MISTAKES

1. Prayer as optional! An addiction.
2. Anecdotal data as research.
3. Assuming. Not getting the facts.
4. Not knowing your next gen retention rate.
5. Not knowing your median age. What is your plan for survival?
6. Not knowing your mission field – real data. Neighbors. A mission field near and far.
7. Assuming congregational awareness and concern over the church mission crisis.
8. Assuming that all attenders are true, praying believers. Not knowing the depth of faith practices in the church.

- <u>Did you also know</u>, that a study across seven denominations, involving thousands of believers, indicated <u>that only about half feel close to God</u>? That many attend church, but do not sense God's Presence? That, in fact, almost 10 percent of those who come have never made a serious commitment to Jesus Christ?

- Don't assume. <u>Know your congregation and your mission field</u>!

MILESTONE FIVE
Planning – Articulating Vision and Mission, Strategy and Tactics

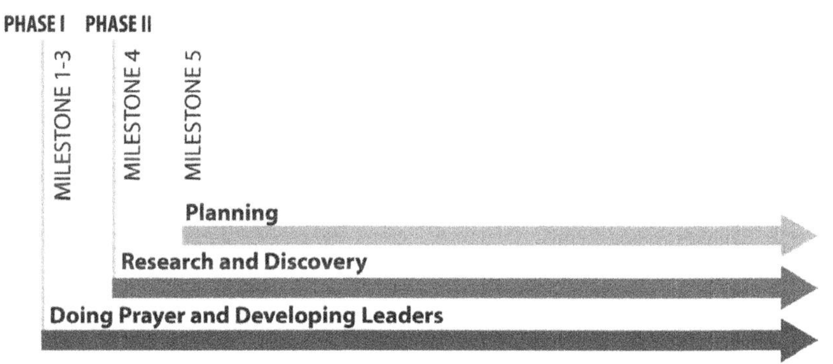

Proposition

Now you must declare your values, purpose, mission, vision, and strategy as well as your tactics. All these are interrelated elements of your effort. <u>This forces you to define and declare what is important</u> (*values*), your reason for existing (*purpose*), and therefore, what you must now do (*mission*). Your *vision* statement articulates a <u>big picture</u> of the kind of prayer ministry you want to see developed in your congregation. Vision imagines what a truly prayer-invigorated church will look like as you mature,

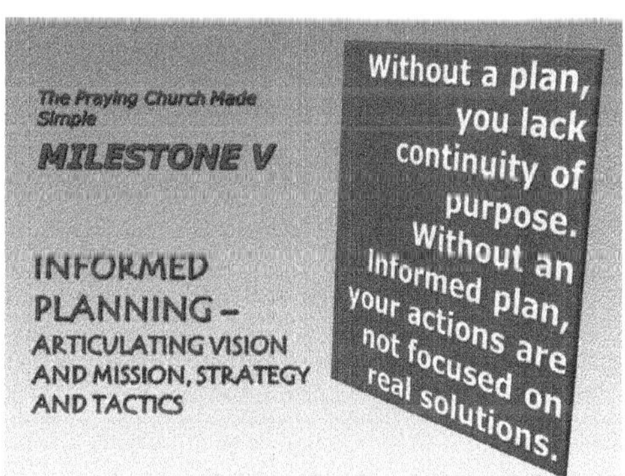

though it might take years to develop. You project a *strategy* (the big picture *plan;* the architectural drawing; the map) out of the *mission* statement with your *vision* in view. Vision the <u>big picture</u>. Dream boldly, and then translate vision into a *strategy,* the <u>big picture *plan*</u>. Unwrap that strategic plan in little pieces, step-by-step, piece-by-piece *(tactics).*

Most ministries operating in a congregation lack coherence. They are not unified by similar values and mission. And their purpose is not clear, biblical or missional. If, for example, the purpose of the prayer ministry is simply to pray, but they do not know the purpose of prayer itself or lack a healthy theology of prayer, they will fail. A Biblical purpose for their prayer effort will help them with a clear mission statement, a big picture vision and a long-term strategy. Otherwise, they will engage in one tactical endeavor or program after another – often calling that a strategy. Most church departments and ministries do just that.

A congregation, to use an analogy, will often invest significant effort and resources to raise up one big prayer domino and watch it fall with little ultimate effect, "This year, we are focused on prayer walking," or, "the family in prayer," or, "building a pastor's prayer team." Those are fine and even necessary, but such efforts are too often single, tactical pieces, disconnected from previous and next steps, and consequently, though noble, they are ineffective because they are disconnected parts of what should be a larger whole. Our problem is systematic. It begs for holistic, rather than a serial, one-dimensional core. Prayer, we believe, is at the heart of every godly function – but it too, must be understood systematically.

With a big picture *plan,* the dominoes of your prayer effort *are strategically aligned* so that a series of learning and doing events each trigger and release their energy, one onto another. That builds momentum. That is holistic dreaming and planning – and that helps you accomplish your objective.

<u>Don't be overwhelmed</u>. And, don't say, dismissively, "We will just pray and God will take care of everything." You are to pray, as we have been emphasizing. However,

not being intentional and strategic causes you to amble along, continuing to deal with single prayer ministry dominoes – parts and not the strategic whole.

Not doing your homework leaves you with an uninformed plan and random prayer programs and practices. The consequence is that the spiritual slide in which we all find ourselves will only accelerate. Look around at the nation. It is clear that our present approach is not working out very well for us. We are losing ground, first, because of our cultural disconnect and denial; and second, due to our failure to discern the degree to which the darkness now characterizes the spiritual atmosphere of the nation and the church. Finally, the degree of lost-ness, the intensifying degree to which believers are abandoning the faith, exceeds all our previous numbers. We need a total realignment of our efforts.

This type of planning is intense. You might find it helpful to commit the details to a task team, and have them bring back their results to the leaders. In a small congregation, one person, with strategic planning skills, might be tasked with developing the initial language and allowing the leadership team to amend the draft in order to own it.

Why, What, How?

If you want your congregation to get on the prayer reformation train, you will need to be clear about your *purpose, your mission and vision*. You must tell them first, your leaders and your congregation, *why* the redoubling of your prayer effort is important. They should have a sense of *what* they can expect as you move forward. You must give them your best answer to *how* you plan to proceed.

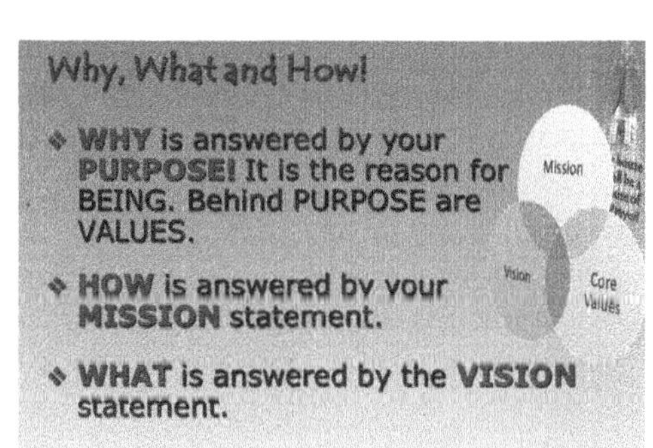

- The 'why' question is answered in your *purpose* statement. It is the reason for *being*. Behind purpose are your *values*.

- The 'how' question is answered in your *mission* statement.

- The *vision* statement answers the 'what' question.

On any journey, you begin with the end in mind. In the case of the church as a house of prayer – there are few models. God is taking us to a place we have not been before. We are living the reformation of the church – the 500-year-old reformation is not finished. You must imagine, *vision*, your end. Your constant reference point is your *purpose*, and its underlying *values*, the *'why'* you began this journey. Your map, the *'how,'* is your *mission* statement – "this is how we plan to get where we are going!" That, of necessity, will be dynamic – you will have detours. Your *vision*, the *'what'* will become clearer as you move along. You have to know where you are going to figure out how to get there!

- Start with *values and purpose* – keep that mountain in sight as you move forward. Vision is your future – you move toward vision. This is 'why' you decided to make your congregation a house of prayer. (See the 10 Prayer Values in the front of this book as an example.)

- Your *vision* is your towering target, your future. It informs where you want to go, what your church will look like when you become a house of prayer.

- To fulfill your vision, you need a strategic plan that will plot your steps forward, and that requires a *map.* The map details the environment in which you are working, what is around, behind and ahead, promises and perils. You get map data from the congregational and community research you did in the discovery process. Without such data, you are proceeding blindly.

- With clear vision and purpose, and with reliable data – you know where you are and where you want to go. That allows you to develop *a strategic, informed plan.* This will be *your guiding architectural plan* (map) to build your house of prayer. Later, the strategic task teams (STT) who take up 'pieces' of your prayer process will hammer out plans for specific focus areas, micro-plans. Now, you want a macro-plan.

- *Mission* is what you *do* – and what you will do to move toward your vision. Your informed *strategic plan*, anchored to your mission, will keep you from losing your way and helps you create a *tactical path* toward your destination – the vision.

- With a *strategic plan,* you proceed down the *tactical path,* updating your data, keeping vision in view and purpose clear. (Example: Your strategic plan may call for you to mobilize fifty intercessors. Your tactical steps are – a recruitment campaign, a night of intercessory prayer, a class on intercession. If these tactics fail, you will not accomplish your strategic objective. You will then need to alter your path to reach your goal. Your plan may need time-line revision as well.)

- Strategy lines up all the dominoes. It predicts the path forward. *Tactics* are the dominoes one-by-one, one prayer effort aligned toward the next. Tactics are the steps you take along the path. Each tactical piece makes progress toward your vision of the church as a house of prayer, proceeding according to your plan, not losing sight of your values and purpose. Tactical plans are your micro-plans, a magnification of your macro-plan in specific areas.

Whether you aimlessly move from one prayer idea to another or up a focused pathway toward a measurable objective will be determined by how well you:

- Fix in your mind your *values* and your *purpose* (the 'why' of your effort)

- Are able to stay focused on the *vision* (your objective, the 'what') before you – a *picture* of what your completed *mission* will look like

- Make use of research and discoveries. This the environment, the mountains and valleys, that inform your missional *map* ('how')

- Develop a strategy (*plan*)

- Translate the *strategic* plan into a pathway of *tactical steps* toward your objective

Drilling Deeper

Let's do it again – for drill.

- PRINCIPLES – *Values* are fixed ideals, beliefs, out of which your working principles are derived. Values are beliefs that define our behavior.

    ✓ Values, by definition, are not things you *declare* as important, but things *you now do* and thereby *demonstrate* as important.

- ✓ In your *discovery* process (previous milestone), you probably determined that while everyone says prayer is critical, it is not a practiced value.
- ✓ Acknowledge the degree to which you now value or do not value and practice prayer, and articulate a new behavioral standard for your congregation.
- ✓ Values describe the culture. They serve as a behavioral compass.
- ✓ This will determine your mission statement.

- PURPOSE – *Purpose* is a crisp, inspiring, reason for your existence.[1]

  - ✓ Purpose is the heart of your intent.
  - ✓ It is the object or objective toward which you strive, describing your function and utility, your essential goal.
  - ✓ It gives focus to mission and planning activities.
  - ✓ It provides for team members the ability to concentrate their primary reason for existing.
  - ✓ While the mission statement, the 'how,' and the strategic path may be amended from time to time, generally, purpose is constant.
  - ✓ When competing ideas emerge and the mission and strategic plan, the tactical next steps are in doubt - a focused purpose statement will provide clarity, and your values will keep you from taking compromising short cuts. They are like a compass.
  - ✓ The purpose statement will be at the center of your activities.

- PICTURE – <u>Vision</u> is your destination, your goal, what your mission will look like when it is accomplished.

- PROPOSED INTENTION – <u>Mission</u> is your vision in

---

1 Dr. John Noseworthy, president and CEO of the Mayo Clinic described how a staff member, when asked what her job was, responded, "I save lives." That's crisp purpose. Clarity of purpose helps your people grasp their role, find meaning in their worship and work for Christ. www.forbes.com/sites/barbaraarmstrong/2012/04/26/the-power-of-purpose-and-values-leadership-lessons-from-the-great-place-to-work-conference/#6d0d5dc02dca Accessed: 4 22 2017.

action, connecting back to your *purpose,* rising out of your *values,* unwrapped in a plan *(strategy)* that moves you toward your vision.

- ✓ *Mission* is what you <u>do</u>; *purpose,* out of *values,* is <u>why</u> you do it.

- ✓ *Mission* unwraps into *strategy; purpose* pervades the <u>culture</u>, the ethos of your missional community.

- ✓ Your team must believe your *mission,* but they must be invested in the *values* and *purpose.*

- ✓ *Vision* will provide focus, but *purpose* fuels passion.

- ✓ *Mission and vision* help you build the church prayer ministry; but *purpose* and *values* help you build community. The former is impossible without the latter.

- ✓ The *mission* is fulfilled brick-by-brick, but the *vision* is the cathedral, and *your values* are the proliferation of prayer in the house of prayer.

- PLAN – Your <u>*strategy*</u> – the big, wide lines for moving forward, drawn on your research map.

- PATH – <u>*Tactical*</u> – the little, diverse, multiple and sometimes simultaneous small lines drawn on your map, steps that follow the strategic *plan.*

Here is a review:

- ✓ **Your values and your purpose** statements <u>*guide*</u> you. Your purpose statement articulates why you do what you do, why your organization exists, and why you serve a higher purpose (your cause).

- ✓ **Your mission** statement <u>*drives*</u> you to accomplish your purpose. It is the difference you determine to make, the change you anticipate. Your mission drives you to fulfill your purpose. Mission helps you do what really matters and eliminate distractions. It unwraps in a strategic plan aimed at results and impact.

- ✓ **Your vision** <u>*inspires*</u> you. It is your aspiration to be. It is prophetic of your future, the results you want to achieve, the measurable impact you hope to make. *Vision* aligns. Your organizational trajectory is on the line of *mission,* between,

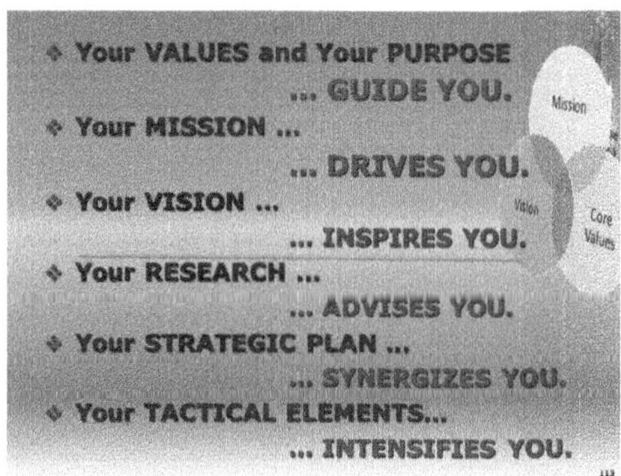

your *value* inspired *purpose* and the most optimistic *vision* of your desired outcome. You are constantly recalibrating mission – aligning organizational function and goals between *values* and *vision*. *Values* ground you; *vision* guides you toward a goal, providing a forward-looking focus that keeps you on course, allowing you to fulfill your *purpose* and yet stay true to your *values.*

✓ **Your research** out of the discovery and exploration process, *advises* you. It warns you and warms you. It helps you remember where the people are experientially in prayer, and where you have to begin, the level of their hunger and resolve and that determines the pace of change. It warms you with stories of prayer in the congregation's history. It advises with regard to the churches with the best practices near you. It reveals the challenges in the mission field around you. It is a written record of what God has said to you.

✓ **Your strategic plan** is designed to *synergize* you, your team, and their efforts. It is a means of alignment. It is beyond cooperation and collaboration. Synergy combines your efforts and energy releasing them in one grand stream.

✓ **Your tactical elements** *intensify* your momentum, being unwrapped one immediately after another, one impacting the other, synergistically.

To some prayer leaders, hammering out statements of values and purpose, vision and mission, distinguishing between the path and the plan, strategy and tactics seems a distraction. However, a frantic rush to prayer activities without serious consideration of the 'why,' the 'how,' and the 'what' is a mistake.

What do you think the disciples did in the week in which they waited in the Upper Room? And why did Jesus send them there, to tarry, knowing it would be at least a week before the Holy Spirit descended? We have no record of those days, but it would not be far-fetched to consider that in those days they wrestled with their values, with what was important to them – their new mission in life; their purpose; what they now had to do, based on the last command of Christ; and how they might move forward.

You have to know *'why.'* You should know *'where'* you are going – *'what'* prayer ministry might look like in a year or two. And then, *'how'* you are going to move forward. The difference is unity around common values and mission, a shared vision, and potential disunity without clarity, without a shared knowing of a joint purpose. Without an agreed mission, vague unstated presuppositions lurk like alligators in the transition waters and guarantee confusion and discord.

Your Purpose Statement

There may not be a better prayer ministries purpose statement than that of Jesus: *My house shall be a house of prayer for the nations!*

Of course, the focus of Jesus in that moment was on what the temple wasn't, so some would argue that the statement is too narrow, it does not include, for example worship.

A worshipping community of believers, praying and serving the world open to the gospel.

That purpose statement begins with worship, infers community and fellowship, then moves to mission. For some, the emphasis will be too much on serving, a reflection of the Great Commandment of love and care, and too little on sharing the gospel, the Great Commission.

The experts define the *mission* statement as an internal matter; and *purpose* as outwardly focused. Purpose puts the people in the shoes of outsiders. "This is what we do for others." Purpose is motivational. It connects at both the head and heart level. It is a kind of "philosophical heartbeat" of the organization. The ING Financial services purpose is, "Empowering people to stay a step ahead in life and in business." The Kellogg food company's purpose is, "Nourishing families so they can flourish and thrive." Craft a purpose statement to inspire your team by expressing the desired impact on the lives of others. Graham Kenny argues that a company's purpose is not

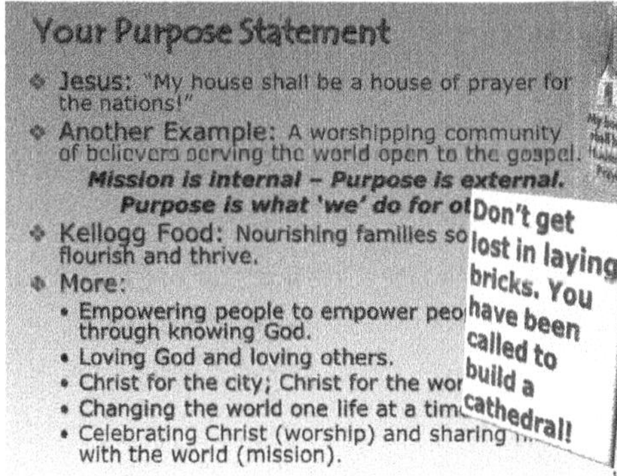

its vision, mission, or values statements.[2] The difference is between a job in which one is laying bricks or building a cathedral. Purpose is 'building a cathedral.' Purpose is "Worshipping Christ and winning followers." Purpose is "Empowering people to empower people - through knowing God." Or "Loving God and loving others." You might consider a missional purpose, "Christ for the city; Christ for the world." Or, "Changing the world one life (family) at a time." Here is another, "Celebrating Christ (worship) and sharing him with the world (mission)."

Values to Mission

Values determine the spirit and manner in which the *mission* is completed.[3] Mission (doing) must be congruent with values (being). Our mission should be to honor the prophetic cry of Jesus in the Temple, "My house shall be called a house of prayer for the nations." If that is our mission (doing) and we are not people of prayer (being), who actually pray for the nations, we will fail in our mission. Simply put, values are behavioral. They involve doing the things that move us toward the fulfillment of our Biblical mission. The mission is what the ministry is *supposed* to be doing! The Biblical elements of mission are clear. How will you integrate those into your mission statement?

- ***The Great Commitment:*** *Pray for men everywhere, beginning with kings, that they might be saved! My house shall be a house of prayer for the nations* (1 Tim. 2:1-4).

- ***The Great Commandment:*** *Love God! Be a passionate Christian – having given your heart to the Lord and committed yourself to things eternal, laying up treasures in heaven. And let your love relationship with Christ be an evidentiary witness to your neighbor! Love God. Love others. This is the incarnational gospel* (Mt. 22:37-39).

---

2   Graham Kenny. See: hbr.org/2014/09/your-companys-purpose-is-not-its-vision-mission-or-values. Accessed: 4 22 2017.

3   Aubrey Malphurs, *Advanced Strategic Planning: A 21st-Century Model for Church and Ministry Leaders* (Baker Books, 2013), 14.

- ***The Great Commission:*** *<u>Preach</u> the gospel. <u>Share the good news</u>. <u>Tell everyone</u>. Get the message to those near (the neighborhood around the church, the city) and those far (the ends of the earth); <u>baptize</u> them, inducting them into the Kingdom of God and His Church; <u>disciple</u> them, teach them to obey the precepts of the Word of God (Mt. 28:19; Mk. 15:15).*

- ***The Great Consummation:*** *After this I looked and saw a multitude too large to count, from every nation and tribe and people and tongue, standing before the throne and before the Lamb. They were clothed in white robes, with palm branches in their hands. And they cried out in a loud voice: "Salvation to our God, who sits on the throne, and to the Lamb!"* (worship, Psalm 66:4; 1 Chron. 16:23-31; Rev. 5:13, 7:9-10).

Remember, the prayer effort is not a simple ministry you are adding on to the string of other existing ministries. There is a veritable reformation of the church taking place across the nation and around the world. The reformation is still on! And a critical component is the restoration of the church to a house of prayer. At this point, this prayer movement - as was the reintroduction of the Holy Spirit to the church, a hundred years ago; and the birth of the modern missionary movement, 250 years ago - is still on the fringes of our awareness. It is being resisted and is not understood in terms of its full implications. Yet, it promises to become a mainstream movement – it is the heart of God that his people pray. (More on mission and values late in this chapter.)

Timing

The <u>timing in this phase is a matter of sequence</u>. It will be counterproductive to merely project a generic plan forward. Instead, <u>you want an *informed* plan</u>. Further, you need a team to lead the effort, a team that believes in the plan, and in fact, has developed the plan. You are praying together – the congregational prayer effort; and identifying leaders who are learning together, thus, you have determined that they are teachable; and they are deepening their own prayer life, determining to meet God daily, and you are evidencing the fruit of that; and, you have explored other congregations and how they are bringing prayer to the heart of what they do – now, you are ready to begin to plan forward.

Resources

Continue to draw from the book, *Transforming Your Church into a House of Prayer – Revised Edition,* also *The Praying Church Made Simple,* but especially, this publication *Milestones.* You will also find the quarterly curriculum in PLCE very helpful in gathering your leaders and processing through teaching, examining fresh tools and most importantly – talk-it-over and assessing your next 3-6 months. In addition, you want to draw heavily from your research and your strategic plan. The newly formed strategic prayer leadership team will need to continue to meet monthly as they did in their learning phase.

Do your major planning effort in a compact manner, a retreat or several nights and a day together. You will lay-out plans prior to and leading up to this major planning retreat. And, the planning team(s) will continue to finalize details of your plan post-retreat. This is a process. But it needs time away and space apart for collaborative and maximum impact.

Duration

You should be able to <u>conduct a prayer planning retreat</u> over a 24-48 hour period. The ideal schedule is something like Thursday evening to Saturday afternoon. You want a lot of time for break-out discussions and planning by teams, then co-planning. Your complete plan will not be completed at this retreat – it will evolve, but you will have an architectural team and a planning team with enough data that they can forge an 'action plan,' over the next few months, for moving forward.

Focus

The focus is on <u>the development of an initial prayer activity plan (macro)</u>. And on the teaming (a culture issue) necessary to move that plan forward. All the 'task team' leaders expected to implement the prayer activity plan should be at the table. Remember, plans matter; but people matter more. Without people, plans fail; without teaming, there is competition and conflict, not unity and collaboration. You are watching two things – the cultivation of relationships and the development of a collaborative prayer plan.

Involvement Goals

You began your prayer leadership development process with a learning group based on the size of your congregation, a group that may have expanded and contracted, but you emerged with a core of committed prayer learner-leaders (Phase I, Milestone Two).

As you entered a research-discovery stage, you invited others to the team. That was your second official leadership team expansion.

Now, as you develop your plan, and possibly conduct a prayer planning retreat, out of which will come a definitive leader and leadership team – you will expand your learner-leaders yet a third time.

CAUTION: THIS IS IMPORTANT, because <u>these people will determine the plan, and the plan demands people invested in the values, the mission-vision and the strategy</u>. Every member added to the team who has *not* been on the learning journey, may weaken the resolve and dilute the sense of the change needed. If your core group is strong enough, they will infect the others with the values they now share out of their learning together. If that fails, those who do not share the prayer theology or philosophy of the core team will color the plan. Changing the culture from humility and teachability, for the sake of 'effectiveness' and quicker results, sacrifices the transformational mission for pragmatic outcomes. Protect the ethos over praxis; the culture against pride and independence, the quality of relationships as much as the quantity and quickness of success.

You have a learning team – a core team of prayer leaders; and a larger team that helped you explore other models and determine the true level of commitment to prayer

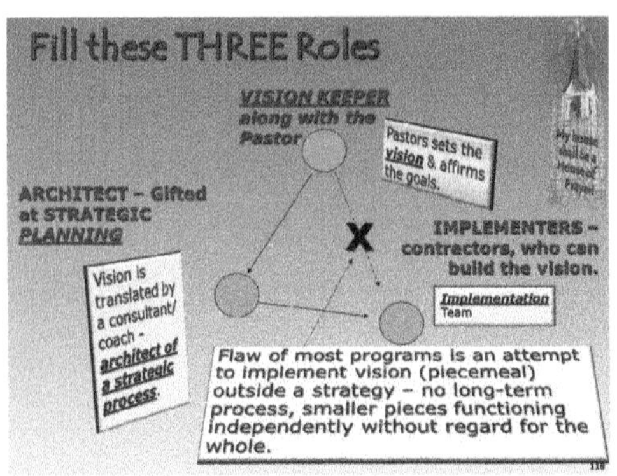

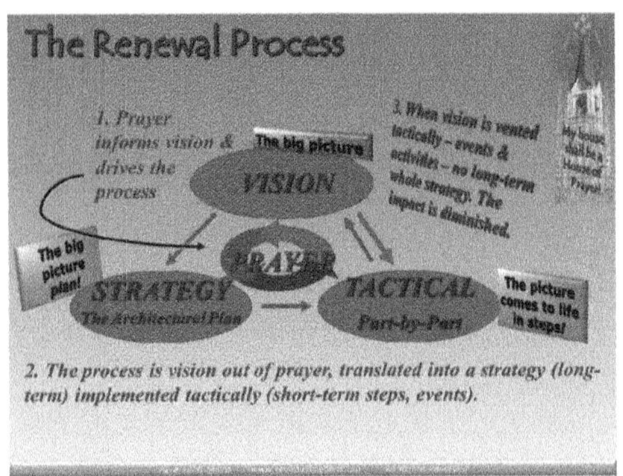

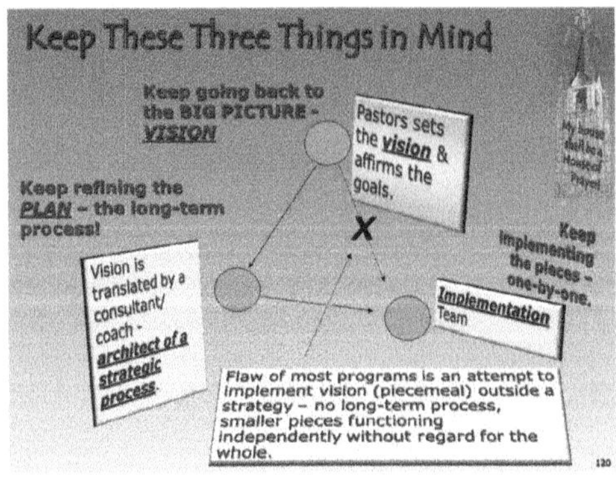

in the congregation; and now, you are adding potential prayer leaders for your planning retreat. That might include elders/deacons/church council members/staff who have not been a part either learning or exploring. They may have strong opinions. <u>Be gracious, but guard your developing core values, vision, and mission</u>.

- **The Vision Keeper** – carries the burden and vision with the pastor about what a "house of prayer" looks like. In choosing this person, it is not enough to look for a person of prayer. It is also a question of leadership and perspective. Who can see the big picture? And articulate it along with the pastor? Who can provide leadership, as an extension of the pastor's ministry, in the area of building the church into a house of prayer?

- **The Architect/Strategic Planner** – "constructs" a process, organizing the ideas, translating the articulated vision into tactical steps one-two-three. This requires a detail person. It is not a matter of just planning an event. You need someone who can strategically plan a 3-5 year development process for prayer ministries. Neither the pastor nor prayer coordinator may be good at drawing maps, nor yet, designing a plan and drawing a path on that map. Find a long-term thinker and planner. The role of this person will be intense early in the process. Later, they will serve as a consultant to the pastor and prayer coordinator. They cannot work independently. They draw what another sees.

- **Implementers** – tactical leaders who will "run with the vision." They must work within the marco-plan. They will gather the resources to accomplish their assigned micro-job – both the people and the materials. And they will get the job done. They are the "sub-contractors!" These hands-on individuals do the work of building the prayer ministry in the four dimensions.

Transition

<u>With adequate data</u> and congruence among leaders, you are <u>transitioning</u> <u>from learning and exploring, through informed planning, toward permanent leaders</u> for your prayer process.

Common Mistakes

The most common mistake is sacrificing the plan for the people; or the people for the plan. A plan will not be effective unless your leaders own it. As someone has observed, no plans survive enemy engagement. Your plan will meet resistance and require resolve. You may be forced to retreat and reteach the values rather than moving forward with a plan that is inadequate or only a mirror of the past. You may also find that some wonderful people, perhaps veteran prayer warriors, cannot make the trip using your new plans. Their wineskins are too stiff for change. You will make a mistake if you anticipate no resistance. It will be rare, if the Evil One does not resist both prayer and prayer plans. You will also make a mistake if you do not encourage the exhibition of humility in the process. Everyone is a learner. No one knows exactly how God is leading. The Holy Spirit must be in charge. All must remain teachable, especially leaders. Humility and the refusal to grasp at a desired outcome, to be manipulative, will create the unity that allows the Holy Spirit to make the group one in their planning. Stop and pray often in the planning process. Don't push forward for the sake of time – wait on the Holy Spirit. Plans belong to the pragmatic side of organizations, but in the kingdom, the ethos, the environment out of which of those plans evolve and in which they are executed is as important as what the plans are designed to accomplish. Remember, culture trumps structure.

Discover the appropriate "level" of intensity for the prayer ministry in your situation. Can you see an aggressive, balanced, integrated prayer process in your congregation, even if it is small? Is there a possibility of having a dedicated prayer room? What about a prayer center? Can you sustain prayer in that center, multiple days a week? A 24/7 prayer process usually requires a church of a thousand or more? It requires 168 man-hour volunteers just for on-site prayer hosts. Most churches should not make constant "24 hour" prayer their top priority. You want to launch a prayer process that is sustainable given the amount of manpower which the church can allocate to it presently. If you invest all of your energy in this component of your effort, you will build a process that is too narrow.

What level do you see your church achieving? What function will intercessors play? What will the interface of prayer and mission (prayer evangelism) look like? How will prayer be organized to support the ministries of the church? And how will prayer be integrated into those ministries?

Adapted Excerpt – Values, Mission, Vision, Strategy and Tactics

The following is an adapted excerpt from *Transforming Your Church into a House of Prayer*.

The Missional Overview

> *A House of Prayer and Worship that catches people up in the love of God, making them passionate for Him and His causes, infecting them with a vision beyond themselves and a caring love for others – especially the unsaved and our neighbors near to us; looking for opportunities to demonstrate the light and life of Christ, to share his transforming love, to lead them into a saving relationship with Him, to teach them the ways of God until Christ is incarnate in them and they have been transformed by the power of the Spirit and principles of the Word.*

This mission statement builds on the Great Commitment – *Prayer*; the Great Commandment – *Love*; and the Great Commission – *the Gospel*. Do you recognize these elements in the mission statement above? It is quite lengthy for a good mission statement.

A more concise version might be:

> *A house of prayer and worship that leads us to love God and care for others, living beyond themselves and looking for opportunities to share light in a way that brings others into a saving relationship with Christ, until His life breaks forth through them.*

Here again, do you see the three elements – prayer,

Creating a Great Commission Church

❖ MISSION STATEMENT:

A House of Prayer and Worship that catches people up in the love of God, nurturing passion for Christ and His causes, infecting them with a vision beyond themselves and a caring love for others – both the distant unsaved and neighbors near to us; seizing opportunities to demonstrate the light and life of Christ, to share his transforming love, to lead others into a saving relationship with Him, to teach them the ways of God until Christ is incarnate in them and they have been transformed by the power of the Spirit and principles of the Word.

Creating a Great Commission Church

❖ A More Concise MISSION STATEMENT:

A house of prayer and worship that leads us to love God and care for others, living beyond ourselves and sharing light in a way that brings others into a saving relationship with Christ, until His life breaks forth though them.

care, share? Here are two additional mission statements provided by Cheryl Sacks in her book, *The Prayer Saturated Church:*

> *Our [mission]…is to encourage and support believers at Grace Chapel to communicate confidently and joyfully with God through all areas of prayer.*

> *The mission of the prayer ministry at First Church is to pray, motivate, and teach others to pray, and to provide prayer opportunities for our church's members, inspired by the Holy Spirit.*[4]

The power of a mission statement is not merely in word crafting. It is in the agreed meaning of the statement. The statement is a forecast of the future of your prayer ministry. This is the reference point to which you will return often for perspective. It will become a guardian. It will keep you from darting down wrong pathways and chasing the vision and mission of others. The mission should be your authoritative mandate. It is what God has called you to do, to build. You can do no other.

The mission statement sets the trajectory. It includes some values and excludes others, purposely. You can change it. Amend it. However, you must always take it and its implications seriously. So, laboring over your sense of what God is calling you to do will force fresh and clear thinking for the future. It will fuse the many minds into one. It will unify and catalyze.

Writing Your Mission Statement

Here is a more technical approach to writing your mission statement. Use the guide below in this way. Fill in each phrase with a substitute phrase. "Your enterprise" will be the name of your church or prayer ministry, and so on:

> <u>Your enterprise…verb/action…adjective & noun/ who/what</u>
> *The Lakeview Church…mobilizes…its people to pray,*

> <u>"and"…adjective and noun…   "resulting in"</u>
> *and…freely share the gospel of Christ…resulting in*

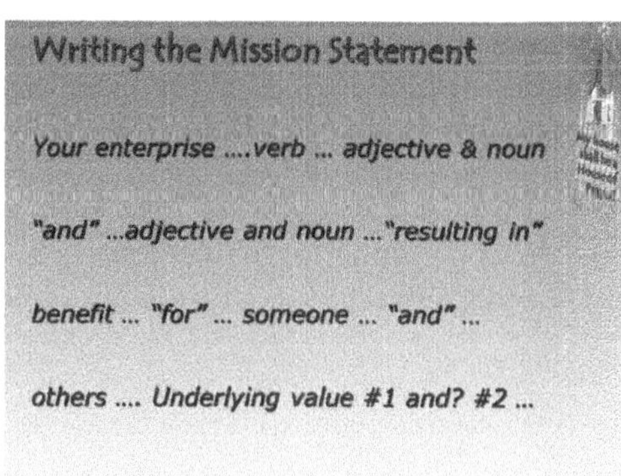

---

4   Cheryl Sacks, *The Prayer Saturated Church* (Colorado Springs, CO: NavPress, 2004) 110-111.

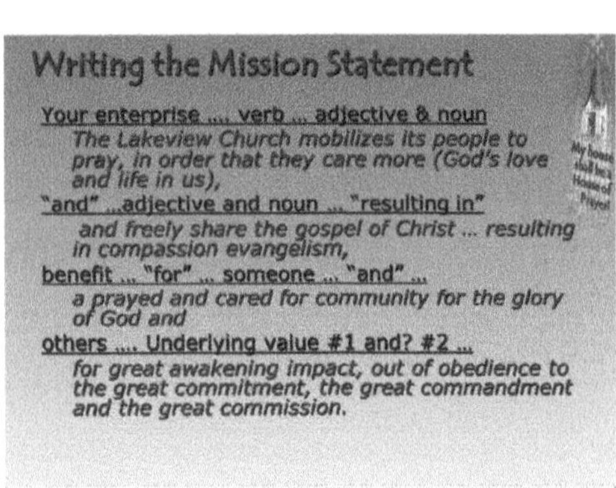

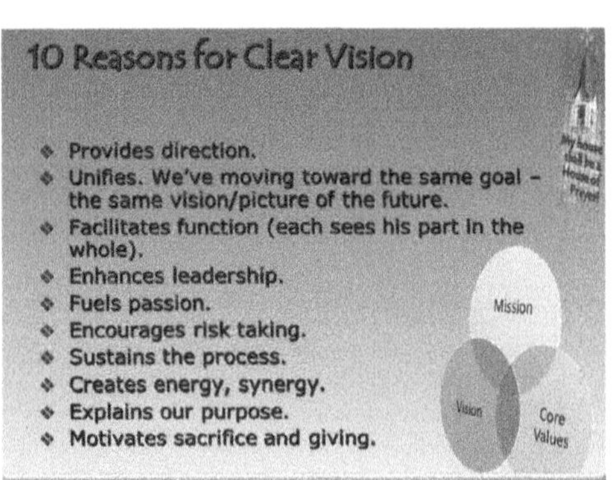

benefit ..."for"...someone..."and"... *a prayed and cared for community...for...the glory of God...and* others.... Underlying value #1 and? #2... *the salvation of the lost...out of obedience to the great commitment,...the great commandment and...the great commission.*

Distinguishing Between Mission and Vision

Mission and vision are not the same. The vision is also an expanded statement, a *picture* of the mission! Mission *feels*. It has passion. Vision *sees* – it paints a picture. Vision answers the question, "What does a house of prayer look like?" It is descriptive of the end result. "When we get there, we'll know because ..." Both the mission and vision statements are directional. Without direction – we wander. We noted earlier that George Barna's research indicates that only two percent of pastors can identify a vision for their church.[5] "Where are we now, and where does God want us to go?" is a directional question that should be visited at least once a year.[6]

As you translate your mission statement into a vision statement, here are the elements of clear vision:

- Provides direction.
- Unifies. We're moving toward the same goal – the same vision/picture of the future.
- Facilitates function (each sees his part in the whole).
- Enhances leadership.
- Fuels passion.
- Encourages risk taking.
- Sustains the process.
- Creates energy, synergy.
- Explains our purpose.
- Motivates sacrifice and giving.[7]

How do you distinguish between mission and vision?

---

5 Barna Research Group, "Seven Paradoxes Regarding America's Faith," December 17, 2000.
6 Malphurs, 18.
7 Malphurs, 28.

Here is a contrast between the two in seven different areas.[8]

CONTRASTED AREA	MISSION	VISION
Definition	Statement	Snapshot
Application	Project a Plan	Communicates
Length	Short	Long
Purpose	Informs	Inspires
Activity	Doing	Seeing
Source	Head	Heart
Development	Science (taught)	Art (caught)

While the mission statement is concise enough for people to remember, the vision statement may be a document.[9] It contains:

- Ministry purpose
- Mission
- Key values
- Strategy
- People needed for deployment
- Location[10]

The vision statement is inclusive. It is a comprehensive statement. Here is an example of a Biblical vision statement:

For the LORD your God brings you into a good land, a land of brooks of water, of fountains and depths that spring out of valleys and hills;

A land of wheat, and barley, and vines, and fig trees, and pomegranates; a land of oil olive, and honey;

A land in which you shall eat bread without scarceness, you shall not lack any thing in it; a land whose stones are iron, and out of whose hills you may dig brass.

When you have eaten and are full, then you shall bless the LORD your God for the good land which he has given you.

Beware that you forget not the LORD your God, in not keeping his commandments, and his judgments, and

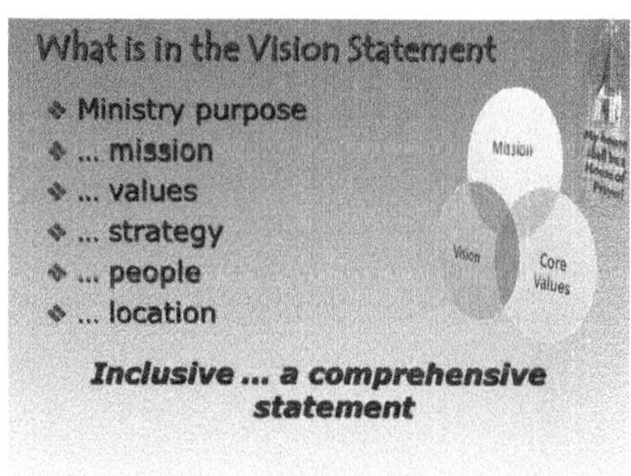

---

8   Ibid, 32.
9   Ibid, 31.
10   Ibid, 75.

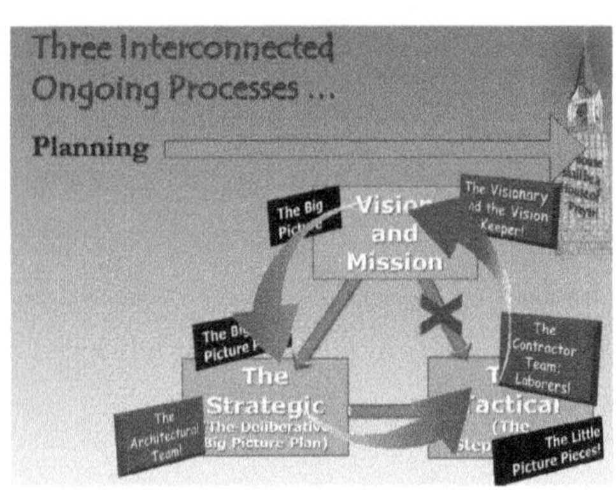

his statutes, which I command you this day...(Deut. 8:7-11).

Notice how visual this prophetic declaration is – how descriptive. You can see it! That is what a vision statement does – it paints a vivid picture of the mission. In the last section, we offered a bit of a vision statement in our description of the Prayer Center. Begin your vision writing process in this way.

Moving Beyond Vision to Strategy and Tactics

Vision is not enough to begin the building process. You may be able to envision your new house on the hill with a walk-out basement, a backyard patio, a pool, and a wide inviting front-porch with a swing. But chances are you will need to hire someone to draw the plans. The *strategy* is architectural drawing of the *vision!* It is an involved process. It is the *structural plan* for completing the mission. *Tactics* are the part-by-part, stage-by-stage unwrapping of the vision and plan.

- VALUES — ***What you currently do!***

- MISSION — ***What you are called to do, what you "should do!" Where are we going? A concise statement of direction.***

- VISION — ***What will it look like? – A clear picture what your church should become!***

- MAP — **The map details the *plot***, not the strategic (architecture) *plan* or the tactical (steps) *path* – but **the environment** in which you will build your house of prayer. The obstacles to overcome or avoid. The challenges you discovered in research; the promises you recovered.

- STRATEGY — ***The long-term plan! The architecture! The big-picture process.***

- TACTICS — ***The short-term steps of the parts of the big-picture process. The steps down the tactical path.***

The strategic process has a number of elements necessary to make it whole. They are:

1. **Research** – An assessment of the spiritual climate of your congregation and community, plus, an appraisal of the effectiveness of existing prayer ministries and needs.

2. **Discovery** - The learning process by leaders – where are the best materials, the cutting-edge models, the better practices for prayer ministries from which we can learn.

3. **Visioning** – How can we best tell the story of the call of God to make our church a house of prayer? What pictures do we need to offer? Whose testimony can we give? What purpose will systematically inspire the congregation to spend time with him, personally and corporately?

4. **Teaching** – What teaching and training needs to be offered, and in what order. And in what venue? How do we get teaching and training to the people, and not merely try to bring them to the training? How do we both organize and deploy our training for effectiveness?

5. **Doing** – How do we mobilize the entire church for prayer? In what component parts, departments, ministries? In what sequence? What is our critical mass point – how many people do we need to mobilize before we change the culture of the church? What different training components do we need in place – individual devotions, family prayer, intercessors training, lighthouses, prayer-walking, a prayer room, and more – and what is our time line for initiating each of these prayer ministries?

6. **Leadership** – How will we structure the mission? Who carries the vision on the prayer leadership team? Who clarifies our focus when we loose perspective? Who can draw maps – to help us get to our destination? Who has, not only a passion for some component of the process, but the leadership gifting to organize and lead that part of the prayer ministry?

7. **Assessment** – How will we measure success? How will you achieve balance in your prayer process: all 4-dimensions, so that it is not exclusively an intercessors venture, or all about church-prayer with little at-home prayer, or bent toward transactional evangelism praying with too little emphasis upon transformational prayer? How will you determine

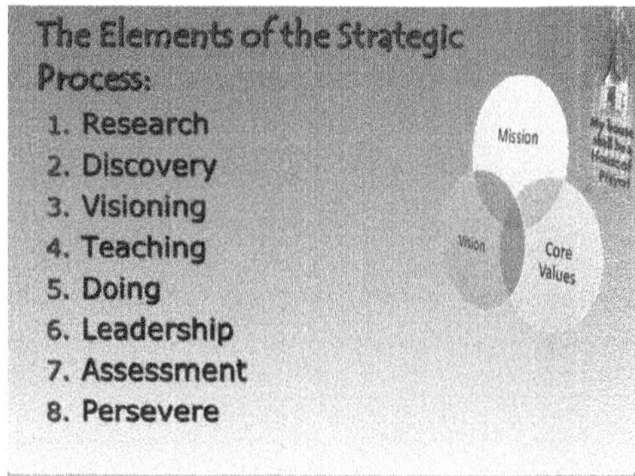

A vision cannot be established by edict, by power or coercion. Articulated? Yes! Legitimized by leaders? Yes! But to become reality – it must be claimed and owned by the important players!

when learning is integrated? And you should now go to the next level? The Prayer Leadership team should probably conduct an annual retreat to plan and assess inviting members of the various prayer ministries as needed for parts of the retreat – particularly if they are playing a key role in implementation or needing encouragement in the development of the ministry they are leading.

8. **Persevere.** Satan considers prayer an act of aggression. Retaliation – spiritual warfare - is common. Spurgeon reminds us, "By perseverance the snail reached the ark."[11]

The Prayer Leadership Team, your core leaders, should continue to meet monthly to provide evaluation and vision for becoming a house of prayer.

Here is a quick review of what we have just rehearsed:

1. *Begin by writing out your prayer values!* To do this, you will need to conduct a survey to determine the "practices" of prayer in the congregation among the members and the various ministries. What is happening in the homes and small groups of your congregation will tell you how much prayer is valued.

2. *Get a group of diverse people of prayer together* – intercessors, veterans believers, prayer-walkers, members with a heart for evangelism, others with a concern for at-home, family prayer. *Dream together.* What is God calling us to do in prayer ministries? What will it look like when we get there? How will it change our congregation? What will be different – behaviorally. This is the beginning of your vision process.

3. *Develop your mission statement* for prayer ministries.

4. Lay out your *strategy, a plan* – Keep in mind all four aspects of a well-rounded prayer process in stages, with time lines.

5. *Translate your strategy into tactical steps* – the programs you will use, the prayer learning and doing events you will conduct, the leadership you need in place to accomplish those goals. These are the small steps, the bite-size goals in sequence.

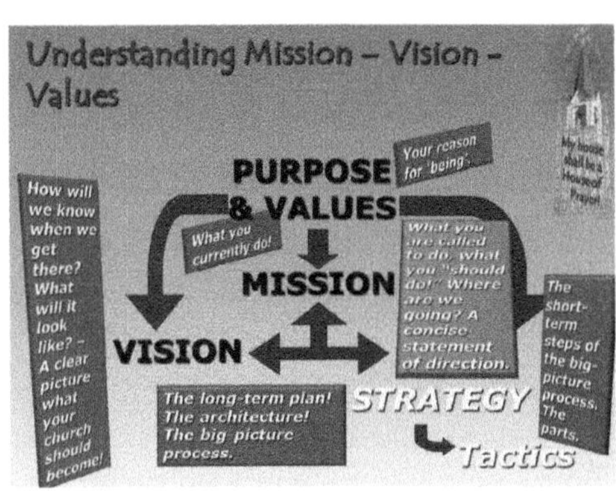

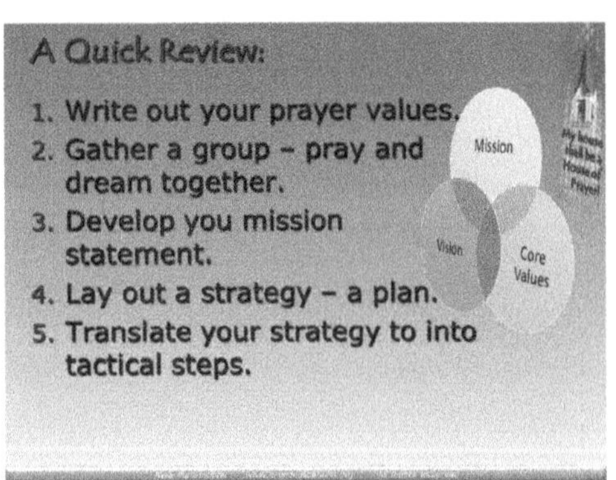

---

11 Craig Brian Larson, *Illustrations for Preaching and Teaching* (Grand Rapids, MI: Baker Books, 1993), 59.

Your goal is to mobilize an entire church to pray. At first, everyone will say, "Yes, let's make our church a house of prayer!" Then the reality of what prayer will cost will become clear. And your initial enthusiasm will fade. Don't be discouraged. Persevere without being punitive toward those who pull back – you'll have some surprises in this area. Refuse to allow a "they don't want to pray!" pessimism to develop among your leaders. It is a subtle form of pride that will paralyze your movement. It leads to a division that immobilizes you. There can be no them--and-us mentality allowed to take root. Your prayer journey is much like a long interstate trip. There are many entrances and exits along the way. Some will leave you and later rejoin the movement. Others will not come into the stream of prayer initially. They may choose another entrance point. For example, not all will respond to a 3-day prayer summit. The idea may be too intimidating for them. Some intercessors will not want to be a part of an Intercessory Prayer Team. Not everyone will attend the church-wide prayer gatherings. No single prayer slice, program, or event will capture everyone. Some will join the parade through the entrance of prayer evangelism. Others will join when you announce prayer training for lost family members. Still others, when you form prayer ministry teams. Some will see a need for family prayer – for learning to bless their children, and that will be the key to their response. A few will join you in support of national concerns and moral issues. Some may have a specific passion to pray daily for Jerusalem. If you expect everyone to come through one door, one event, or one training model your prayer process will fail. It must be broad and long-term. Keep offering different entry points into the journey.

This means that you have to create side-doors into prayer. As the prayer leaders work with department leaders to help them integrate prayer into every aspect of the life of the church, the members will inevitably be exposed to new prayer styles and models, literature, and language. Don't expect them to come to you – to either prayer training or doing events. Take prayer to them. Push it into every seam of church life. This will happen as the leaders of

Sunday School classes, small groups, men and women's ministries, children and youth leaders, couples and singles – all are trained themselves as prayer leaders. Insist: To be a leader of any ministry in this church, you must be a prayer leader. No ministry can be led without prayer.

Forewarning

At West Point, there is a saying, "No plan survives contact with the enemy."[12] Unpredictable things happen outside your control. The army has a crisp, plain-talk statement stamped on all its orders – called a CI. That is code for the Commander's Intent. It is a reminder not to get lost in a battle plan (tactics) and lose the war (the big picture plan). It is permission to improvise, on the spot, as long as the ultimate strategic objective is in mind. The details, the tactical steps, are subordinate to the overall strategy, and the strategic plan itself has its roots in the ultimate mission and vision. Strategies and tactics change – the mission and vision, the values that drive them and inform them are constant.[13] It is the core idea, the 'Commander's Intent' that is important.

12 Chip Heath and Dan Heath, *Made to Stick: Why Some Ideas Survive and Others Die* (New York: Random House, 2007), 25.
13 Ibid, 26.

MILESTONE SIX
Affirming Leaders (Leadership Structuring and Affirmation)

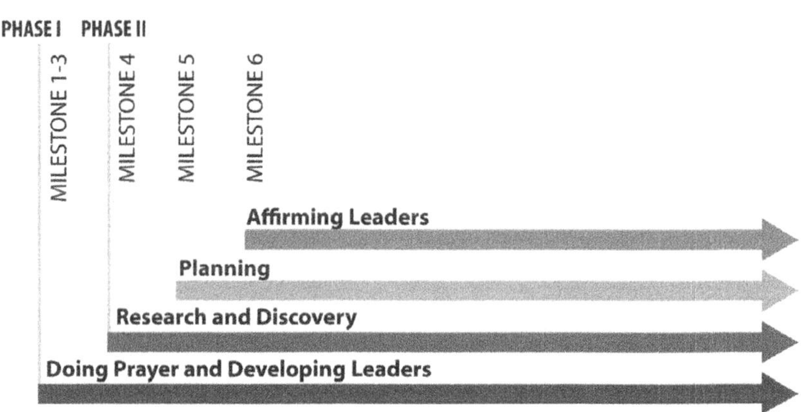

Proposition

The prayer effort moves forward on two legs – *learning and doing*, and then comes *leading*. You started *doing* prayer in your church-wide prayer effort; and quietly developing learning-leaders who themselves, have not only learned together, but also, prayed together. In order to plan, you entered into a discovery and research process, gathering data on your congregation, the prayer needs of your congregation and community. You then conducted an extensive *planning* retreat and projected an informed plan.

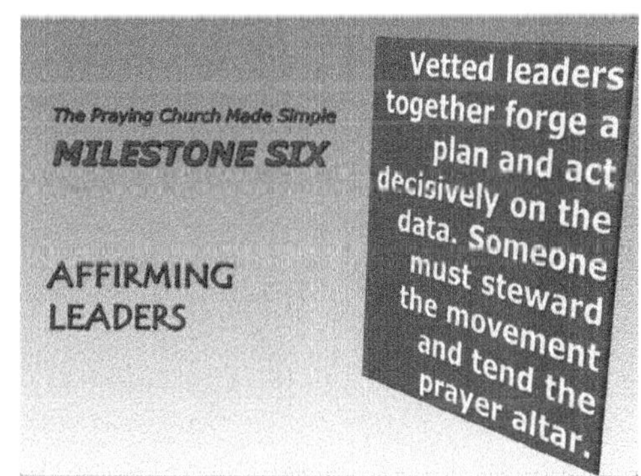

Now, more than ever, you are moving into the execution phase. What was on the edges of congregational life will now be front and center – you are ready to call your congregation into a full-blown encounter with God in prayer. From your learning team, explorers and planners, <u>you will now set forth a leadership team</u>. You have seen them under pressure. You have measured their willingness to learn and their flexibility; both are important. You have a sense of those who are tactical and those who can think strategically. You have also heard them pray – and not merely 'pretty praying,' but with passion and depth, scope and vision, Biblical roots and balance. You have seen them mature, and among them, you have observed those who bring others to consensus and those who repel; those who serve as glue for the group and those who are at times sandpaper. It is time now, from among these, to set forth a prayer leadership team.

Timing

<u>This transition from learners, to explorers, to planners and now to leaders might occur as early as 9 months or take as long as 18-24 months</u>. The typical transition will probably be between 15-18 months occurring in the second quarter of your second year. More important than linear time is sequential time – you have prayed and learned together, you have explored and planned, and now you are ready to lead.

Resources

This is the point at which a leadership planning retreat might be very helpful. A curriculum that you might find useful is based on the book, *Transforming Your Church into a House of Prayer – Revised Edition*. It has a schedule for a rather intense weekend leadership planning retreat. You can adapt the schedule for an in-town experience. During the retreat, you will review critical conceptual materials. You will also unwrap the data from your discovery exercises and surveys, and you will begin the process of projecting your on-going strategy and your next steps.

Continue to draw from the book, *Transforming Your Church into a House of Prayer – Revised Edition,* also *The*

Praying Church Made Simple, but especially, this publication *Milestones.* You will also find the quarterly curriculum in PLCE very helpful in gathering your leaders and processing through teaching, examining fresh tools, and most importantly – talk-it-over and assessing your next 3-6 months. In addition, you want to draw heavily from your research and your strategic plan.

As noted earlier, you will find an annual leadership retreat, or extended thinking-praying-planning event helpful to keep you focused. The newly formed strategic prayer leadership team will need to continue to meet monthly as they did in their learning phase. Continued participation in the PLCE quarterly gatherings will also be a great benefit.

Duration

The prayer leadership team will need three-to-five years to begin to transform the culture of the congregation. The group can be expected to expand as the ministry goes forward and grows, but the core of team should remain constant. Frequent leadership changes will destroy the foundation that you laid.

Focus

The focus now is on implementation of the plan. It is important, in the initial plan development, that it rise out of learning, out of the exploration of the original learning-discovery team so that it is an informed plan, and out of the planning retreat, so that it is owned by the larger prayer leadership team and key congregational leaders. It is also important, that in the drawing of the map, the final plan developed by the Prayer Leadership Team, that pastoral input and affirmation is clear. The plan must be his plan, his vision, his mission, reflecting his values, informed by his learning and growth, as well as the research process. The prayer coordinator and the pastor must be on the same page. The architect's great challenge will be in developing a plan that is both a valid expression of the pastor's vision and reflective of the various dreams and plans of the learning-exploring-planning team. And yet, it must be strategic and not merely a string of unrelated tactical ideas, or a collage of prayer ministry ideas unwrapped serially. Neither the pastor nor the prayer learning-discovery team can be betrayed. Nor with integrity, can the architect draw. Nor with integrity, his own plans. Without involvement in the process, the typical pastor, whose approach is most often single-dimensional, serial and tactical, will say, "Keep it simple." That may destroy months of research and planning. As noted earlier, the problem of prayerlessness is pervasive – it affects everything. The failure of the church is systematic in nature, therefore the solution required must be systematic. The plan must be multi-faceted in scope, systematic in nature, and designed to be rolled out over a three to five year period. It must be simple enough to be clearly articulated but not simplistic. It must reflect the input of those who carry out its details.

Involvement Goals

First, the goal is to <u>solidify the key leaders</u>. Then, <u>enlarge the prayer leadership team as new layers of prayer are added and new emphases implemented</u>. The goal is to engage the entire congregation in a movement of prayer:

- At-home, personal and couple's prayer, family prayer
- At-church prayer, beyond a church-wide prayer meeting, a process that embeds prayer at the heart of every church ministry effort
- The identification and mobilization of intercessors;
- The turning of prayer's energy outward onto a broken and lost world
- On-going training and teaching that addresses all the various aspects of prayer and the prayer effort, systematically
- The development of a prayer room, center (in a larger church), or some physical focus for prayer and evangelism

You started with a small group. You called the church to participate in a congregation-wide prayer meeting. You chose a small group of learners, and expanded it to explore the depth and breadth of prayer in your congregation, and examine the prayer ministries of other churches.

You forged an informed plan. Now you have a permanent leadership team. From one, to a small group, to a prayer meeting crowd, to the Sunday morning gathering – you are incrementally engaging the church in a call to pray.

Transition: The transition is now <u>from the planning team to the leadership team</u>.

Common Mistakes

<u>The most common mistake is to appoint leaders before they are learners, before their theology of prayer is stretched and reshaped, before they are exposed to research inside and outside your congregation. Doing so, you short-circuit the process</u>. Don't take short cuts. You must battle reductionism. If you don't, you will accept a small vision, a doable man-sized mission and plan, rather than an impossible God-sized plan. You will appoint leaders whose prayer theology and ideas have not been stretched. That will mean more trips around the old prayer mountain – not a new worship-fed, transformational prayer model ready to energize mission.

Leaders will, in a sense, self-select. They will be commended by their peers as a result of their gifts, their temperament, the collegiality, their evident leadership skills, and, their permission to lead, which is the influence factor. It is important that the pastor stay connected to the learning and exploring phases. In a small congregation, he may lead these efforts – and that is ideal. He is building around himself and the church, the most important and critical group to the congregation's success – certainly equal to the elders and deacons, and, to any staff, paid or volunteer. In a large congregation, if he does not lead the learning-exploring process, he must stay connected to it. In short, he too must learn. Otherwise, the prayer effort will default to his underexposed theology of prayer and his insufficient information about prayer trends and models. The work of a valiant prayer learning team will then be frustrated, perhaps, aborted. It is important that the process work, that true prayer leaders bubble up, that the exercise not be a pretense – with predetermined leaders and a model secretly written in advance. Trust the Holy Spirit.

Note: You have now crossed another major threshold. You have informed leaders in place, in a larger group of leaders – a group that has prayed together, learned and explored together, a group that both respects and loves one another. They are poised to lead the congregation forward in prayer, and to expand the effort.

YOU ARE NOW AT A CHECK POINT!

Going Public: Feeding the Prayer Fire and Finding Leaders

Phase III

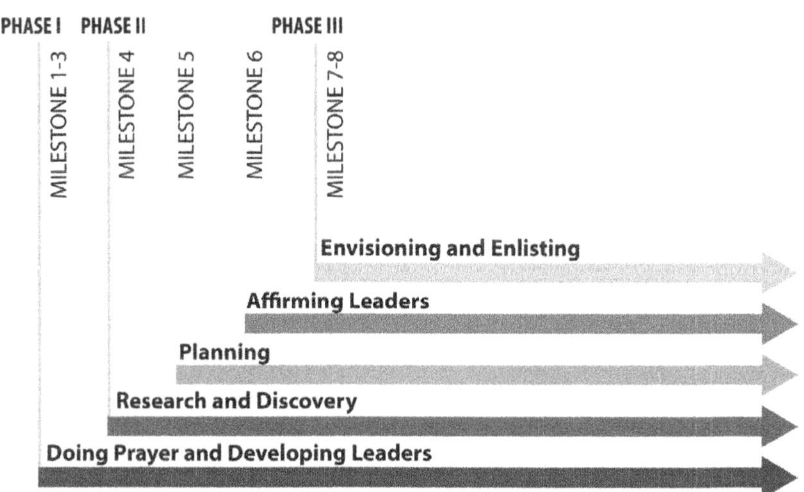

Congregation

You have been quietly praying and learning, while focusing on developing a group of leaders. A slice of the congregation is praying. You have explored and discovered the depth of prayer and prayer models. You have projected plans for moving forward. Now, a vetted leadership team is in place. At the very least, you have in place, the bare bones of a strategy to move you forward. It is not that you have been hiding your prayer effort. Everyone has been consistently invited to the weekly prayer meeting. You have quietly recruited leaders to your learning team meetings. You have encouraged daily time with God. In the exploration and discovery phase, you again recruited as you did for the planning retreat. It is time again to

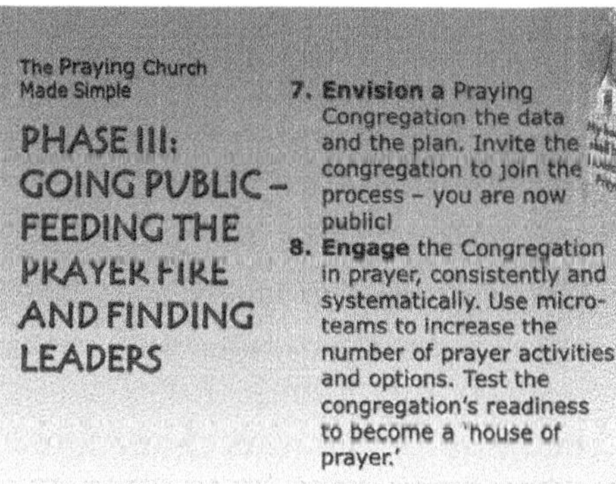

expand your circle of prayer leaders go public with your effort.

You are attempting to build the fire you have started. It is not yet burning – throughout your congregation. Fires are usually started with materials that have a low combustibility factor – paper, twigs, kindling. Those substances start a fire, but alone, they can't sustain it. The fire is only sustained when its intensity and combustibility levels consume small, dry pieces of wood, the larger and harder ones, than a cold, wet log. Certain woods are unmoved by the combustibility level that overcomes paper. To mainstream prayer, your prayer-fire levels must intensify, and you must mainstream prayer. You are now giving light prayer-fire in almost every area of congregational life. Your intensity and combustibility levels will increase, all to the end, that the congregation embraces prayer fire. Caution: To be successfully, you must be sincere. No 'strange' fire. It must be God's fire, and not merely enthusiasm. As you envision the church as house of prayer for the nations, and engage them in a variety of prayer experiences and exercises – pray for fire to fall on the altars you are building.

Say to the congregation, "For some time, a small group in the congregation has been meeting and praying about how to bring prayer more fully to center of all we do. We want to be a 'house of prayer for the nations.' We have been collecting data on the state of prayer in our congregation, looking at what other churches are doing, and studying the needs of the community and city around us – and we have discovered in some rather specific ways, how desperately both we and our city needs God. Our profound congregational need for revival, we believe begins with prayer. We need God for our sake and the sake of the community. We need a revival in the church, that leads to a spiritual awakening in the community.

Of course, you want to encourage the entire church to embrace the new prayer paradigm – to pray daily, to join the weekly prayer meeting, and you want to expand your prayer leadership team. You especially want to encourage elders/deacons, staff – lay leaders and paid, who have not been engaged in the effort thus far, to join the prayer

---

In the planning stage, you must *"Shrink the change."* Make the change small, incremental, and increase the possibility of success. In shrinking the change, and granting a sense of success, you grow the people, build faith, change habits and rally the herd for the next challenge, preserving your unity and momentum.

— Chip Heath and Dan Heath, *Switch: How to Change Things When Change is Hard* (New York: Broadway, 2010), 134.

reformation train. You want to gently probe resistance without demanding participation – this has to be an inner-outer work. It can't be mandated, and yet, unless leaders lead, and do so by example, the effort will stall.

Individuals

Previously, your call to pray was general. Now you are specifically looking for intercessors, prayer evangelists, those with an interest in youth and children's prayer, the family altar, prayer partner ministry and other prayer focus areas you might develop. You are looking for prayers, that's critical. You are also searching for those with a capacity to lead some aspect of your expanding prayer ministry.

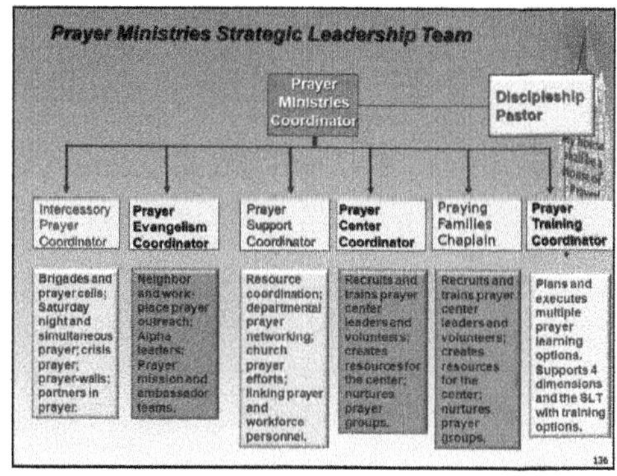

Leaders

In this stage, the learning-leaders will now crystalize into a strategic prayer leadership team. From among them, your most catalytic leader will emerge; and alongside that leader will be those who probably will lead some component of the prayer effort. Around your core leaders (SPLT) will emerge a prayer council for your congregation. The earlier learning process was designed to take leaders deeper; now you must take them wider, broadening their scope.

Focus Areas

Prayer Task Team Coordinators

This prayer ministry leadership model focuses on eight areas.

1. ***Prayer Ministries Coordinator*** – *Developing a culture of prayer* – the critical and most important function of the prayer ministry: *a praying people.* This is the over-arching leadership role.[1] In this role is the area, not noted in the diagram, of developing praying homes. In a larger congregation,

---

1   For a comprehensive job description for the Prayer Ministries Coordinator, see the *Praying Church Resource Guide.* You will find other job descriptions for the other key prayer leadership roles there as well.

a Family Ministries pastor might take that role. Family prayer is foundational – don't forget it.

2. ***Personal and Family Prayer Coach*** – *Nurtures personal daily prayer,* encourages prayer closets, the practice of couples praying and the re-establishment of the family altar, the cultivation of the missional family.

3. ***Department Support Coordinator*** – *Nurtures the role of prayer as a central component of every ministry in the church.* This may be the role of the Prayer Coordinator in the smaller congregation. This is the person who interfaces with each ministry department – seniors, family/couples, men, women, college and career, singles, youth, children, etc.

4. ***Intercessory Prayer Coordinator*** – *Recruits and structures intercessory prayer cells.* Helps build PIT crews. Mobilizes, trains, deploys, and debriefs intercessors.

5. ***Prayer Evangelism Coordinator*** – *Builds the "great commission" dimension of prayer ministry.* In the smaller church, intercessory prayer mobilization and prayer evangelism may be combined.

6. ***Marketplace Coordinator*** – *Identifies members in the workplace for prayer and evangelism mobilization.* With less than twenty-percent of the population in church on any given Sunday, we must develop a more intentional 'go' strategy. The first step is to encourage members to take prayer to work with them – and pray for those who work around them. Every city needs a workplace prayer and evangelism, salt-and-light strategy.

7. ***Training Coordinator*** – *Builds a curriculum, recruits and trains trainers for prayer ministry;* an ongoing training process in all four areas. This may be the role of the Prayer Coordinator or may often be the role of the Discipleship Pastor. It also could be the role of the Department Support Coordinator, who works with the various church ministries to identify resources for them to teach and train in the area of prayer ministries. Of course, each prayer ministry leader (Intercessors, Prayer Evangelism, Prayer Center) may also be training.

8. ***Prayer Room/Center Coordinator*** – the prayer

center will become the nerve center of the church. (In the smaller church, this will probably be role of the Coordinator.) This role develops the prayer life of the congregation beyond the weekly pastor-led prayer meeting and the Sunday experience. It seeks to make the church 'a house of prayer' – seven days a week. Around the prayer room/center, the prayer group ministry will revolve, as well as, the integration of prayer teams into various ministries and the proliferation of prayer throughout the congregation, even the community.

In the typical church, your core prayer leadership team will lead these efforts, and probably wear two or more hats.

Prayer Ministries Council

This is a gathering of all your prayer ministry leaders – everyone that leads a prayer ministry effort in the congregation – men and women's prayer, the intercessory ministry, prayer evangelism, coordinator of any prayer groups that you have established, youth and children's prayer leaders, prayer trainers and prayer chain mobilizers. They fill out your prayer effort, around your Strategic Planning Team, whether that consists of your core leaders or others plus that original group of learners. You cannot lead the prayer ministry alone. The goal is the entire congregation aflame in prayer.

Each of the focus areas are actually a cluster of various tactical *prayer ministries*, each needing a leader. You will need additional leaders, beyond a Strategic Leadership Team (SLT) around core leaders. In many cases, your core leaders will be your SLT, each of them taking a focus area and serving as the coordinator. In a typical congregation, they probably served as the 'task team' leaders when you introduced various prayer activities in the most recent phase. Now they will need to recruit effective members from their task teams or others to develop a team to assist in their focus area of responsibility. These are referred to earlier as Strategic Task Teams, contrasted with your Strategic Leadership Team (core leaders). They gather individuals who will lead slices of

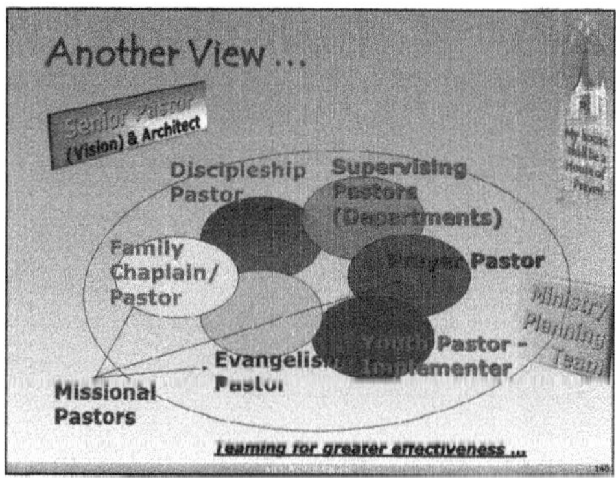

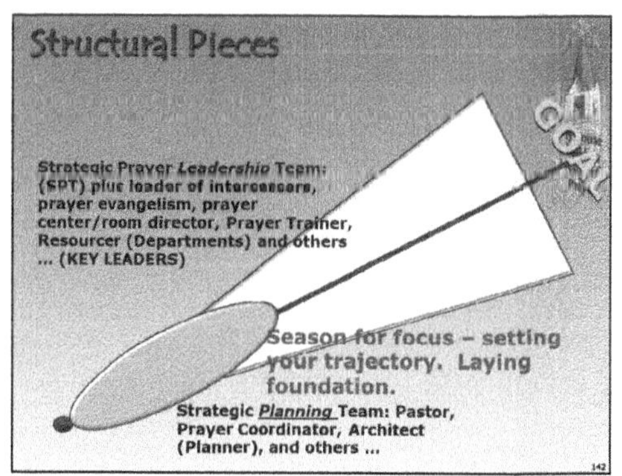

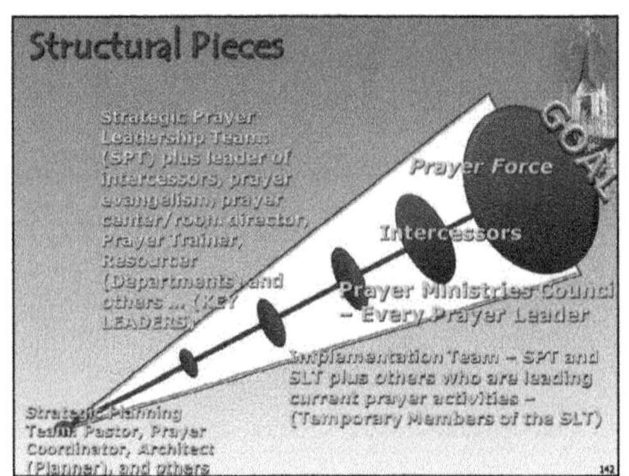

prayer. For example, the prayer evangelism coordinator may be looking for a coordinator for neighborhood prayer. Someone else might have a passion to start prayer groups for the lost at workplaces. Another might lead regular prayer mission teams into the community. Some individual might serve as a liaison to a local school that the church has adopted for prayer, to police or fire personnel that also been adopted, etc. Each strategic task team will consist of those who lead various tactical prayer endeavors in the sectors of your prayer effort.

All these tactical prayer ministry leaders will then serve on a Prayer Council that integrates every prayer ministry effort into one of the many areas stewarded by the SLT. The Prayer Council brings all the strategic and tactical leaders together. This group should be convened at least twice annually for prayer, dialogue, envisioning, and teaming. You should consider, at least in the early years, an annual prayer leadership retreat or an annual Prayer Training Conference.

The kind of STT prayer ministries these people might lead, include:

- Adopt-a-cop in prayer; or a fireman. Shield-a-badge
- Altar Prayer Response Leader
- Annual Prayer and Evangelism Conference Coordinator
- Children's Prayer Leader
- Coordinator of Prayer Groups
- Father and Son Prayer Experiences Coordinator.
- Healing Teams Leader
- Intercessory Prayer Teams
- Intercessory Issue/Cause Groups
- Intercessory Coordinator for Community Leaders – matching intercessors with community leaders for prayer! Intercessors in public hearings, courtrooms, especially when church-state and faith issues are decided.
- Leaders for the Prayer Center
- Mother and Daughter Prayer Experience Coordinator
- Neighborhood Prayer Evangelism

- Nursery Prayer Coordinator – Blessing the babies, not just baby-sitting
- Pastor's Prayer Partners
- Prayer Ambassador Ministry – teams of positive, priestly pray-ers sent out to bless community leaders, both those who are believers and those who are not
- Prayer-Care Teams – ministry to shut-ins and others in need
- Prayer Chains and Watch Organizer
- Prayer Coordination for the Shepherds of the City
- Prayer for Unsaved Family and Friends
- Prayer Mission Teams – overseas /out-of-town prayer deployment
- Prayer Missions – in the city, focused on specific places
- Prayer Partner Ministry
- Prayer Retreat Coordinator
- Prayer Support for Missions – missionaries, UPGs, nations, the 10/40 window
- Prayer teams - focused on dark places in the city, social pain
- See-you-at-the-pole – School Prayer (4th Wed. of September at the School Flagpole)
- Senior Prayer Partners of Youth
- Systematic Prayer Walking
- Workplace Prayer Evangelism
- Youth Prayer Leader

Intercessors

Intercessors comprise one of the focus areas. However, they also constitute the bubble of prayer support in which the prayer ministry itself operates. Everything, even the prayer ministry itself, should be bathed in prayer. So find ways to wrap every effort in prayer. It seems strange to suggest that we should "pray about prayer!" But if we are not careful, we'll replace God's direction for our prayer ministry with good ideas.

Prayer Force

The whole of the prayer effort - every individual who is praying at home or is an identified part of the one of the prayer efforts – constitutes *the prayer force*. The total prayer force of your church is determined by the number of people you can quantify as being a part of some aspect of the congregation's prayer effort. For every stream and type of prayer in the church, how many are you mobilizing for prayer? How many homes are signed up as praying for their neighbors? How many are doing the work of intercession? How many are taking a watch shift at the prayer center? How many are using the prayer center – by personal visit, email contact, or phone-call? How many are now praying daily?

The ideal would be – every member a part of the prayer force! The practical goal in this phase is to mobilize and involve at least 50% of the church in some exercise, some prayer ministry endeavor – learning or doing, in the course of the year!

The Envisioning Evening Example Schedule

7:00 p.m. Welcome – Begin with expressions of thanksgiving and praise.

7:10 p.m. Share your vision, as pastor, for prayer ministries in the church based on your research and discoveries.

7:25 p.m. Show one of the shorter Transformation Videos. I use Transformations II (the Preview Clip). It is about 17 minutes.

7:45 p.m. Share stories of what is happening in other congregations that have become intentional in developing a prayer ministry.

8:00 p.m. Pray...Sharing is great! But you also want to hear those present pray! Use the verbiage outlined previously. Gently remind everyone, "Don't share it...pray it!" Keep everyone vertical. It may be uncomfortable at first, but the dynamic of praying something is different, than sharing the same thing. Listen not only for content, focus also for heart.

8:15 p.m. Break into small groups (4-7). Ask each member to share – "What is your passion for prayer and prayer ministries?" Organize everyone in at least these four groups:

1. Church-wide prayer. Prayer meetings. Prayer groups. Pastoral prayer support. Personal Intercessory Teams for church department leaders, staff members, mission endeavors, etc. How do we make our church a house of prayer?

2. At-Home Prayer. Daily Prayer. Personal and family devotions. The power of praying with and for our children. The restoration of the family altar.

3. Intercessors and Intercessory prayer. Priestly and prophetic intercession. Mobilizing and teaming intercessors, directing and debriefing intercessors, etc.

4. Prayer-Evangelism. Prayer for the lost. An external focus on prayer. A mission near and far. Prayer for the city. Prayer walks and prayer missions. Prayer ambassador teams.

5. Additional groups might form around – youth and children's prayer, developing a prayer room/center, praying training, prayer events, etc.

8:30 p.m. Refocus the group – ask them this question   "What is God saying to us about prayer in our church and community?"

8:45 p.m. General Sharing. Wrap up and summary by the leader.

MILESTONE SEVEN
Envisioning the Congregation

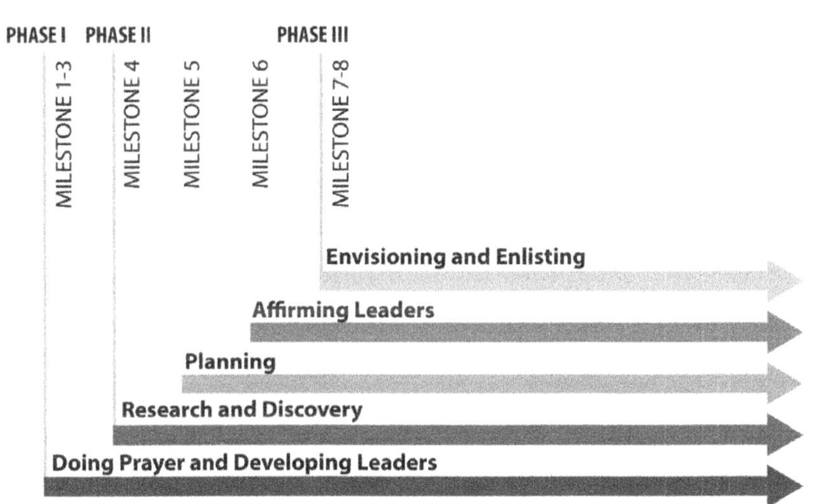

Proposition

For more than a year, you have been conducting a congregation-wide prayer meeting. You have not been primarily concerned with numbers – and that is an important consideration. At times, in a small church, you may have gone to a prayer meeting in which no one showed up – but, you were there, and you prayed, and you persisted. At other times, those in attendance might have consisted only of the small group of leaders with whom you had also been meeting separately. <u>The bottom line is this –</u>

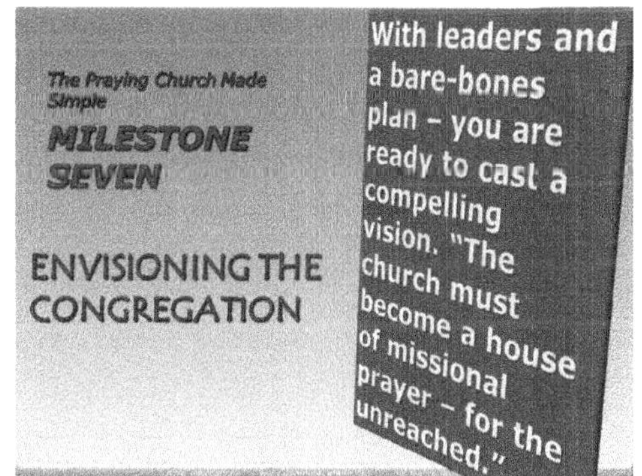

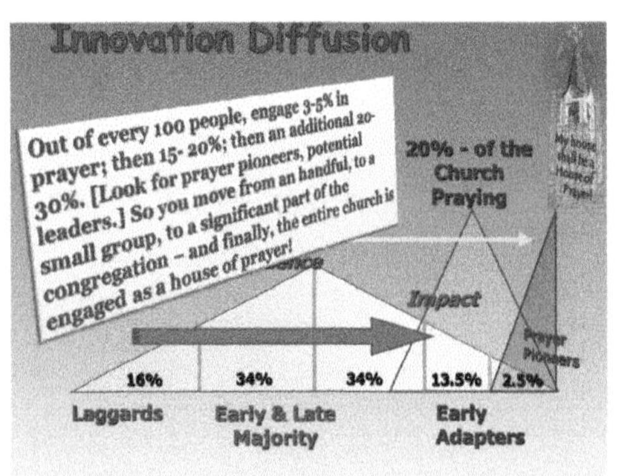

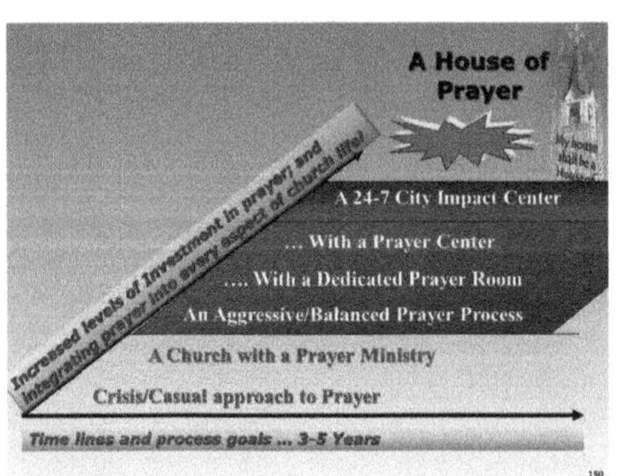

you persevered; and, hopefully, you have begun to forge a model for your prayer meeting that is effective, even if that has been primarily with your learning team. You should have also had occasional Sunday prayer experiences. You may have exposed the congregation to various calls to prayer: National Day of Prayer, Seek God for the City emphasis, Pentecost Sunday, January Prayer and Fasting. In each case, you have not been concerned, to this point, with numbers – the calls have served to uncover those with a heart from prayer, provide opportunities to expand prayer's focus from self-interested praying to kingdom prayer purposes. That is enough to have served your purpose at this point. It may have revealed the abysmal lack of interest in prayer, especially in prayer that was not self-interested, but even that is helpful – it gives you your baseline. It's your reality.

Now, you are ready to *envision* the congregation with the mission, that it become a house of prayer for the nations. Then, in the next phase, you will *engage* the congregation. You have no alternative. Jesus wants his people to be a praying people, his church, a house of prayer for the nations. Previously, you recruited for your learning team quietly and privately. Then you added others in the discovery-exploration and planning process.

Now, you will openly recruit to your effort. Make an announcement on Sunday morning. Build interest, "Those interested in seeing our church become a house of prayer; join us from an evening of prayer and vision." Put on the coffee. Conduct the meeting in your fellowship hall around tables. Share findings from your research and exploration. At some point, designate certain tables for interest in various aspects of your effort. At each table, a member of your prayer leadership team will be able to inform and recruit volunteers to some aspect of your expanding prayer effort. The focus areas, and even potential prayer exercises that you may have identified in your planning retreat, should be at the top of your discussion list. In smaller churches, combine the table discussions – personal and family prayer, prayer at and in the congregation, intercession and prayer evangelism. Keep the seven marks of a praying church in mind in the process.

You now want to permeate your congregation with

prayer until you have a worshipful prayer ministry with mission at its edge. The depth of your foundation determines the height and weight it can carry. Going deep is critical to moving forward and higher. If you have chosen to follow the model, as you have worked quietly, under the radar, you have had ups-and-downs, comers and goers, breakdowns and breakthroughs – but you persisted. You learned, explored, and you have now projected an informed plan. You have affirmed and confirmed a SPLT.

All along, you have laced prayer experiences into your Sunday worship. Your prayer theology is healthier – at least your leaders believe that prayer is at its heart, worship, and at its edge mission, and in between, God meets our needs. It is a relationship with a holy God in the context of love and grace that calls for change – in us, our churches, and our world. This is a view of prayer you want the entire congregation to come to own. You are ready for the entire church to catch prayer fire.

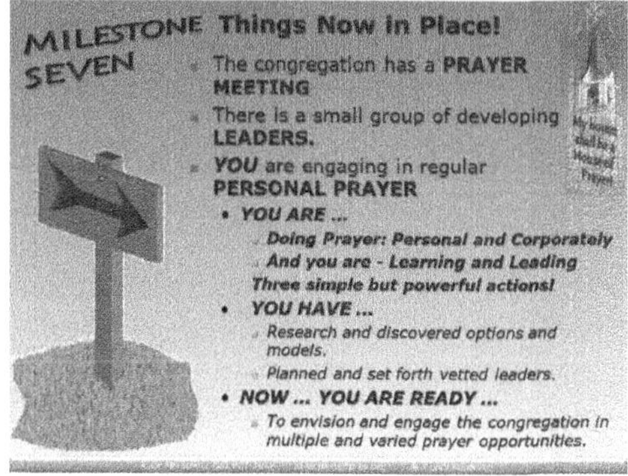

Focus

The focus is vision - the congregation as a house of prayer for the nations. Not only a house of praise and preaching, but a house of prayer; not a place primarily for nurturing and encouragement, but a place of mission and engagement. Mission need not displace nurture, nor prayer, praise, and preaching – but a new balance is needed. You are informing and yet, allowing members who have not been involved in the process, to express their desire and heart for the effort moving forward.

Timing

This is your recruitment moment – a call to the entire congregation to embrace the prayer effort. You have leaders in place. Even though you have conducted your planning retreat, remember, your vision always expands, your strategy will be redefined, and your tactics reconfigured, all this, over and over again. This is a big idea, a major congregational paradigm shift. You may discover that you need a series of vision evenings. If necessary, take a year to envision and engage the congregation in specific aspects of your prayer cause.

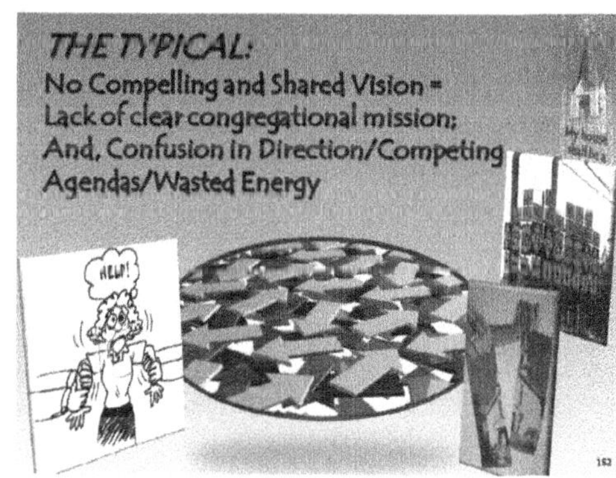

Resources

There is a resource for the envisioning evening available in the *Praying Church Resource Guide - Section 1*. *Read more and download a Power Point file at: projectpray.org/become-a-praying-church.*

Duration

The envisioning evening requires advanced planning, promotion and specific recruitment to the event. The meeting should be planned for a couple hours; and if, due to interest, people tarry and talk, rejoice. Just make sure you release those with child-care needs and concerns so that they do not have to leave unceremoniously. You may choose, as an alternative to do a Saturday morning or Sunday evening envisioning session.

Involvement Goals

Elders and/or deacons should be in attendance. Other key leaders and staff, should be present as well as the recently engaged SPLT, learning team, explorers and planners, your developing prayer council, and prayer leaders. Your minimal goal for this meeting is twenty-percent of your Sunday morning crowd. If you have more in attendance – rejoice! That is good sign.

Keep in mind, catalysts and pioneers rarely number more than three-to-five percent. In a small church, that may be only a couple of committed believers. Your early adapters will number no more than 12-15 percent. To arrive at a congregational majority of 30-to-35 percent engagement will take 3-to-5 years. The late majority, another 30-to-35 percent, will have to be convinced, repeatedly and graciously engaged – 5-10 years. Expect resistance, mostly passive. It will take time, years, to move the entire congregation to daily, personal, Christ-centered prayer – years.

Don't allow excitement and enthusiasm to be mistaken for deep, transformational prayer. At the other end of the continuum, as many as 5-15 percent may always resist your prayer effort. Superficial resistance will be due to style and philosophy differences. You must counter this with patience and teaching. Profound resistance will be due to carnality. The flesh hates true prayer; it resists repentance. It battles change. It struggles to hold on to tradition and comfortable old patterns that do not challenge it.

Your goal is your entire congregation involved in your prayer effort. Prayer cannot be a sidebar endeavor by a spiritually elite group of specialists. Prayer is the best friend you have to humility and unity, to a servant spirit in your congregation. The carnal run from prayer or attempt to control it. The immature are intimidated by it, they have to be helped across the creek. The truly spiritual and godly hunger for it. A praying congregation is God's tool for a community transformed.

The Congregational Envisioning Evening.

Your first efforts were by-invitation to the prayer meeting and the learning-leader team; and then to the exploration team; and the planning team. This is a 'whosoever-will' gathering. You may still need to 'compel' some key potential leaders to the evening. The goal of the evening is to explore what it would mean to make prayer a higher congregational priority – to bring prayer to the heart of church ministries, to renew personal prayer, to encourage family altars, to identify and mobilize intercessors, to push prayer beyond the boundaries of the church.

Have this meeting in a warm area that encourages conversation. Do it around tables if possible. Put the coffee on and have some light snacks. You may need to have Power Point projection capability, perhaps, a marker-board and an informal atmosphere.

Out of this group, you will begin the process of recruiting to your various prayer ministry leadership teams – first for the prayer activities you will conduct in the next year, and then, to the prayer processes those activities represent. People will self-declare their interest in prayer related to children or youth, men or women, families and singles, intercession and prayer evangelism, missionaries and unreached peoples.

You can find stories in the books, *Transforming Your*

Church into a House of Prayer – the Revised Edition, Entertaining God – Influencing Cities, Intercession – the Strategic Critical Middle, and also, *Prayer – the Heart of it All.* Or, you can google prayer stories and find wonderful inspirational stories to share.

The shorter of the transformation videos is called *Transformation II, Preview Clip* and is available from George Otis, the Sentinel Group. Or, you can obtain it by calling Alive Ministries: PROJECT PRAY, 855-842-5483.

Lead a conversation about the need for prayer. And then share your vision for an expanded prayer ministry in your congregation. And, pray. Ask specific people to pray. Have each table pray. Have them pray one at a time – and then ask, "What is God saying to you?"

Poll the interest of the group in various prayer ministry areas (just an example):

- Intercessory Prayer
- Family prayer
- Church-based prayer groups
- Establishing a prayer room
- Integrating prayer into the ministries of the church
- Prayer training
- Youth/children's prayer
- Prayer Evangelism
- Beginning Prayer groups
- Establishing a pastor's prayer team

Invite members of your learning team, your core leaders (PMLT), those who assisted in the exploration and planning phases, to briefly share significant findings and plans.

Transition

This is the critical transition. <u>A new congregational paradigm is being proposed. It is carried forward by the pastor – a vision for a praying, missional church. A burgeoning group of leaders have learned, explored, and projected a potential plan. Now, the congregation must own the vision.</u> Their decision <u>cannot be in the form of a business session</u> – that would be a fatal mistake. God's plan is for His church to be 'house of prayer' and that is not up for vote; and yet, the vision and mission must be owned by the people. You must provide a context for discussion and engagement in which the Holy Spirit can change hearts. The visioning evening is an event; but on-going envisioning is a process that may require years. The typical time necessary to change the culture of the congregation is three-to-five years – and that may be optimistic.

Common Mistakes

A common mistake is <u>ignoring the delicate dance between the ownership of the congregation in the prayer vision and the learning and exploring of the emerging team</u>. The team cannot race ahead. It cannot force its conclusions on the congregation. Truth and love must travel together. <u>To lead, the emerging prayer team must have permission to lead, by the congregation's grasp of the vision</u> and its commitment to integrate the prayer values into congregational life. The strategic plan and the tactical path are subordinate to vision ownership. Don't get lost in the plan and the details. Keep vision and values foremost. You can develop your mission, your strategic plan, your tactical steps forward, but only vision will compel people to embrace change and follow the new path. The people need to 'see' the vision you hope they will 'own.' Be patient. Seeing the kingdom is the work of the Holy Spirit.

MILESTONE EIGHT
Church-Wide Enlistment

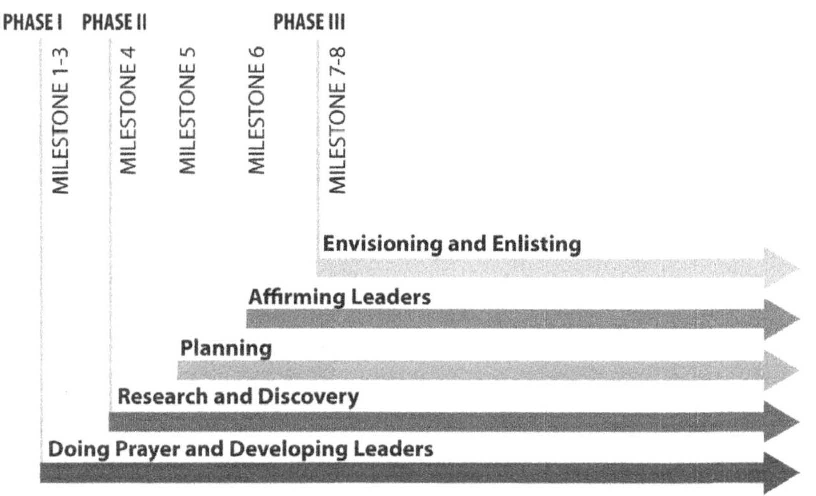

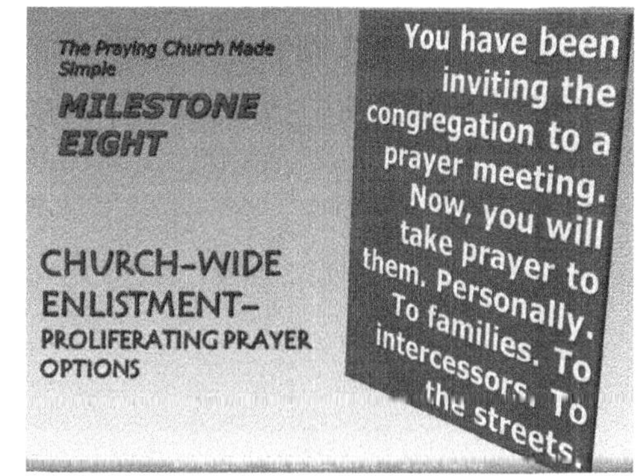

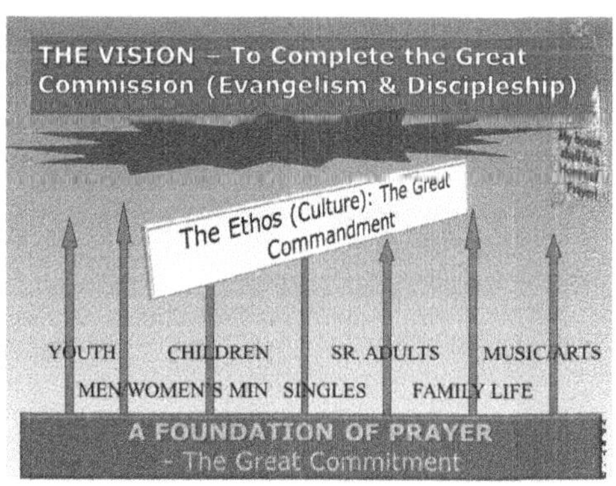

Proposition

In your visioning evening, you had an open discussion about the church as a house of prayer. <u>You should have exposed the congregation to the 'Seven Marks of a Praying Church,' and your values, perhaps adapted from the 'Ten Values of a Praying Church' resource. The envisioning evening is not to set the trajectory. It is, however, to affirm congruence between the perceptions of the congregation, what they see as the essential elements of a house of prayer, and the informed plan of your leaders.</u> You might find surprising congruence, but typically, you will

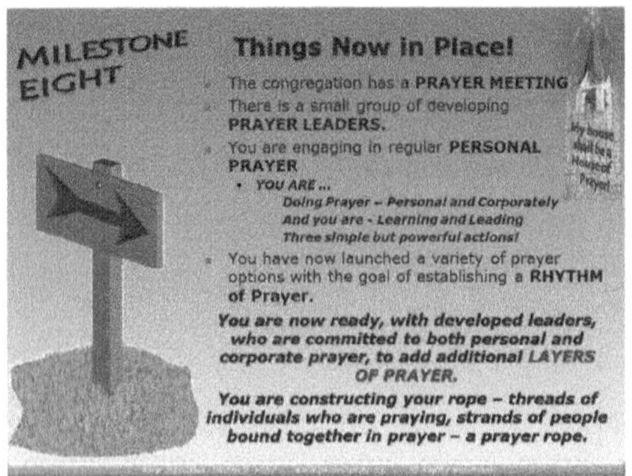

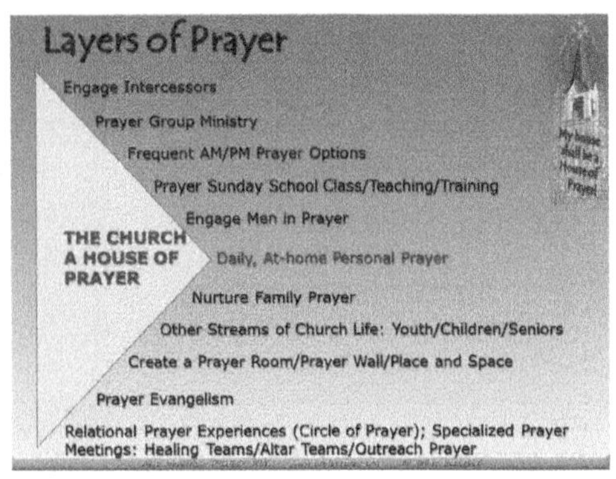

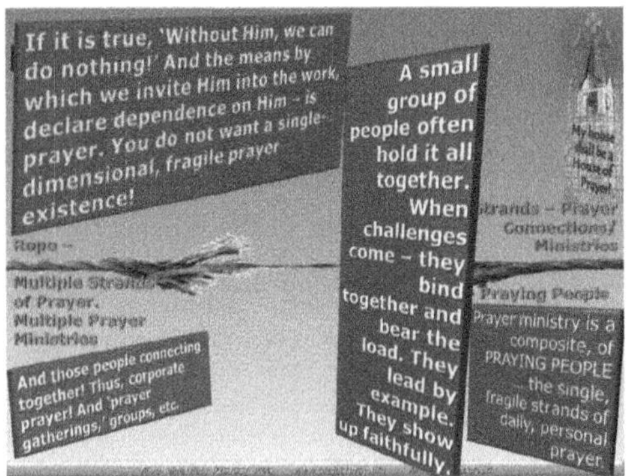

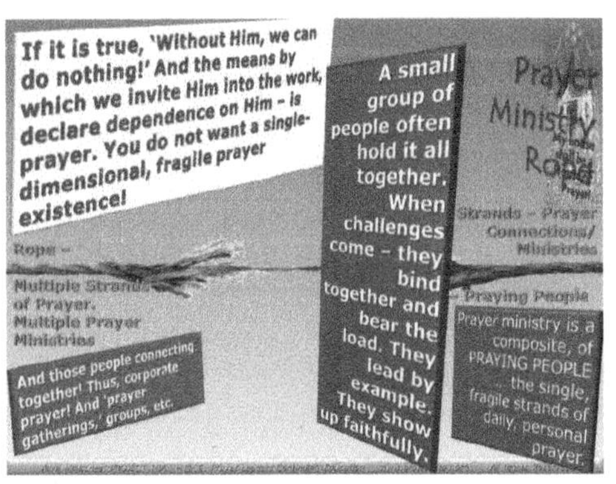

find significant distance between the two visions. You will need to teach and train into those gaps. The evening will help you determine your pace, how quickly you can move forward or how deliberately you must plod onward. Your envisioning evening may leave you thrilled by the interest and affirmation of the congregational participants. Or, it may leave you disheartened by the dissonance and confusion, by the degree of commitment to a narrow prayer theology. Be ready for either response. If necessary, plan a series of envisioning experiences.

You are learning from your members and stretching their vision. This is a marathon, not a sprint.

Focus

Your prayer effort is now public. Your goal now is congregational engagement. <u>Get 'em praying</u>.

Involvement Goals

<u>Enlist and engage the entire congregation, in segments</u>. Your first step will be more congregational prayer. Go slow. Yet, promote the church-wide prayer meeting more aggressively.

Offer additional prayer options. Again, pay attention to the levels of enlistment and engagement, but don't worry excessively about the numbers. Don't abandon the effort because prayer does not seem to be as popular as you desire. Prayer is never popular when the godless appetites of the culture are egregiously high and are bleeding into the church – and we are at a low cultural tide, morally and spiritually. You must persist. It is the only way out, the only pathway to spiritual awakening. Your core leaders (SPLT) should be more determined now more than ever. So, gently expose the congregation to various prayer emphases – personal transformational prayer, family prayer, intercession, prayer evangelism – and to various prayer themes – prayer for revival and awakening, prayer for the nation, for the lost and the never reached. As you expose them to lost-ness, to the needs of the city and the world, you will discover that information is fuel for prayer fire – and that is the value of your research and discovery phase. The Holy Spirit will open their eyes and inspire prayer.

Timing

Plan to take at least a year in <u>introducing various new prayer initiatives and exercises</u>. Look for existing national and international prayer resources that are easily imported and adapted. Don't make the mistake of just filling the calendar with prayer options. Be strategic. Keep thinking in terms of the 'Seven Markers of a Praying Church,' inside of which are the four dimensions – personal and family prayer, congregational prayer engagement, intercessory mobilization, and prayer and mission.

<u>Select activities that touch each of these areas</u>. Here is a sample:

- Personal/Family Prayer - Conduct a *family prayer* night. Do a family prayer revival. Review the resources noted earlier for personal and family prayer.

- Congregational Prayer - *Encourage the congregation to pray* beyond themselves.
  - ✓ The Call2Fall Sunday, an opportunity to get a congregation on their knees to pray for the nation occurs on the Sunday nearest July 4th annually (www.call2fall.com).
  - ✓ The International Day of Prayer for the Peace of Jerusalem, the first Sunday of October annually (www.jerusalemprayerteam.org and www.idop.org).
  - ✓ The International Day of Prayer for the Persecuted Church (idop.org and www.opendoorsusa.org), the first Sunday of November annually.

- Intercessory Prayer. Discover your *intercessors.*
  - ✓ Promote the 21-day virtual prayer meeting in January (www.amcrciapray.net).
  - ✓ The National Day of Prayer unites intercessors and patriotic Americans all across the nation on the first Thursday of May (www.nationaldayofprayer.net).
  - ✓ The Global Day of Prayer unites nations on Pentecost Sunday (www.globaldayofprayer.com).

- ✓ Cry Out America/Patriot Day is always on September 11 (sponsored by www.awakeningamerica.us and www.nationaldayofprayer.net).
- Prayer Evangelism. Great *prayer evangelism* tools and opportunities are found in:
  - ✓ The *Seek God for the City* guide (a 40-day prayer tool used in the season of Lent, www.waymakers.org).
  - ✓ The International Day of Prayer for Unreached Peoples (billion.tv/networking/prayer/) is the last Sunday of October annually.
- A *gathering of youth* at their schools around the flag pole occurs on the 4th Wednesday in September each year (www.syatp.com).

Integrate prayer opportunities into the life of the church regularly and systematically – family prayer engagement, intercession, prayer evangelism, the congregation praying corporately. Community prayer.

Project Pray and the Billion Soul Network produce monthly materials for use in prayer for Unreached Peoples (A bulletin insert and Power Point). These are available at projectpray.org/praying-for-unreached-people-groups. Church of God congregations can download resources at praycog.org/finish-challenge.

Build your prayer effort with the level of intensity that you feel appropriate for congregational engagement.

Resources

You will find resources for praying throughout the year in Section 8 of the *Praying Church Resource Guide* and online at www.projectpray.org/prayer-throughout-the-year.

Project prayer experience options for the next twelve months.

- Do some simple things to raise the profile of prayer ministry!
- Do a bulletin insert on prayer – monthly (Or, use one created with a focus on prayer evangelism for the unreached. You can retrieve it at projectpray.org/praying-for-unreached-people-groups.)

- Suggest books on prayer – make them available to the congregation.

- Show videos on prayer ministry to the congregation. The Sentinel Group has a whole series of videos on how prayer is changing the face of cities and in some cases nations. Check out teaching and training videos on at the ProjectPray YouTube channel.

- Do some teaching and preaching on prayer.

- Pray – form spontaneous groups for prayer after or during the Sunday service. Groups of five-or-six may be more comfortable than prayer-triads at the beginning.

Duration

<u>The duration of this phase is one year</u>. You are introducing devotional and missional prayer to the Sunday morning congregation. Each subsequent year, you will modify this prayer menu, adding, and in some cases, subtracting various emphases. You want to encourage a rhythm of prayer – daily prayer, weekly prayer as a congregation, participation in a prayer group, special monthly prayer engagements, quarterly prayer that might involve a gathering with other churches, and an annual day of prayer – National Day of Prayer, Pentecost Sunday, or a Solemn Assembly.

Focus

<u>Congregational</u> prayer engagement. Every member. Every family. All ages. Gentle calls to prayer with resources, "Teach us to pray!"

Involvement Goals

Incrementally, <u>more and more of your congregation</u>.

Transition

The critical transition in this stage is <u>intensifying prayer engagement</u>. Currently, Sunday morning is almost exclusively, for praise and preaching. If your congregation is like most others, when prayer is offered, especially in smaller churches, the immediate expectation is that prayer will be for personal needs – prayer requests. <u>Helping your congregation transition from narcissistic, self-interested, pragmatic praying is the hurdle you must transcend.</u> Prayer requests have their place, but not at the center, either of your corporate or personal prayer effort. Gently help the congregation move to worshipful prayer expressions.

Currently, we use the term 'praise and worship,' at least in Evangelical-Pentecostal congregations, to refer to singing. This narrows worship. Worshipful prayer and praise cannot be reduced to a songfest or a clap offering. It demands verbal expression. Cultivate a language of worshipful praise. Emphasize songs that are really prayers – don't merely sing the words; sing them as prayers. Expand the worship prayer time to include a pastoral prayer, missional prayer for nations, the unreached and loved ones, all without completely displacing personal prayer needs – which is an affirmation of God's love for us – or praise and preaching. Promote prayerful worship, elevate intercession for the lost and subordinate personal interests to worship and missional prayer. Don't condemn – it has taken years for the church to drift into such self-obsessed praying and worshipping. Gradually make the journey back to a Biblical center. It won't happen overnight unless you have a divine invasion, a kind of God-quake. And it won't happen without some resistance. Keep explaining the 'why' of what you are doing. Be patient. Teach, then do; then reteach into learning gaps.[1]

Common Mistakes

The great mistake will be in <u>failing to adequately engage the congregation</u>, and in underestimating their hunger to pray, to be led in prayer; or, in pushing too hard, too quickly.

<u>Look for early successes!</u> Celebrate them. Don't cross

---

1   A helpful resource here are chapters in *The Praying Church Handbook, Volume III – The Pastor and the Congregation.* In Search of a Pentecostal Liturgy, Chapter 11 and Shallow Contemporary Worship, Chapter 15. Available at www.alivepublications.org.

the creek at the widest spot! <u>Introduce prayer experiences that will be received most readily, most naturally</u>. Carefully discern your congregation. Don't shock them with a "spiritual warfare" conference when they are struggling to learn conversational prayer! Find out where they are at, and take your prayer ministry to them.

<u>Go slow</u>! Babies learn to walk with support – and they take one step at a time. They fall a lot too! As you call the congregation to prayer, you may be in for a shock. Many Christians are not so excited by prayer – unless it is for them. <u>Too much change, too fast and you will set your prayer ministry efforts back</u>. <u>Teach, then do! Then, assess</u>. How well did we do? How many participated? Are we ready for the next step? Do small events for those who are ready to move ahead more quickly. Keep developing your leadership and working toward a tipping point.

Additional Ideas

Call each segment of the church to prayer. Hold special nightly prayer gatherings: youth, the leaders and workers, singles or seniors, with men and then with women, and then couples. It works best to process these separately first (Men, then women, then the couples together). These gatherings can be small living-room gatherings. Or, it can be at the church facility. Just meet and pray – don't just talk or preach about prayer - pray.

Introduce prayer into the life of the church:

- Children's prayer initiatives
- Encourage participation in city-wide, regional and global prayer events and initiatives
- Neighborhood prayer evangelism ministry
- Prayer partners for public safety officers in the community, police and fire, etc.
- 'Prayer Shields' for the staff, ministry workers in the congregation
- Prayer retreats
- Prayer walls/chains
- Prayer walks and missions

- Simultaneous Worship Service Intercessors – praying while the service is in progress
- Youth prayer initiatives

Simple Suggestions for Corporate Prayer Enrichment[2]

Here are some simple ways to raise the practice and profile of prayer at-church, in the context of worship:

A concert of prayer. This is different from 'concert prayer' – a term that denotes many voices simultaneously raised to God as one. In this model, worship, prayer, and thanksgiving are woven together. Voices are raised to God one-by-one with others silently agreeing. It can very simple and almost unstructured, or very structured and orchestrated. For example, in a 60-minute prayer service, you might choose six themes and allot ten minutes for each theme. Anchor each prayer segment with Scripture. Allow assigned participants to then come forward and read the passage, followed by prayers. Or you can do this spontaneously. Say to the congregation, "We are going to reach Scripture and pray about each of these themes! One at a time, I am asking you to come to the open microphones on each side of the church. Pray about the issue on which we are focusing. Please, limit your prayers to about a minute or two. No long prayers." Use microphone monitors to hold the microphone. If someone goes too long, a few "amens" from the prayer leader sends a gentle message. Transition each section with music, and move to the next passage. Mix in some small group time. Make time for silence. If the Holy Spirit descends on one of the segments – stay there all night. Throw the schedule out.

An evening of "thanksgiving" prayer. Spend an evening reading the psalms or other thanksgiving narrations. Read – then pray. Plan some thanksgiving prayers. Develop a thanksgiving liturgy. If you have a small congregation, do some 'open mic' thanksgiving prayers. Share testimonies.

---

2 P. Douglas Small, Excerpt from *Transforming Your Church into a House – Revised Edition* (Kannapolis, NC: Alive Publications, 2017).

A night of missions praying. Do it in the same way you would organize a concert of prayer. Pray for your church's missionaries. Mention the state of the nation in which they work. Acquire some footage of their work or other challenging missions work. Focus some of the prayer segments on unreached people groups. Stimulate visionary praying, "God, we do not know what it be like to be in a culture that had no Bible! No churches! That had never heard the story of the resurrection of Christ! Challenge the church to pray against that backdrop. – "Church, imagine with me, what that might mean? Let's pray this way – 'it would mean ___________!'" Have them fill in that blank. Stepping into an alien situation is largely the role of intercession. Help your congregation begin to step into the needs of people without Bibles, without the gospel, without missionaries or even the necessities of life!

A prayer banner service. Even if you do not have colorful banners, you can create posters around various themes: Revival, Souls, Holiness, the Schools, Government, Families, Drug Addiction, Purity Needs, and more. The list is almost endless. Place these all over the congregation. Invite people to prayer at them, not to them, but around them with others who share their burden. Encourage them to pray aloud – but necessarily loudly. Encourage them to pray prayers of agreement one with another. And Project Pray has affordable prayer banners in three sizes. Go to www.alivepublications.org. You can order them with your logo. Stands and cases are included.

Add a "pastoral prayer." Most congregations look forward to this time of *pastoral blessing.* One pastor encourages each worshipper to scoot-to-the-front-edge of the their pew, and surrender the back of their pew to the person behind them. This encourages active participation. Too often, prayer can be such a passive time. Or it is a time for moving around in the sanctuary. This exercise provides focus and reverence. It draws the congregation together for prayer.

Assign different families or *intercessors to "pre-service" prayer,* though you might open it to all. Rotate the duty to bathe the sanctuary in prayer each Sunday. Be careful that you do not encourage a style of prayer that is not consistent with your worship!

Bring the children into the congregation several times a year, and let them pray. Seat them around the front. Give them the microphone. Their prayers are often so direct. So simple. One child prayed, "God I pray that the mommies and daddies will stay together!" – this sensitive subject gently mentioned. "God help the people stop fighting on the television!" You will find wet eyes filling the house, when you release the children to pray.

Call the men forward – pray a prayer of blessing over them as the priest of their homes. Ask them to form a circle and pray one for another. Charge them with the privilege of leading their family in spiritual matters. Grace them with forgiveness for their failures in this area and for the guilt that keeps them from feeling worthy and spiritually qualified to lead their wife in prayer and bless their children. After prayer, ask their wives to come and join them, to stand with them at the altar. Lead them both in a blessing prayer, "Men, would you pray with me, 'God, I bless my wife. I thank you for her companionship and partnership. I pray that we will walk together in greater unity than ever before honoring you and one another, that I will love her, sacrificially. That together, we can discover your will for our lives and open the doors of blessing and favor on our home and our children.'" Continuing, say, "Wives, would you prayer with me, 'God, I bless my husband. I release him to lead our family in godly ways. I pray that he would be a holy man of God after your heart. That he would be, by your grace, an example of strength and humility to our children. I thank you that you have given him to me and that I am his wife.'" Of course, you can wordsmith your own pastoral prayer of blessing. As couples stand together and pray one for another, expect tears. Expect some discomfort. For many, such spiritual closeness is not a common thing. You model it at church, in order to encourage it at home.

Choose a different church in the city to pray for each week. Encourage the members to write that pastor a note (provide note cards in the pew or bulletin) and place their card in the offering. Mail it to that pastor. In the same way, mention a handful of nations each Sunday in prayer, and keep mission praying in front of the people. Rotate the prayer focus for each Sunday on different ministries in the church needing prayer support.

Coach the music director! Have him choose at least *one congregational song or hymn – which is really a prayer!* Cultivate awareness in the congregation – that they are singing a prayer. Occasionally, have someone sing a special prayer song! Choir selections should be chosen and offered as prayers. Don't merely sing the words; sing prayer. In the Revelation, the incense, a type of prayer, is translated into a song (Revelation 5:8). The words of earth's prayers are set to music in heaven. What an idea – let's join heaven's prayer songs.

Conversational, summit-style evenings of prayer. Ask people to sign up for the special prayer experience. A group of 25 or more is a great beginning and assures a reasonably vigorous prayer event. Put the chairs in a circle. Eliminate empty chairs. Begin with a brief explanation: "Tonight, we are not going to focus on any specific needs, except our need to know God more fully and be conformed to the image of Christ. Please, no sharing. If you have something to say, 'Pray it!' Let's stay vertical. Brief prayers, one after another. I'll coach us along at times. Also, feel free to read a passage from the Bible – that is the way God speaks to us in prayer. And everyone here is a song leader. So, we pray, and read Scripture, and sing, and pray – and follow our hearts in seeking the face of God. Let's begin with some prayers of thanksgiving." Move then to prayers of praise, then to worship – until you sense the presence of God. In the presence of God, prayer should take on a special dynamic. Focus simultaneously on God's transforming love and His Holiness. Don't fear silence. And don't let silence rule the meeting. If necessary, frame the prayers, "Let's imagine Christ came into this room and walked right over to you. What might he say? Could you pray that back to God? 'Jesus, I think you might say _______'."

Choose *one service a week* in which you announce *a brief 15-30 minute prayer session prior to the service.* In many congregations in Mexico, they fill up the altar before the service begins. Sometimes, after a service begins, they quietly come to the altar and kneel, refusing to be seated in the sanctuary until they have knelt before God. In small churches, a group might gather in the front of the sanctuary for prayer. In larger churches, the entire sanctuary might be given over to prayer. At Brooklyn Tabernacle, a New York congregation, known for prayer, when the doors open for their Tuesday evening prayer meeting at 6:00 p.m., the early arrivers will find the sanctuary lights dimmed and soft music playing. A few years ago, while in attendance there, I noticed that the movement into the prayer meeting at 7:00 p.m. was seamless. Suddenly, instrumentalists are present and the congregation was worshipping. That directed prayer service continued for 90 minutes.

Create a collage of pictures of lost loved ones – some churches put it right in the sanctuary and call it their "wailing wall!"

Encourage some people to pray silently in the congregation while the pastor is preaching, and others to go a special room for *simultaneous intercession*.[3]

Family Prayer Day – Encourage the families that we so often split apart in our church activities, to be together, at least for a part of a service. Lead them in a prayer exercise. Have fathers come to a microphone and pray – as in a concert of prayer. Have mothers do the same. Then, spend some time having the family pray one for another in a circle of prayer.

Feature prayer in your worship event. One pastor uses light control to dim the lights of his sanctuary. He kneels in front of his pulpit and intercedes for his congregation. During this time, the sanctuary is quiet, agreeing with his prayer. Some folks slip quietly to the altar and kneel during this time. Most stay in their seats. After he prays, the congregation is encouraged to softly pray as a worship team sings. Elders and deacons meet people with prayer needs at the altar. The prayer time flows naturally into the next portion of worship.

---

3   For more information on simultaneous, see chapter five.

Feature prayer testimonies as a part of the regular service. To control time issues and keep the testimony focused, do them as brief interviews.

Invite the entire congregation forward for prayer. If that is not possible, engage them in a short prayer response to the preaching. Tell them you want them to settle in for a season of prayer. Have them complete this phrase in prayer, "God, this morning, as our pastor brought the Word, I felt that you were saying to me ____________." Encourage the use of a phrase. But don't inhibit divine surprises. Someone might erupt with something exploding in their soul and touch the entire church. Move from the *personal* to the *corporate*, "God, I sense you are saying to our church that __________________." These can be incredibly powerful times in which the congregation is being challenged to discern the word of the Lord that has just been preached to them, and not only to them, but to the corporate church. Most people observe the preaching and listen to the message - passively. This moves the ball to the other side of the court, asking, "What did you hear from God today?" It creates participants out of passive observers. It calls for us to consider what obedient action is appropriate

Pentecostals are accustomed to "concert prayer" – unlike a "concert of prayer" mentioned earlier. *Concert prayer is when everyone prays aloud together.* The Scripture says, *"They raised their voice to God with one accord!"* (Acts 4:24). Many Evangelicals have not been accustomed to praying in this manner. Here is the irony. As Pentecostals give up this Scriptural practice, Evangelicals are encouraging it. Al VanderGriend, from the Reformed Tradition suggests, "Ask everyone present to pray aloud at the same time, focusing on a specific request or area of prayer."[4] Many churches are introducing passion into their prayer times by using *concert prayer,* calling it the "Korean Method of Prayer!" Dr. Paul Cho, the Pastor of the 850,000-member Yoido Full Gospel Church in Seoul, South Korea, is Pentecostal. He says, "When I hear people praying, it sounds like the forceful

---

4   VanderGriend, *The Praying Church Sourcebook,* 50.

roar of a mighty waterfall. We know God must hear the sincerity of our prayer because we are praying in unison and unity!"[5] If you are a Pentecostal Church – don't let this passionate prayer style die! But don't *exclusively* use this style of praying. People hide in the noise of prayer and never really learn to pray. If you are not a Pentecostal congregation, try it.

Prayer Request Time Needs an Overhaul

- *Change the atmosphere of the prayer request time.* Daniel Henderson warns that "sharing the trials and traumas of people in the church can easily downgrade to inappropriate chit-chat. Sometimes the devil is in the details." Henderson says, "A strong worship-based prayer time tends to eliminate loose lips."[6]

- *Change the way in which you receive prayer requests.* Rather than a long litany of individually called out needs, have your people offer the needs spontaneously, but prayerfully, "Congregation - as we bow our heads in prayer, mindful that God hears us and cares -would you prayerfully call out the needs of loved ones?" After spontaneous needs are called out, lead the congregation in prayer for those needs.

- *Collect the prayer request beforehand.* They are given to the pastor, who will often call many of them out as he prays for the congregation, "Lord, today, we offer these people to you in need – John, recovering for surgery; Ann, needing a job; our youth, and their summer mission trip – and so on!"

- *Give thanks for answered prayer!* After you have prayed for those in need, the pastor might continue the prayer time in this way, "Congregation – would you now respond spontaneously to God in thanksgiving for answered prayer? God, this week you answered my prayer by ________." Have the congregation fill in the blank, encouraging them to use no more than phrases or sentence prayers. Keep the prayer responses moving around the room! Repeat them if necessary, so that all can hear.

---

5   Paul Cho, *Prayer: Key to Revival,* 101-102.

6   Henderson, *Fresh Encounters* (Colorado Springs, CO: Nav-Press, 2004) 39.

- Have *a prayer request box or chest*, and at prayer meetings, members come forward and take the requests out of the box by the handfuls. They go to a quiet place and pray through the needs, returning them to the prayer chest at the end of the prayer session. The prayer meeting usually begins with a general charge and some instructions. Conclude with thanksgiving and praise for answered prayer.

- Have people who will *take home prayer requests* and pray for them during the week.

- *Keep a record of answered prayer!* Make a book. Sometimes we are so overwhelmed by the sheer number of prayer requests that we fail to see any of the answers. John Hyde, the son of a pastor, is often called the apostle of prayer. Affectionately known as "Praying Hyde" (1865 – 1912), he recorded 50,000 specific answers to his prayers.[7]

- *Put up prayer requests on a screen* during your prayer time.

- *Note: Alive Publications has a great resource called, The Great Exchange – Why Your Prayer Requests May Not be Getting Answers, by P. Douglas Small. There is a book, a study guide with a 'group-it' section, Power Point, a companion video series and a teaching guide. It connects witness and prayer requests, joy and peace in the midst of personal deprivation and need.*

Preach on prayer. Better yet, have the pastor pray the pastor's sermon! Teach a section, then model "praying it!" Let the congregation respond with bite-size prayer responses.

Project a corporate prayer on the screen – one that is not merely recited, but prayed by the congregation. Read a section – then pause. Allow for bite-sized spontaneous prayer in the context of the planned corporate prayer. Which is the main thing? Reading the prayer on the screen, or encouraging heart-felt focused praying?

Re-establish the tradition of the altar. Let people tarry in the presence of God. Occasionally, bring the entire

---

7 Philip Graham Ryken. *When You Pray* (Wheaton, IL: Crossway Books, 2000), 20.

congregation forward for a season of prayer at the altar. Insist, with as much grace as possible, that *all* come forward. Be sensitive to the elderly and the infirm.

Show short video clips on answered prayer – or prayer inspiration points.

Take time for small group prayer during your services. It encourages 'whole church' participation. Most people sit passively during congregation prayer times – the tradition of coming forward to an altar or even kneeling at one's pew has almost vanished. Small groups influence people toward participation. The newer your congregational prayer emphasis, the more caution you need to use here. Larger small groups forecast less peer pressure to participate, less relational intensity, psychological distance for those who may be uncomfortable in praying aloud. Smaller circles of prayer, triads for example, are intense, and probably should be reserved for a more prayer savvy congregation.

Expanding Leadership Teams and Long-Term Planning

Phase IV

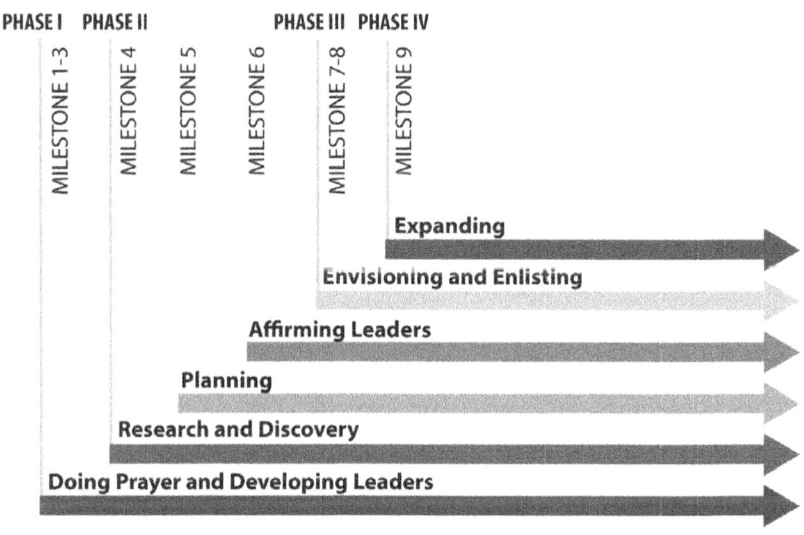

The Praying Church Made Simple

PHASE IV: EXPANDING LEADERSHIP TEAMS AND LONG-TERM PLANNING – DEEPER AND WIDER

9. **Expand:** Create multipl[e] leadership teams to expand and widen the prayer process into the four dimension. Experiment with prayer activities.

10. **Plan:** Develop multiple micro-plans to move the process forward that embrace the Seven Markers and the Four Dimensions – expand your ongoing teaching and training.

Congregation

Prayer is intuitive – it must be taught: the ideas are contradictory. Prayer is intuitive, but it is too often superficial and self-interested. There is a world of prayer in which all of us need experienced guides. To proliferate prayer, you must teach in-depth different facets and aspects of prayer, different applications and contexts for prayer.

In Phase I, you started a congregational prayer meeting and looked to see who showed up. Your emphasis was on developing key praying leaders and your prayer meeting was a laboratory.

In Phase II, you cast a broader vision, explored the prayer ministries of other congregations and surveyed the congregation's prayer habits to determine the level

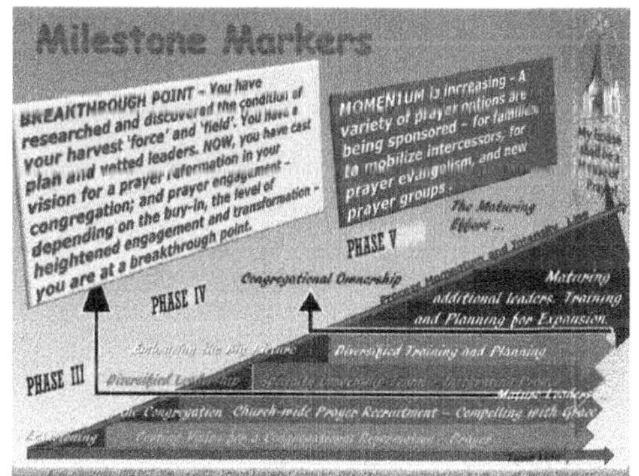

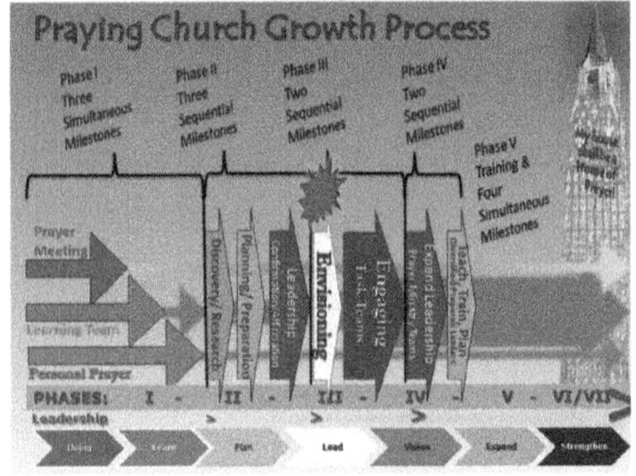

of actual prayer engagement, all to develop an informed plan. You emerged with informed, praying leaders (SPLT).

In Phase III, you stretched your congregational vision. You went wide with your call to prayer, and in the course of the months that followed, you created 'task teams' that offered a collage of prayer engagement opportunities, in areas where you planned to develop prayer ministry. You did that in addition to continuing your congregational prayer meeting. In the beginning, you watched those who came to your church-wide prayer meeting. And some you tapped for leadership. Then, you watched who showed up to pray, for example, on family prayer night, or to practice prayer walking, or for an intercessors gathering, etc. They were demonstrating an interest in some specific focus or aspect of prayer. You may want to tap some of them for your track-specific STTs or to serve on your prayer council. You offered a variety of prayer events and opportunities with the goal of launching a prayer process. Activities were not your only goal; they were a means to your goal. The 'task teams' that led those various prayer activities that sought to *engage* the congregation, further testing its resolve and its appetite for various prayer activities, will now be the teams that morph into leadership for a deeper, long-term process in each of the focus areas.

In Phase IV, your year of engaging the congregation allowed time to lay the foundation to build focus-specific strategic prayer leadership teams along the lines of the four dimensions of the praying church. (See the diagram for Prayer Ministry Leadership structure, and adjust it to your needs). These STTs will not only lead prayer activities, going forward, but will plan a process of transformation. They will coordinate and train in their 'focus area' – teaching, training and doing.

For example, you offered family prayer engagement (Phase III) – and from the 'task team' that led those efforts, you identified a permanent 'family milestones prayer team' to lead that effort. You offered intercessory prayer options (Phase III), and you formally organized and expanded your intercessory prayer ministry by appointing leaders for that segment. You engaged in prayer evangelism, then you identified the passionate and the interested, and established a permanent team to lead that effort. These are your Strategic Task Teams (STT), extensions of your SPLT (core leaders). You have an SPLT. You have now named STTs, a specific aspect of prayer, to set forth a plan specific to their area of specialization. These are now your permanent strategic task teams. (Their names may vary.) They must now develop a prayer teaching and training plan, in addition to prayer engagement in each focus area.

People

In personal prayer, God shapes our hearts. Every prayer life should share the same basic components – worshipful devotion (communion with God); petitions of dependence; intercessory engagement; gratitude and praise. Beyond these basic elements of Paul's theology of prayer (1 Tim. 2:1-4), there are variations. Some will major on prayer as a means for spiritual formation. Some are *called* to intercession. Further, some intercessors are called to 'watch' in prayer, not only over souls, but also over nations. Some will come to know the travail of prayer. They will taste lament in prayer and the resolve that rises out of such moments. Some will tend to prophetic intercession and others to priestly intercession. These diverse intercessory perspectives will clash at times. The prophetic intercessor dances with truth; the priestly intercessor with mercy. Both are critical to balance. This can make intercessory prayer ministry and teaming intercessors challenging, to say the least.

The 'gifts' (enabling) of the Spirit will enhance and color the prayer lives of the people, as will their motivational gifts. Some may pray with the 'gift of faith' resulting in gifts of 'miracles' and 'healing.' Some may have their discernment amplified to painful proportions. They may develop an extraordinary sensitivity, not only to the Holy Spirit and his voice, perceiving his will and way, but they may at time, become acutely aware of the presence and work of evil spirits, and indeed the intent of men – the nature of their motivations, good or evil. Discernment is a means by which the 'spiritual' nature of an angelic, demon or human, or even a place, is decoded. It allows, at times, by divine disclosure, a prophetic intercessor to know the subliminal attitudes and spiritual dispositions of others, hopefully, with a gracious and non-malignant intent. Divine disclosure (knowledge and wisdom) is a gift, a gracious bestowment, but it can also be an extraordinary encumbrance. Spiritual enablement should be an aid in prayer. With insight comes anointing; the God that reveals also directs.

Like Daniel, some intercessors pray for nations. Like David, some weep over a lost son (Psalm 3). Like Jeremiah, some weep over a backslidden nation (Jeremiah 2). Some, like Zechariah, may see visions (Zechariah 1:8). Some may pray out of their personal pain (Hosea). As people move beyond prayer basics, to prayer as a ministry – your congregation and its prayer ministry will expand.

MILESTONE NINE
Multiple Leadership Teams

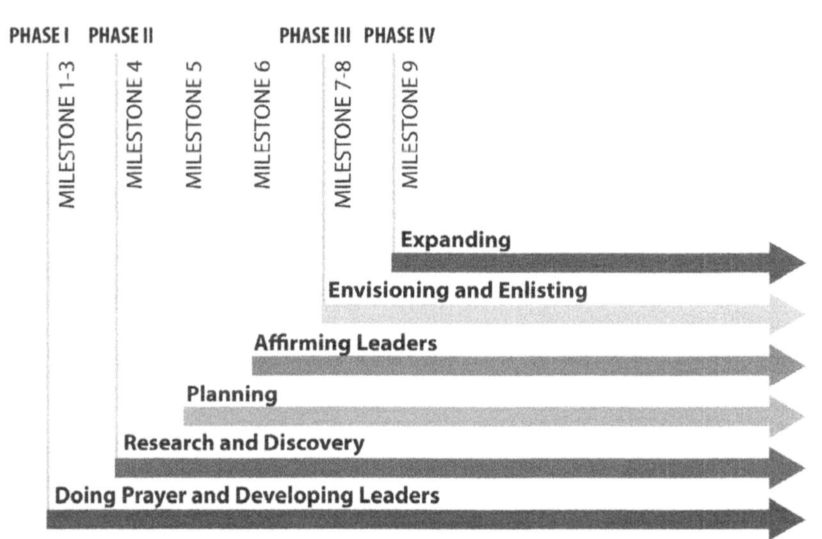

Proposition

Your model is a matrix in place of dysfunctional silos. You want an integrated community of prayer and mission! You started your effort by calling your congregation to participate in a regular prayer meeting, and from those who responded, you chose potential leaders who were willing to learn. You met with them, prayed with them, stretched their vision, urged them to explore different praying churches around them. You then, with those core leaders and others, entered into a discovery-research process. Out

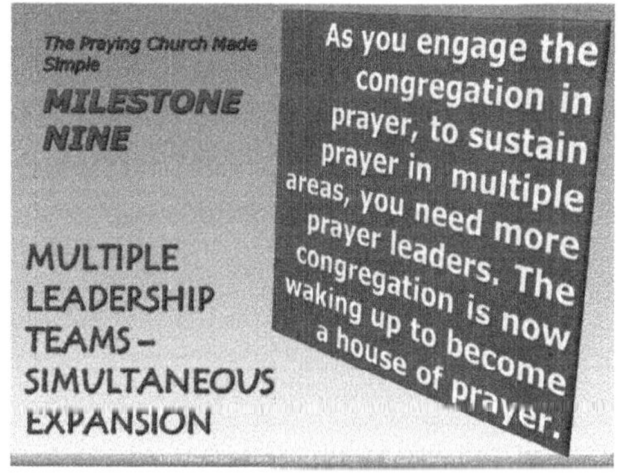

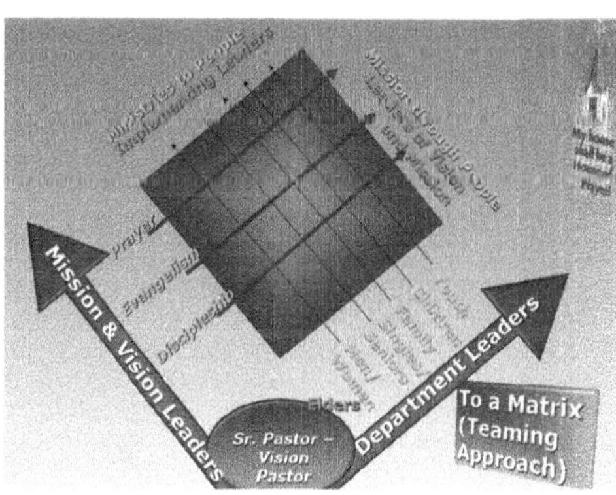

of your discoveries, you projected a broad informed prayer plan for your congregation. You confirmed, from your core leaders and others, a Strategic Prayer Leadership Team. You then cast vision for the church as a 'house of prayer.' For six months to a year, you offered the congregation a sample of prayer options. You appointed 'task teams' to lead these prayer activities and experiences in the congregation – all the while, testing the waters, increasingly calling for the embrace of prayer. You are now in the process of not only offering additional prayer items on the congregation's menu, but of launching simultaneous processes – deepening and widening the prayer stream throughout congregational life. Your temporary task teams will now give birth to permanent Strategic Task Teams, each leading various segments and aspects of your prayer effort.

Your goal is a congregational culture of prayer. That will require more than prayer activities – it will require daily personal prayer, at-home, by couples and families. It will require a new level of intercession by mature intercessors, trained and teamed, mobilized and focused on prayer evangelism rather than merely reacting against the darkness. It will require systematic missional praying, prayer groups, ongoing prayer teaching and training, and perhaps, the creation of a prayer room/center or at the very least, some prayer focus – a prayer cross or wall in the sanctuary itself.

You are now entering into a new level of learning by expanding your process and creating Strategic Task Teams (STTs), around your SPLT. They will meet, learn and pray together, explore possibilities that have been developed by your learning-leader (core) team and then project an informed plan. Previously, you had a general plan – for the church. Now, you are moving in multiple directions at once – deepening personal prayer; building family altars; mobilizing intercessors; proliferating prayer in the ministries of the church; turning prayer outward onto a lost world; and teaching and training.

These teams will need to engage in their own planning. They will not leave the earlier research. You developed a plan to increase the level of engagement, and 'task teams' led that, but now, they will need to more carefully develop plans for the area of prayer that they are commissioned to lead. Earlier, you did macro planning, Now, these teams will complete the planning process at the micro level. This will require <u>a subset of leaders for each of the areas of prayer ministry that you hope to develop</u>. Additional examples include prayer groups; embedding intercessors into every ministry; prayer partners for pastoral and ministry leaders; prayer with and for youth and children; a prayer crisis line, and so on. In a smaller congregation, (actually the typical church is about 75), combine these areas. Forge your own plan. Form interest groups and teams around the areas that you want to explore going forward.

Your core leaders or SPLT members may take roles in one or more of these focus areas to provide leadership with a small team of two or three others. The 'vision' remains the same – the church as a house of prayer for the nations. Each STT will develop a parallel plan and path, moving simultaneously, and non-competitively. These will be coordinated by the SPLT. Plans and paths may change in the process. You will run into people and problem blockades; detours will be necessary. Stay focused on the ultimate goal. Ask God for wisdom to get you there.

Timing

<u>All along, you have had a growing team of leaders who have helped with discovery and planning, and they then served on your 'task teams.' Now, you are now ready to form and release the STT that will build out the seven markers of a praying church and the four dimensions</u>. In a small congregation, teams may be two to three, or three to five individuals. In some cases, members may serve on more than one team, and the team itself may cover more than one aspect of prayer. For example, the same team may serve to mobilize intercessors and the prayer evangelism-mission effort. Another team might serve to catalyze prayer in congregational life and manage the prayer room/ wall. The leadership team may also be the training team. One team might work on nurturing prayer among families and organizing prayer groups. Be creative, adaptive.

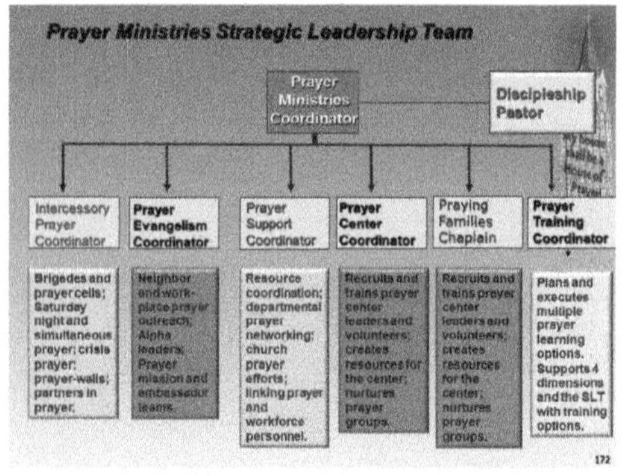

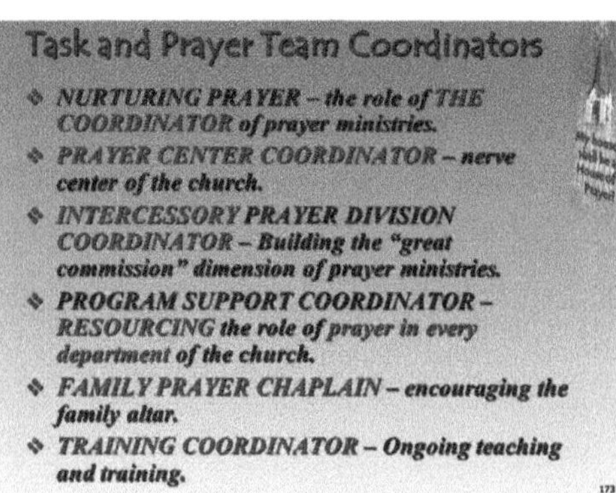

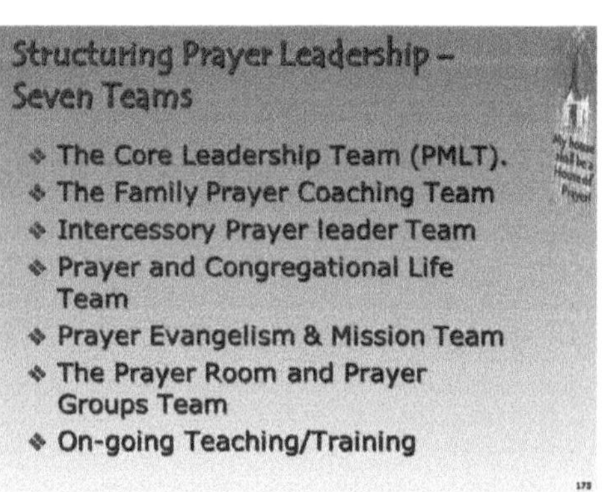

Figure out what works for you. Keep purpose in mind, and remember – the path and plan change, the objective doesn't.

Ideal:

- The Core Leadership Team (SPLT)

STTs

- The Family Prayer Coach/Team
- The Intercessory Prayer Leader/Team
- Prayer and Congregational Life Team
- Prayer Evangelism and Mission Team
- The Prayer Room and Prayer Groups Coordinator
- Ongoing Teaching and Training Coordinator

Above, you have seven teams or leaders. In a smaller church, this might be collapsed to five.

- The Leadership and Training Team (SPLT)

STTs

- The Family Prayer team
- Congregational Prayer Leader Team
- Intercession and Prayer-Evangelism/Mission Leader Team
- The Prayer Room/Center and Prayer Groups Leader Team

And with only three teams (example):

1. Combine – Leadership and Training
2. Combine – The Nurture of Family Prayer, Congregational Prayer, the Prayer Center/Room and Prayer Groups
3. Combine – Intercessory Prayer Mobilization and Prayer Evangelism

In many cases, the primary leaders of the various components of your prayer effort will be the Core/SPLT, each taking a leadership role in the area for which they have a burden (STT).

Now as you did in the beginning, these teams will need to explore, set forward an information track-specific plan.

<u>Give these teams as long as a year</u> to meet together, pray and learn, explore and develop an informed plan for

their specific prayer focus. That year can be simultaneous to your year of envisioning and engaging the congregation. Out of the work of the task/implementation teams, work, create, a 'personal and family prayer enrichment team,' and an 'intercessory prayer team and an evangelism leadership team.' Each area demands informed and inspired leaders.

Resources

Each STT will find helpful resources in the *Praying Church Resource Guide*. They will also benefit from being a part of the *Prayer Leaders Continuing Education* quarterly training meetings.

Duration

These STTs will coordinate prayer in their focus area for the long term. Their initial learning and exploration phase will last from three months to a year. Don't hurry the process. You may need to stage the introduction of each new aspect of the prayer process to prevent too much change, too fast. That will set your effort back. Be patient. Go as fast as possible, but go more deliberately than faster, more deeply than broadly.

Focus

Each group will be focused on its specific area of passion. They must do this collaboratively, and not competitively. Some efforts will engage smaller slides of the congregation. Others, like the recovery of personal, daily prayer, must embrace everyone. This is why the early emphasis of humility and a shared philosophy, values and mission, and a mutually valued strategy will pay enormous dividends.

Involvement Goals

Eventually, you want to engage the entire church in each of these areas. For example, you want prayer in every home, between every couple. You want a spirit of intercession to pervade the entire congregation. You want

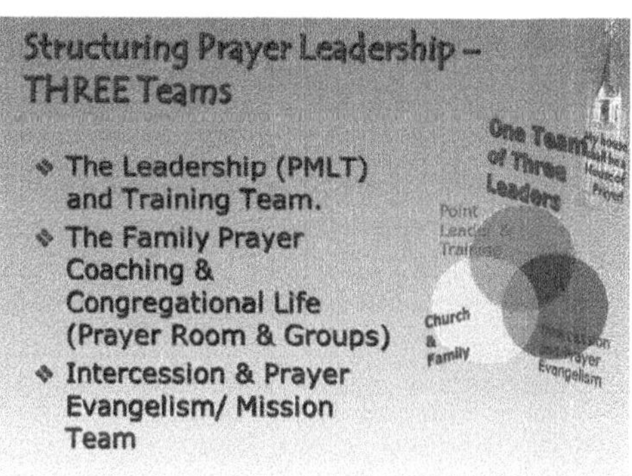

every member praying for lost people, aware of unreached people groups, adopting nations, praying for a mission field near, and one afar. You desire to see a proliferation of healthy, focused prayer groups, seven for every one-hundred, at least five in the typical church of 75. These are small, focused prayer groups that adopt some cause; none more than a dozen in size. They are designed as places where people can learn to fervently pray for a cause about which they care passionately. They are ostensibly prayer groups for a presenting cause; and, simultaneously, prayer laboratories. At least half your congregation should be involved, eventually, in a prayer group.

Transition

Each of these areas represent a prayer specialization, a specific focus. Each is critical to your overall success. As you engage each of these areas, you will find both your greatest challenges and your greatest breakthroughs. This is where you may meet your first most significant resistance. The most difficult stakes to drive are those which are closest to our daily practices. Each prayer planning team will need to embrace change personally, as they call the entire congregation to follow them in the implementation of prayer in each specific focus area.

Common Mistakes

Dare not move through this phase too quickly. As your family prayer team meets and learns, they are not only exploring personal and family resources, they are enlarging their practice of prayer at home. As intercessors learn more about intercession, it should affect both their prayer theology and practice. In every area, potential micro-prayer teams are learning, growing and changing, preparing themselves to lead the entire congregation into the various dimensions of a praying church – and that requires time, not only to learn, but to develop a team culture.

MILESTONE TEN
Diversified Training

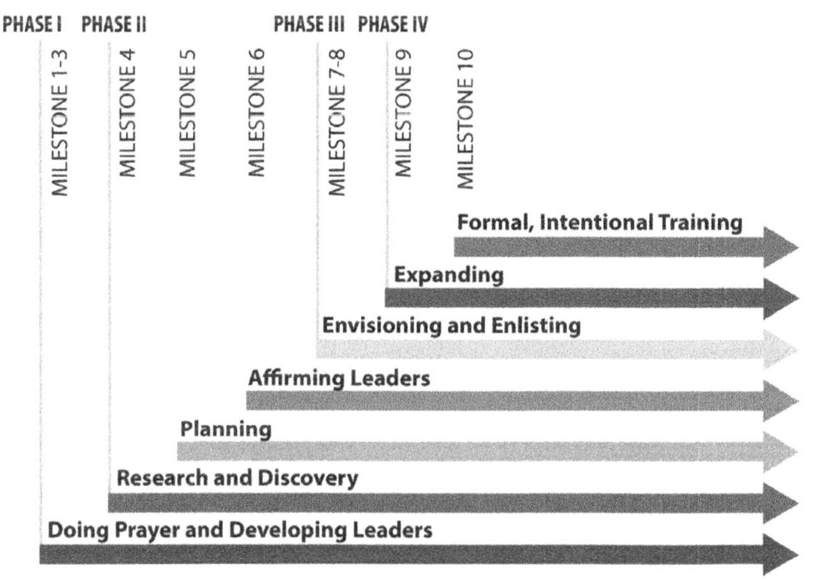

Proposition

Now you are strengthening your effort – with systematic training. This will help your families with their family altar. You will identify intercessors, train them, mobilize them for prayer evangelism, and then establish prayer groups. Prayer is something <u>we never stop learning</u>. Like any relationship, it always has challenges, seasons and stages. It is multifaceted. Now, you must do more than teach and train on prayer generally. You

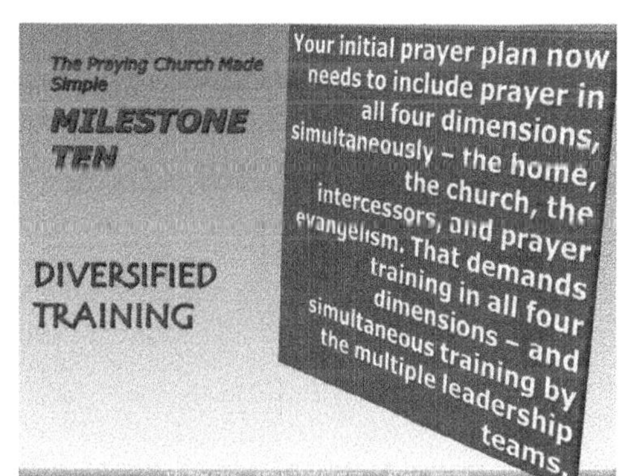

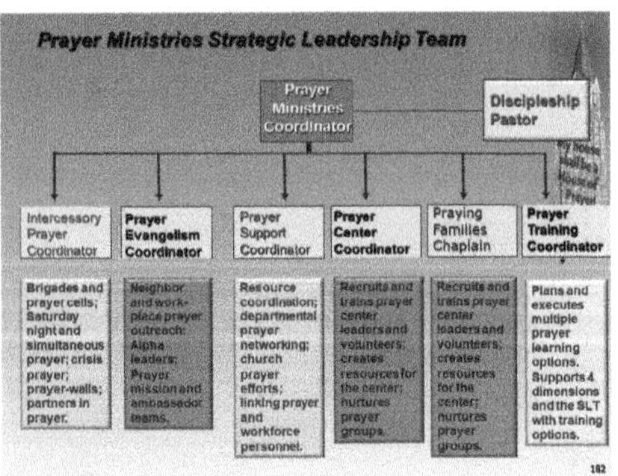

Prayer Ministries Coordinator				Discipleship Pastor	
Intercessory Prayer Coordinator	**Prayer Evangelism Coordinator**	**Prayer Support Coordinator**	**Prayer Center Coordinator**	**Praying Families Chaplain**	**Prayer Training Coordinator**
Brigades and prayer cells; Saturday night and simultaneous prayer; crisis prayer; prayer-walls; partners in prayer.	Neighbor and work-place prayer outreach; Alpha leaders; Prayer mission and ambassador teams.	Resource coordination; departmental prayer networking; church prayer efforts; linking prayer and workforce personnel.	Recruits and trains prayer center leaders and volunteers; creates resources for the center; nurtures prayer groups.	Recruits and trains prayer center leaders and volunteers; creates resources for the center; nurtures prayer groups.	Plans and executes multiple prayer learning options. Supports 4 dimensions and the SLT with training options.

must teach specifically. Fathers must be taught, as well as mothers, and singles. Children and youth must be taught. Elders and deacons must learn to meet and pray together, over the business of the church. Then teaching and training is area-specific.

Timing

Every discipleship department or Sunday School should offer <u>regular training on prayer</u>, at least one new class every quarter. The discipleship effort should include regular training in the area of prayer. Elders and deacons should be trained in prayer – regularly. Every department should be penetrated by prayer – and prayer training.

Resources

Prayer training should be broad – personal prayer, praying scripture, prayer and meditation, prayer and heaven's courtroom, the power of entertaining God, intercessory prayer, watching in prayer, lament and prayer, prayer and evangelism, models for prayer, prayer for direction and guidance, prayer missions and treks; there is so much about prayer to learn.

What are the ways and means by which we will teach and encourage personal-devotional prayer? This may be anything from bulletin inserts to additional congregational prayer exercises. It may also include prayer experiences, continued teaching of prayer both at the church-wide level and in the discipleship arena. How will the church develop a prayer discipleship, teaching-training plan? How and what will you teach intercessors? How will you train in prayer evangelism? What training will you offer prayer group leaders?

Training objectives:

- Every prayer leader should attend an annual department prayer leader training, or in the small church, a church wide training event. (If you are in a small single-cell congregation, you will benefit by being a part of a PLCE effort with other congregations, even if all those congregations are small, as you are. And together you can do joint training, annually, that you would never be able to do alone.)

- Train every prayer leader to lead a basic prayer discipleship group. (There are School of Prayer Resource materials available from Project Pray, www.alivepublications.org, complete with books, study guides, Power Point, teacher's guides, some with video components – all designed to help you disciple in prayer.)

- Emphasize prayer "learning" and prayer "doing" events.

- Teach in the areas of:
    - ✓ *Personal Prayer* including spending an hour with God; praying scripture; transformational prayer; praying through the Tabernacle, etc.

    - ✓ *Family Prayer* – effective prayer and spiritual times in the home; building a family altar.

    - ✓ *Intercessory Prayer* – what is an intercessor, how to do intercessory prayer, the focus of intercession: *the lost!* Launch into the deep – touch on lament, the power of watching in prayer.

    - ✓ *Prayer Evangelism* – the need to pray unsaved people open to the gospel; the plan for prayer for friends and family.

    - ✓ *Theology and Philosophy of Prayer* – prayer as communion with God; prayer as petition – offering our requests to God; prayer as intercession.

    - ✓ *Prayer Leadership* – This training rehearses values and purpose, vision and mission, strategy and tactics. It reviews the Seven Markers of a Praying Church. It assures ongoing congruence in a diverse prayer effort.

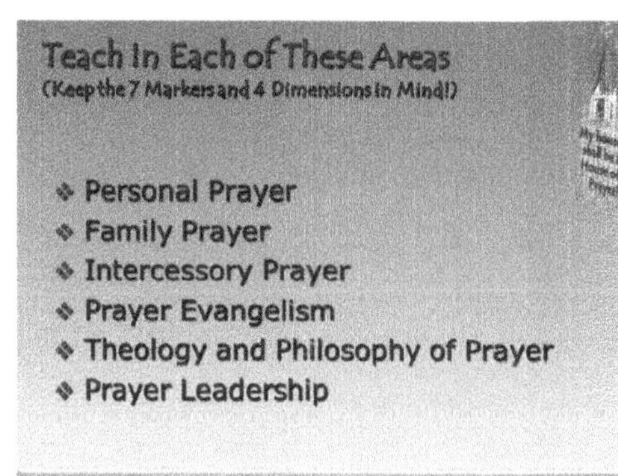

Duration

Ongoing. Cyclical. Relentlessly. Persistently.

Focus

Diverse. All across the prayer ministry continuum.

Involvement Goals

The entire church needs teaching and prayer training. Every congregation adds new members as it grows. You

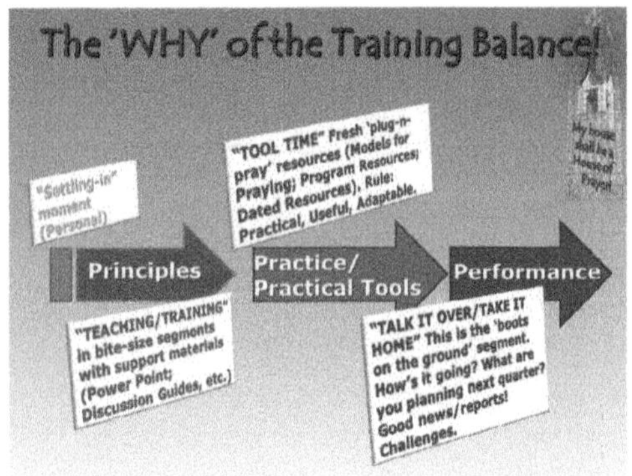

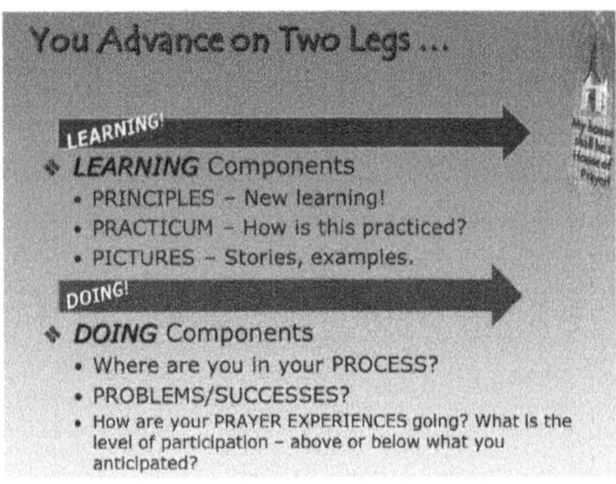

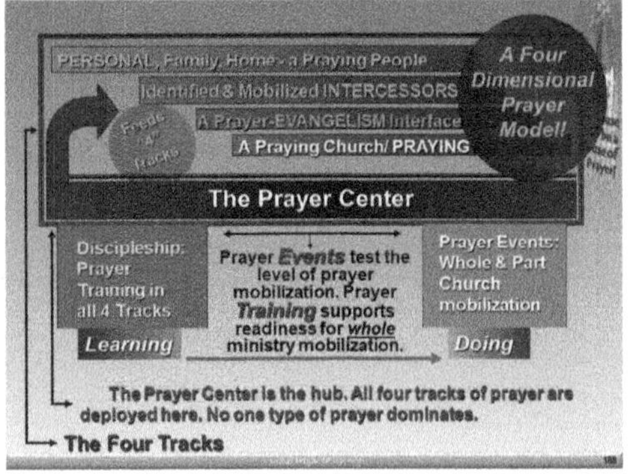

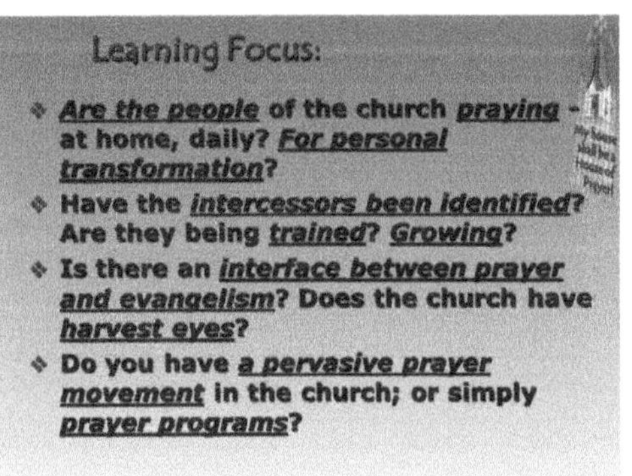

must be visioning those newcomers to protect the developing others of the congregation.

Transition

You will now transition from teaching and training on prayer. When there is a hunger to learn and embrace the discipline of prayer; and not merely prayer as acquisition, prayer for personal enhancement, or narrow self-interested prayer. You have achieved cultural change.

Common Mistakes

Offering popular prayer teaching and training only perpetuates narcissism and shallow pragmatic prayer. Quick-fix prayer formulas, 'Step 1-2-3 to your miracle,' praying feeds the unhealthy obsession with self, and self is what must die for spiritual growth to occur.

Testing Your Effectiveness

Prayer training (teaching) must be balanced by prayer events (doing). The power is not merely in the cognitive learning, but in the obedient doing. Prayer events test your capacity to mobilize a part of the congregation or at times the whole congregation for prayer. So you *learn*, and then you *do!* Train, then test the power of that learning by doing what you have taught. Without being intentional, without testing your prayer training, we are only deceiving yourselves in believing that you are making progress in your prayer ministry. These are the two legs on which the four dimensional prayer process advances. Learning and doing. Doing and learning.

When you call for **prayer events,** you discover the degree to which you can effectively mobilize the church. How many show up when you call a prayer meeting? If they do not come, why not? Have they learned the value of prayer by the experience of answered prayer? **Prayer events** allow "learning by experiencing" the various aspects of prayer. **Prayer training** is for the purpose of application and mobilization for prayer events. No training should stand apart from implementation. Every teaching, training event should be "applied!"

Assessing Your Effectiveness

After you both *teach* (prayer training) and then you *do* (prayer events), you must *assess* the doing (prayer leadership). How well did your people integrate the teaching? Are they comfortable in the practice of the principle? Do they understand? How effective are they? In some cases, such as prayer walks or prayer missions done corporately, you will be able to see the *"learning gaps!"* That will tell you where you need additional training. It may take some courage, but the prayer trainer will have to speak to the *learning gaps*. Avoiding training and teaching in the *"gap"* areas will guarantee the failure of the prayer ministry.

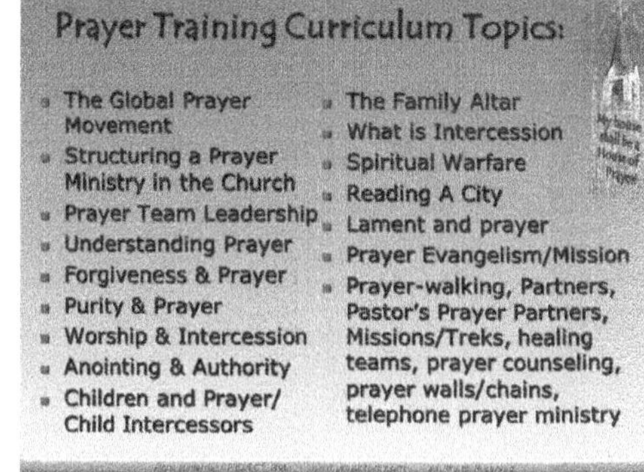

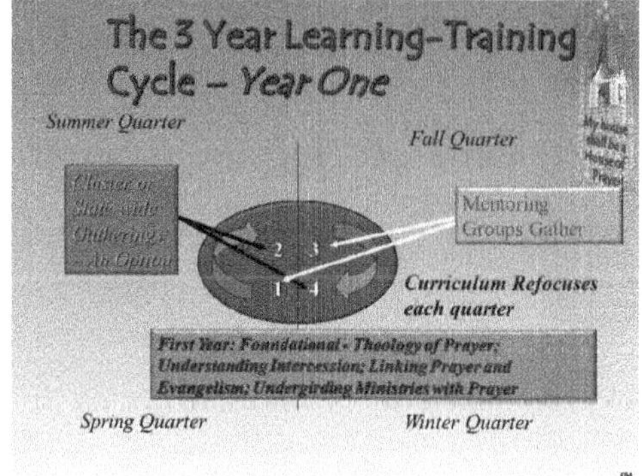

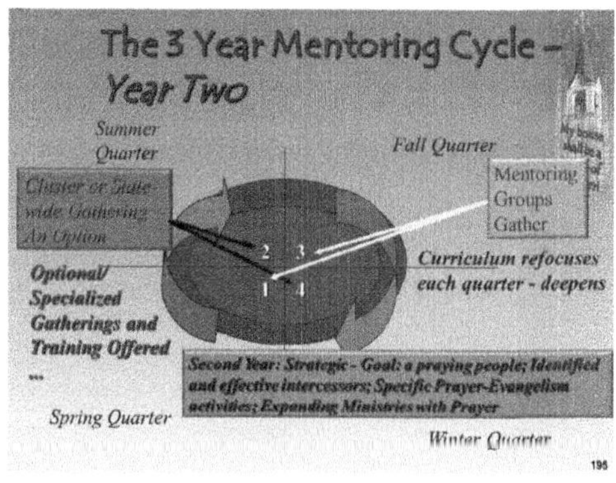

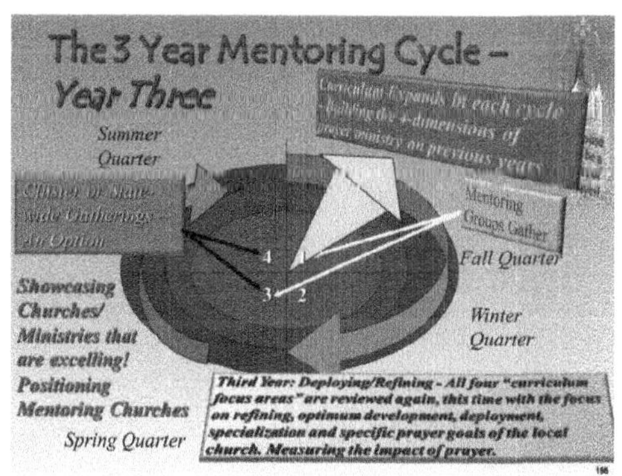

Engaging the Four Dimensions

Phase V

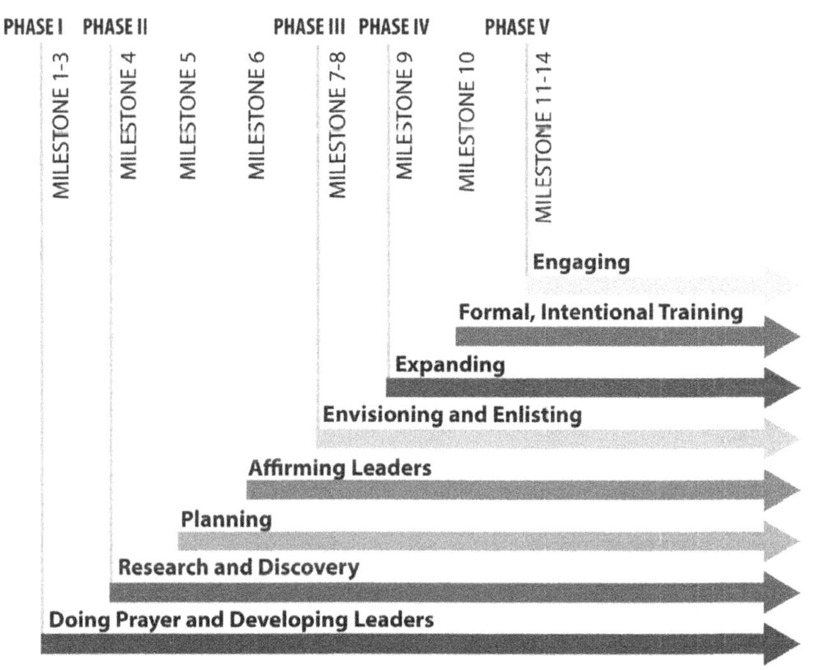

Congregation

You want a balanced prayer process in your congregation – not merely pet prayer ideas and exercises. Yet, some will be drawn into prayer more quickly through one door than another. This is why it is important to offer simultaneous ways to engage the congregation. Before, you offered sequential prayer activities in various areas. You probably found folks who showed up to 'prayer walk' who had no interest, for example, in healing teams; some who wanted to learn to pray their Bible and others who

The Praying Church Made Simple

PHASE V: ENGAGING THE FOUR DIMENSIONS – THE CONGREGATION, THE FAMILY ALTAR, INTERCESSORY PRAYER AND EVANGELISM

- Integrate Prayer – change habits and transform the culture the congregation.
- Make the Seven Marks and the Four Dimensions your template – expand teaching and training.
11. Emphasize the Family Altar.
12. Mobilize Intercessors.
13. Engage in Prayer Evangelism.
14. Organize Prayer Groups and Teams.

wanted to know more about prayer evangelism. There are various prayer callings and they often follow our line of interest. Now, you are offering numerous simultaneous doors – personal and family prayer; prayer groups; intercession; prayer evangelism, etc.

Leaders

Ideally, you have maintained a culture of learning and humility among your leaders. You have retained among the leaders those who were a part of your original learning team, those who served with discovery and initial planning. From those who served on your 'task teams' – and from that vetted group, you now want to form and empower the focus-teams (STT) that will each build some aspect of the seven markers of a praying church.

The teams will work separately together. You want a seamless prayer process, but the vision is larger than any one person or team can direct or track alone. The key leader of each focus team is a member of your Core Leadership Team, each taking a leadership role in the area for which they have a burden.

People

Don't lose the person in the big picture. The bottom line is the transformation of the individual person into a man or woman of prayer. Churches change as their members change. Keep asking – Are the people praying? Are they meeting God daily? Are families praying together? Is the difference evident in their lives? Are there small groups of prayer? Is the congregational prayer meeting affecting the spiritual life and health of the congregation? Are intercessors engaged? Are we praying for the lost? Whether or not the church becomes a house of prayer will depend on how many members become people of prayer.

Grow your people in prayer; and you will grow your congregation. Fail to grow your people in prayer, and the spiritual life of the congregation will grow shallow. As your people learn devotional and transformational prayer and embrace the delight of daily prayer, they will begin to live out of God's presence. The quality of their spiritual lives will explode with love, joy and peace.

MILESTONE ELEVEN
The Family Altar

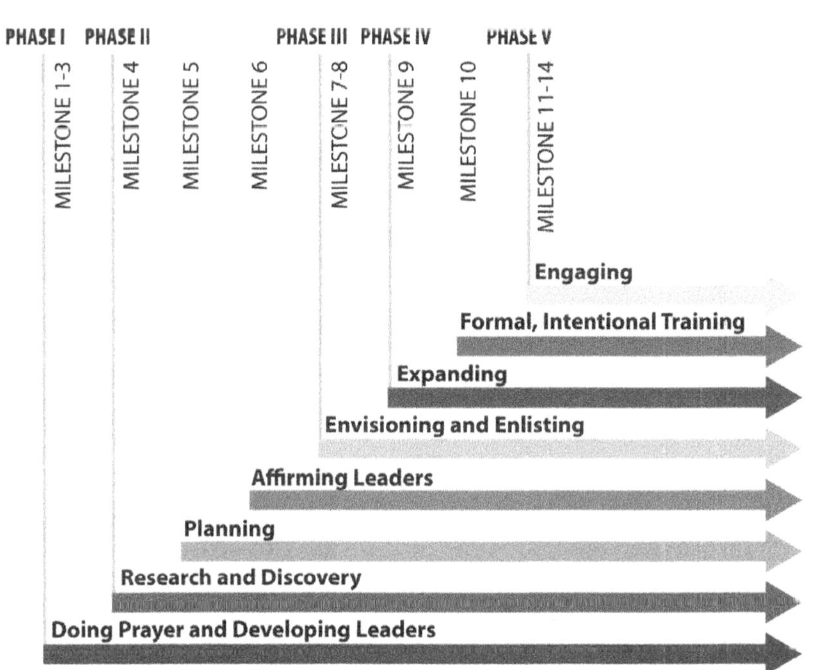

Proposition

There are two great blessings in the Bible – the blessing on the home, on Adam and Eve (Gen. 1:28), and the blessing of Jesus as he left the earth on the church. That 'blessing' was fulfilled in the coming of the Holy Spirit on the day of Pentecost (Luke 24:50; Acts 2:1-4). In that moment, the church was constituted; just as the blessing of the Father

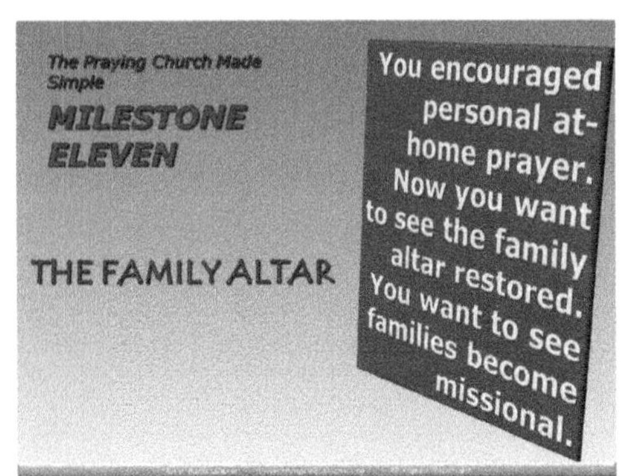

constituted the family in Genesis 1. These two great blessings are the means by which God's purposes move forward. They do so on the back of these two great institutions, the home and the church.

The word bless, *barak*, means knee, it implies prayer. By prayer, we secure God's blessing on both our homes and our congregations. A praying church requires praying homes, and praying homes will also ensure a praying church.

Timing

As one of your first steps, you emphasized personal prayer. That is the anchor of daily prayer at-home. <u>You want to encourage the expansion of personal prayer to couple's prayer, the family altar</u>, fathers and mothers praying spontaneously with sons and daughters, formal blessing events, all moving to missional prayer, out of each member's personal time with God. In Phase I, you encouraged daily, at-home prayer. In Phase II, your Task Teams set forth a number of prayer exercises related to personal prayer, family prayer, and perhaps engaging men and women in prayer. At the end of Phase III, you named strategic task teams and these led various aspects of your prayer effort, including family prayer. You recognized one of the first needs was leading and training specific to the family.

Resources

There are a number of family devotional materials that might be used here. (See the earlier resource listing.)

You have already emphasized at-home, daily, let-Jesus-be-Jesus-in-me praying. <u>Call the men to pray</u>! And really pray. There is perhaps nothing which will skyrocket your prayer effort more than praying men. Have communion. Wash feet. Encourage them to begin to pray with their wives. Have a plan for some type of weekly family spiritual experience. Introduce the importance of family prayer in your prayer meeting, among your prayer leaders and eventually in the larger church.

Amazingly, men will pray with other men when they will not pray in a mixed group. And often before they will pray with their wives. There are few things that are more powerful than a room full of men who lift their voices and begin to cry out to God. Men are led by other men. Just the experience of being together and praying, of breaking into small groups for prayer, can be a starter for men in prayer – not too small or they intimidate; not too large, or the individual is hidden in the group and excused from prayer engagement.

Emphasize the importance of couples praying together. This may be one of the things most fraught with spiritual warfare, most resisted, most uncomfortable. However, on the other side of praying homes – is a praying church. And there is no praying church, without praying homes. The absence of prayer in the home is more damaging than is the absence of prayer in the church.

There are a number of reasons we resist family prayer times – fear, the uncertainty of knowing what to do when we pray together, what family prayer time looks like, and resistance from the business of family life itself, and most often, guilt on the part of the parents, especially the father. The ability to experience the grace of God in our primary relationships, to feel forgiven and made worthy by God to come into His presence is probably demonstrated no more clearly than when those who know us best see us kneel and pray.

Praying Homes

- The number of Christian couples who pray and read Scripture together is only about 4%.
- Among clergy, it is only 6%.
- A century ago – the family altar was normal!

Duration

The goal is the transformation of the culture of the home to a praying home! Think in terms a two to three month period of teaching on the various aspects of personal, couple and family prayer. As you did before – teach, then do, and teach into learning gaps, leading change.

Focus

Personal and family at-home prayer and communion with God.

Think in terms of seven levels of family prayer.

1. Personal, daily, Christ-be-Christ-in-me praying. Focus on transformation in prayer, not merely transaction.

Seven Levels of At-Home Prayer

1. Person prayer.
2. Couples in prayer.
3. The family altar.
4. Personal/Spontaneous prayer moments – now, the culture of the home is changing.
5. Formal blessing ceremonies, rites/stages of life passage, Seasonal faith celebrations.
6. The family as an intercessory, prayer evangelism unit.
7. The family as a sending/going agency – now, the family has become missional.

2. **Pray as a couple** together.

3. **The family altar** [Focus: worship and discipleship] - prayer and worship as a family. Choose at least one meal a day that the family will attempt to share together around a table, regularly. Add a spiritual component that goes beyond a table blessing. It may vary, breakfast on Saturday, dinner through the week, and Sunday dinner. There may be some exceptions, but a regular meal together, at which you share some level of faith experience and do more than merely bless the food, will pay dividends. Turn off the TV. Make talking and sharing with one with another mandatory – but gently and graciously so.

   Once a week, not less, do a family prayer-worship experience. It does not have to be long. The fact of it is, in the end, it is more important than the immediate content. This could be a daily function – but it should never be less than weekly. Years ago, no family would have been considered a Christian family that did not have daily family prayer.

   Add to these seasonal prayer efforts. Conservative Jewish families celebrate the Sabbath with a weekly family prayer gathering. They also celebrate the Biblical feasts seasonally, some corporately in the synagogue and others in the home. That festival calendar had encoded in it the progression of the salvation story – redemption, renewal, cleansing/purity of life and home, spirit-empowerment, repentance and recalibration of values with self-examination, judgment, and eschatological hope.

4. **Informal Prayers.** These personal prayer moments are most often spontaneous, in which either parent prays with a child, often for a need. This weaves prayer into the daily fabric of life. It teaches children dependence on God. It provides God an opportunity to reveal Himself to our children in answer to their prayers. All of this happens in the context of *'loving the Lord with all one's heart'* (6:5). This includes nighttime prayers and off-to-school prayers. Seize opportunities to pray. Engage the power of the informal blessing and incidental prayer. Deuteronomy 6:7-9, urges diligence in our leading our children to encounter God in their daily lives – "*... talk of them [God's commands, His word], when you sit*

in your house, when you walk by the way, when you lie down, and when you rise up." Here is a godly culture. Prayer and conversations about God should be regular and natural. God is a member of the family, spoken of and to throughout the day. *"You shall bind them* [the commandments, God's word] *as a sign on your hand, and they shall be as frontlets between your eyes. You shall write them on the doorposts of your house and on your gates."* Signs on the hands and frontlets between the eyes aside – the point is, that on the body of the child, carried with him, are reminders, "You belong to God. He loves you. He cares about you. You are in a family that has a covenant with Him!" In and about the house are also reminders of our godly heritage, of who we are as people.

5. Now, **formal blessing times** will have more power - baby dedications, a house dedication/blessing, coming of age blessings, the giving of a 'promise ring' or some other token of fidelity to God, baptismal blessings, first communion blessings, leaving home blessings, marriage blessings, first and subsequent grandchild blessings.

In addition, consider holidays – holy days – and how you can lace prayer and family faith traditions into those experiences. Add Biblical holidays – the Jewish Feasts to the family calendar. You will find wonderful examples of how to celebrate Biblical holidays in your family on-line.[1]

Every father and mother should dedicate his or her child as an infant, but child dedication is largely parent dedication. It is the commitment of parents to raise their children in the ways of the Lord, to expose those children to godly principles. When

---

1   Resources: www.faithformationlearningexchange.net/uploads/5/2/4/6/5246709/best_practices_in_family_faith_formation.pdf;   http://www.familylife.com/articles/topics/holidays/featured/christmas/10-great-ideas-for-christmas-traditions;   www.faithgateway.com/christ-centered-family-easter-traditions/#.WPUVg4jyvIU; www.crosswalk.com/family/parenting/6-things-a-godly-dad-does.html;   www.crosswalk.com/family/parenting/10-lenten-traditions-to-enrich-your-familys-easter-celebration-11566549.html;   http://www.keeperofthehome.org/family-traditions-that-keep-christ-at-the-center-of-christmas; www.focusonthefamily.com/parenting/spiritual-growth-for-kids/faith-at-home/faith-at-home.

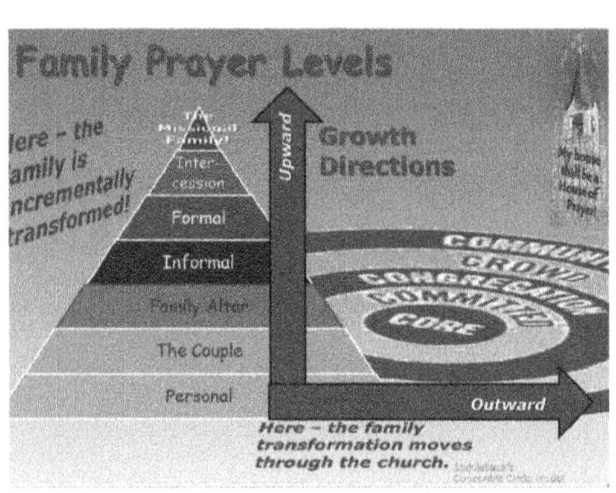

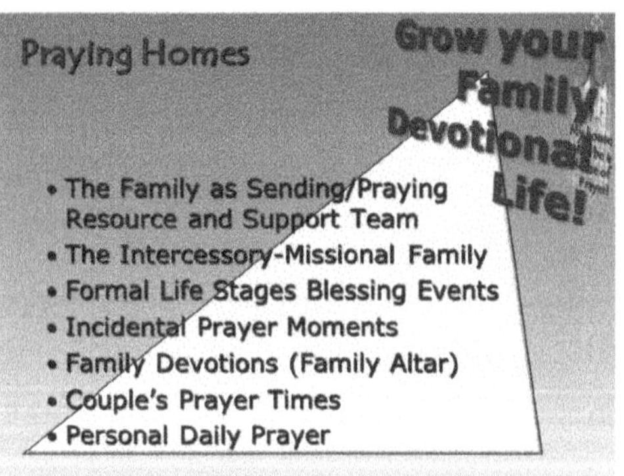

the child reaches the teen years, the mantle of responsibility has to pass to the child and parents have to assume a supportive and less commanding role. The parent moves from prescribing to proposing, from directing to suggesting. There may be moments that require a proverbial line in the sand, but a parent's influence in such moments will reach back to godly family faith practices. Against such a backdrop, the blessing ceremonies can be powerful incentives to discover God's will and ways with supportive parents. The goal is to assist the child in making wise decisions for themselves.

6. **The family as an evangelism prayer force.** Engage the family in prayer beyond themselves, for example, for neighbors – physical neighbors who live next door; family as neighbors; friends and acquaintances as neighbors; work/school associates as neighbors; and finally, using the analogy of Jesus and the Samaritan, the need to be neighborly to those who God places in our path. Teach compassion, beginning with prayer for others. Teach prayer as a gift – wrapped in tangible gifts of mercy to the hurting and the needy. Start a prayer list for neighbors and family. Make it a part of dinnertime daily prayer. Some families have a jar or dish with names. They draw out a name and pray for another family daily.

7. **The family as a missionary prayer force.** As a family, adopt a nation for prayer. Adopt an unreached people group. Adopt a missionary for prayer. Join prayer support teams when short-term missionaries are sent from your church. Then, pray for the sending forth of a family member on a missions trip, and then, for each family member to be involved in a missions trip, and finally, for the whole family to go on mission together, whether it is a stateside endeavor or an overseas excursion.

Remember God's original plan was that Israel was to be a 'kingdom of priests' to the unreached people and nations around them. Every family, then, raised 'priests.' The firstborn son of every family was to be given to God for full-time priestly service (Ex. 13:2; 34:19). Israel rejected that idea. Aaron and his sons were then substituted for the first born from every family.

However, God's original plan should remain a benchmark – every family should produce sons and daughters given to the work of God. Some may end up in full-time, professional ministry. Others might be judges or doctors, teachers or scientists, laborers or loan officers, but all should live from the family faith root system, all should live their lives for the glory of God.

Take a family mission trip – it will be unforgettable. Pray. Raise funds. And together, take the entire family to some mission field for service. Solicit prayer support. Journal the experience. Your children will learn to care for the less fortunate. They may see suffering up close and be touched with the compassion of God for others. They will come to care. They will share the gospel – together. Such moments change people forever.

The transformation of our families will not occur overnight, but the vitality of families who move from level one to level seven will radically influence your congregation. As those families move upward on the scale of prayer engagement and the family prayer movement expands to and through your congregation, you will experience the power of a 'tipping-point' at every level.

As you move forward, encouraging family prayer transformation, mentor families in these seven ways to engage children in prayer:

1. Let them _pray creatively_, playfully, less religiously and more naturally – with their eyes open, etc. Don't worry about religious rules, the goal is spiritual sensitivity.

2. Use _imagination_ in prayer – imagine the story line of scripture. Act it out, and pray it.

3. Use _visuals_ – a globe or map, pictures, cut-outs, rocks and trees, etc. See and pray, touch and pray.

4. _Model_ simple, direct, heart-felt prayer.

5. _Avoid stifling_ their 'free' prayer with adult rules of right praying.

6. _Memorize_ Scripture with them, and then pray it. Teach them the Bible as a prayer-book.

7. *Take them to prayer meetings.* Even if they get restless, trust the Holy Spirit. The atmosphere itself is often contagious.

Involvement Goals

Every home, a praying home. Every family member – the individual, the couple, kids and parents, the family altar, the family in missional prayer, the family in mission. Consider the family, an intercessory unity. Consider inter-family prayer experiences. Offer training on the family altar.

Transition

The transition occurs when prayer becomes spontaneous and natural in the home. When kids urge, could we pray about this? When the family regularly stops and prays – as needs arise and the Lord directs. Informal prayer is powerful; but it rises out of, it is informed by, formal times of prayer. From those experiences, we adopt the 'form' of prayer – praise, thanksgiving, petition, intercession, lament, silence, worship, and more.

Common Mistakes

Failing to see the critical need for daily prayer, couple's connections in prayer, the family altar – the omission is deadly. No prayer ministry at church can survive without roots in personal and family prayer.

Additional Considerations:

God said to Abraham, *"... in you all the families of the earth shall be blessed"* (Gen. 12:1-3). It is the desire of God to bless families, all families, throughout the earth! What an amazing idea. Individuals were not the focus, but families. The blessing of God comes on families, in families, and through families. It is rare to find blessing that is not in some way connected to families. Our society has digressively moved to an anti-family culture of hyper-individualism. We are now redefining family. The divorce culture is a culture of rejection, not acceptance; of convenience, not covenant. Satan divides and destroys.

The phrase 'to bless' is *barak* in Hebrew.[2] It means to kneel before someone. It is the image of one standing over another. And thus, the idea on the part of the one receiving the blessing of humility, and the recognition that the one who blesses is to be revered in some way. So humility and respect are conveyed in the moment of blessing. The impact of the blessing is to empower one to prosper. The Greek verb 'to bless' is *eulogeo.* It means to 'speak well of' and 'to exalt, or to honor'. It is a spoken form of praise. It is a derivative of *logos*, which means *word,* but is better understood as the conceptual framework, the ideological mindset out of which words emerge. 'To bless' is to convey a mindset that empowers one to succeed. A blessing ceremony is a formal expression, a culmination of something deeper, that has been slowly building. It marks the turning point, the launch into some new level of confidence and grace. It was not until the Father's blessing, that Christ began his ministry (Luke 3:22). He did not receive the full empowering of the Spirit for mission until that blessing came, "This is my beloved Son in whom I am well pleased." The anointing for service and the blessing come together.

Craig Hill in his book, *The Power of a Parent's Blessing,* offers six critical points in a child's life when he should be blessed.[3] These times are at (1) conception, while in the (2) womb, at (3) birth, in (4) infancy, at (5) puberty, at the time of (6) marriage and in an (7) older age. The seventh, he says, is when the children return the blessing, and bless the parents. These are drawn from a study of Hebrew culture. Craig notes, "It would have been virtually impossible for someone growing up in the ancient Hebrew culture to miss out on being blessed...the culture was structured in such a way that both ceremonial and day-to-day blessing occurred naturally in most families."[4] Two critical factors emerge from the blessing and they relate

---

2   Strong's Exhaustive Concordance, 'barak,' OT: 1228; See also, W. E. Vine, An Expository Dictionary of Biblical Words (Nashville, TN: Thomas Nelson, 1985), 'berakah, OT: 1293; and 'eulogy', NT: 2127.

3   Craig Hill, *The Power of a Parent's Blessing* (Lake Mary, FL; Charisma, 2013), 6

4   Ibid, 6-7.

to identity and destiny. They answer the questions that most haunt moderns, "Who am I?" and "Why am I here?" The first is the core of the person's self-perception; and the second, their sense of function and significance.[5]

These special period blessings were underpinned by weekly Sabbath moments in the home at which the father blessed his wife, in front of the children, and then each child received a blessing. The culture of the home was that of blessing and affirming, enabling and empowering. Many Christian homes manifest faith in the form of prohibition, "Don't do that…go there…stop that." A blessing environment is not framed in the negative, but in the positive. "You are special…God is with you…You will succeed." Someone said that a Christian family sends their kids off to school with the warning, "Be good today!" And a Jewish family sends their kids off urging, "Do something great today." If you are attempting to do something 'great,' you rarely do something 'bad,' at least, not deliberately. The difference is worlds apart.

Existentialism and hedonism mute the quest for greatness. The contemporary generation reasons unreasonably, "I am a cosmic accident, no more and no less, on a planet that mysteriously, by chance, had the right circumstances to produce the form of life known as humans. At some point, the same random forces that produced my life will destroy it. There is no eternity. No afterlife. No destiny, except what I make for myself here and now. I must enjoy life. I only live once. So I choose to live it up." It takes massive reinforcement to counteract the cultural bias. It comes from every side. It seeps into the home via the television. It comes on the wings of peer influence, public school values, music, dress and social media.

Americans spend almost a third of their free time watching television. Nothing else competes. The time invested is more than the next ten popular leisure activities combined. For teens, the television is a primary companion and teacher, a social tutor and a values regulator, one's pseudo family and source of idols. Reaching the age of 18, a teen has logged 350,000 commercials, and as

---

5   Ibid, 11.

many as 100,000 were enticements to drink beer with the subtext, 'life is party' and the implication, 'you're missing out.' Monitoring the TV is more difficult, since 54 percent have a personal set in their bedroom, often hooked to cable. And 44 percent admit, that alone, they watch what they do not, what they would not watch with their parents. Twenty-five percent of them choose MTV. Sixty-six percent, aged 10 to 16, acknowledge the impact of the tube on their peers. Sixty-five percent of teens favor shows that model disrespect of parents. Seventy percent of girls attempt to model the female body images they see in media, TV and magazines. Boys are attracted to steroids for body enhancement. Sociologists and psychologists say a stimulating three-minute audio-visual encounter is adequate enough to negatively influence self-esteem.

A group of researchers interviewed kids aged 12-to-14. After two years, they interviewed the same group and discovered, those most exposed to sexual content in media (movies, music, magazines and TV) had now had sexual intercourse; they had acted on the media images at a rate 2.2 times higher than their peers.

A third of songs popular with teens contain explicit drug and alcohol references.[6] That means in a typical hour, kids get 35 nudges toward substance abuse. We are desensitizing a whole culture and lowering social empathy. TV accounts now for ten percent of youth violence.[7] Even the American Psychiatric Association admits, "The debate is over...For the last three decades, the one predominant finding in research on the mass media is that exposure to media portrayals of violence increases aggressive behavior in children."[8]

In a home where there is no prayer, no Bible reading, no devotional life – and just church on Sunday, a child or teen in America does not have a chance! Even in so-called 'Christian' homes, kids are battling a flood of immoral,

6   The Archives of Pediatrics and Adolescent Medicine.
7   Leonard Eron, Senior Research Scientist at the University of Michigan.
8   www.parentstv.org/ptc/facts/mediafacts.asp;   well.blogs. nytimes.com/2008/02/05/under-the-influence-of-music/;   www.cbsnews.com/stories   /2006/04/03/health/ webmd/main1464262.shtml

godless influences that sweep them up into the spirit of the age. A home without a family altar is not a Christian home! It has already ceded to the world.[9]

Before the Industrial Revolution, Craig Hill points out, "every child had a father, a family, and a future." The families prepared their children "to fulfill a destiny, not just to have a job."[10] Of course, not every family was so noble. Consider Max Jukes. He was an atheist and he married a godless woman. Some 560 descendants can be traced to Max. Here is a profile of how the seed of the atheist turned out – 310 died as paupers (more than half), 150 became criminals, seven of them murderers, 100 were known drunkards, and half the women who descended from Max were prostitutes. It is estimated that the family of Max Jukes cost the American government some 1.25 million dollars. On the other hand, consider Jonathan Edwards, one of the preachers who sparked the First Great Awakening. He and Max lived in the same time period. Edwards married a godly woman. Some 1394 descendants can be traced to the preacher. Here is a profile: 295 graduated from college, 13 became college presidents, 65 became professors, three were elected as US senators, three as state governors, 30 were judges, 100 were lawyers, one became the dean of a law school, 56 were physicians, one was the dean of a medical school, 75 were officers in the military, 100 were either missionaries, ministers or authors. Another 80 held a public office of some kind, three were mayors, and one was the comptroller of the Treasury Department, another Vice President of the United States.[11] So will your family be like that of Max Jukes or Jonathan Edwards?

---

9   Look for more information and practical helps in the *Praying Church Resource Guide*, Section Three: Personal Prayer and the Family Altar.

10 Hill, 49-50.

11 Ibid, 50-51.

MILESTONE TWELVE
Organizing Intercessors

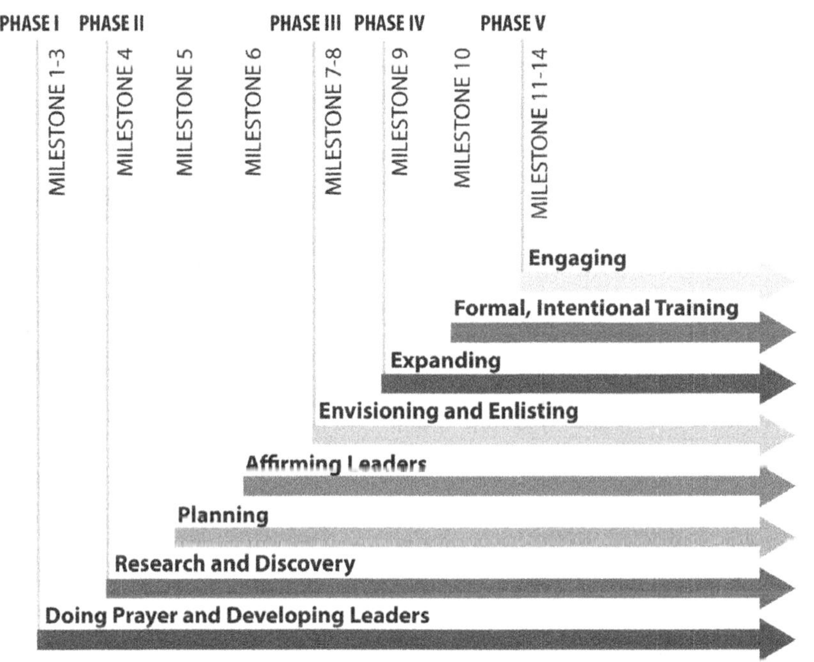

Proposition

Intercessory prayer is critical to mission. However, intercessory prayer cannot be the center of your prayer ministry. Intercession is a *utility* of prayer. It is prayer as duty, not delight. It is the work, the labor of prayer.

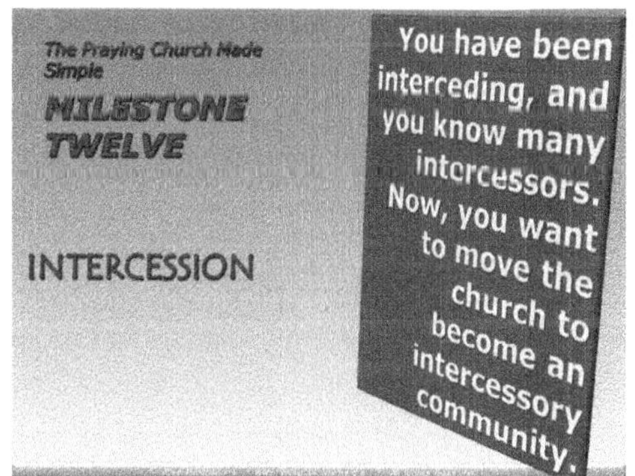

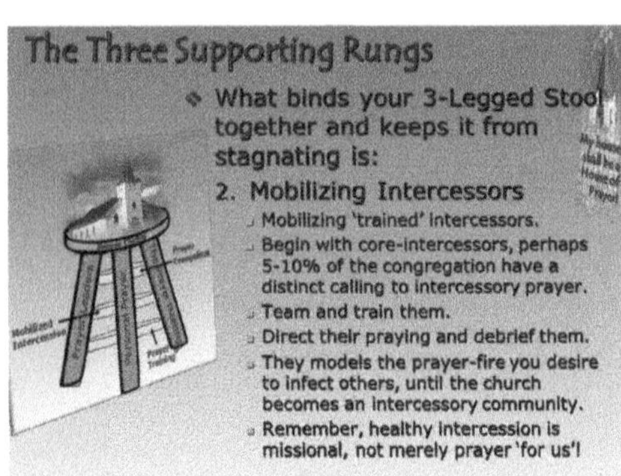

It is the edge of prayer, between light and dark, saved and lost, inside and outside. It is on the line or the wall, where some advance of the kingdom of God is sought, or some push back by the Evil One is occurring. It is the means by which God opens closed doors, enlightens blind hearts, opens ears, empowers the witness of an evangelist or missionary. It is fraught with warfare, but its heart is not warfare, but reconciliation of the lost to Christ. Intercession and intercessors need the tethering of worshipful communion. Mobilize intercessors after you have established an understanding of healthy corporate prayer aimed at transformation, after you have articulated a sound prayer theology.

Timing

Intercessors are typically the ones praying at home – but not always in healthy ways. And, they are often the ones who will show up at church for a prayer meeting. Note those who have supported the prayer effort. With teachable intercessors on your leadership team, you are now ready to identify and mobilize them across the congregation. The identification and teaming of your intercessors will depend on their level of trust, as will your capacity to teach, train and retrain. Directing the intercessors is also a matter of trust and training – most have never been teamed or directed. Getting them to adapt ministry and mission causes for regular systematic prayer will be a new idea for many. To create a successfully dialect between debriefing and redirecting intercessors in prayer will take special training and teaching and time for trust to develop between these watchmen on the wall and elders at the gate.

Resources

Alive Publications has released a small book called *Intercession – the Critical, Strategic, Middle*. The book, *Entertaining God – Influencing Cities* is also a great resource. It emphasizes 'hosting the presence of God' as the key to intercessory influence. There are also materials for training intercessors in the *Praying Church Resource Guide*.

There you will find a great deal of material on intercessory prayer. Make sure you use material that does not emphasize spiritual warfare as 'the essence' of intercession; nor material that denies its reality. <u>You want to develop worshipping intercessors who know their strength is in communion with God</u>, not railing at the darkness. You want intercessors who see God as the warrior. His warfare, in behalf of His own purposes, allows us to do our most effective work as intercessors – between Him and lost people.

Most people have heard of intercessory prayer, but many have a confused sense of what it is. Some see it as belonging to an exotic handful of the more spiritually elite pray-ers. So they distance themselves from intercession. Some see intercession as a 'spiritual gift' – and they are sure they do not have it and are grateful. There is scant evidence that intercession is spiritual *gift*, especially one limited to a handful of fervent pray-ers. That being said - there does appear to be a group of believers who have a special *call* to intercessory prayer. Estimates are that such Christians compose 5-10 percent of believers. However, all believers are invited into the role of intercession; it is the noblest use of prayer. In intercession, we stand between God and another, perhaps in behalf of their greatest need – to become a follower of Jesus Christ.

Preach on intercession. Teach on it. Identify those who feel a call to the ministry of intercession. Meet with them. Pray with them. Begin to trust them with assignments for prayer. Debrief them.

Eventually, you want to look at teaming your intercessors. See the *Praying Church Resource Guide* for suggestions. Each intercessor should be assigned to a virtual prayer team (VPT) of 3-5 or 5-10 depending on your congregational size. These are not PIT Crews, focused on or attached to some ministry effort for prayer support. That is different. Each ministry will recruit prayer partners and some intercessors will serve to provide prayer support for a given ministry. However, these VPTs are the *primary way* in which you organize your intercessory effort and stagger prayer assignments. This is also how you direct intercessors, debrief them, team them for greater effectiveness, and keep them encouraged.

Create a means to convey prayer requests, needs and news to your intercessors through these virtual teams. You might use email, twitter, texting or old-fashioned telephone chains. At times, you may want to do prayer exercises – prayer chains, prayer conference calls, etc.

Do prayer walking and prayer missions to various sites in the community. Hold extended prayer times. Conduct a 24-7 prayer weekend. Identify your mission field and engage intercessors to pray into and over that mission field. Take them there. Study the neighborhood around your church. Create prayer points for your church neighborhood and city. Cultivating a caring church starts with prayer. Care without prayer is humanitarian work. It is noble. But what sets the church's care apart is that it invokes God's blessing on the gift, and it invites His Presence to go with the gift. It is Presence that brings a consciousness of the greater need, which leads to personal conviction by the Spirit, which leads to conversion. Don't do care without prayer! For more ideas see *The Praying Church Resource Guide*, Section 7 – "Prayer Evangelism."

Duration

Training intercessors is perpetual. They will be trained best 'on the wall' in the act of interceding. The Holy Spirit will teach them. If they pick up bad habits and theology, you must be brave enough to teach into their learning gaps. Exotic intercessory practices can quickly infect your intercessor team. Be patient. Remember, these people are the ones who have bullets whizzing around their head. One of the mistakes has been leaving intercessors to themselves – and isolation is not healthy for any believer, especially those caught between heaven and hell so often.

Focus

Identify your intercessors. Offer training. Team them. Direct them. Debrief them. Get them engaged in missional prayer, proactively praying, not merely reactively praying. Affirm them.

Involvement Goals

It is estimated that <u>1 in 20, about five percent of believers</u>, have a calling to intercession. The number of these staunch and committed intercessors is rarely thought to be more than ten percent. The number is about the same for those who have a gifting for evangelism. However, both called intercessors and gifted evangelists are exemplary – not exclusive. Both are the core of your intercessory-evangelism effort – the heart. <u>From them, others will catch the spirit of intercessory prayer</u>. In truth, all believers are to be intercessors, to pray for others, for believers and especially for non-believers; all believers are to share their faith. That is your goal, the entire church as an intercessory-evangelism force. The driving force of that effort will be healthy, engaged intercessors.

Transition

<u>The transition comes when teachable intercessors have been identified and engaged; when intercessors are affirmed and their 'prayer hunches' are taken seriously</u>. Directing intercessors can also be affirming, "Would you pray about ..." This makes intercessors a part of the pastoral team. Identifying trusted intercessors who are complimentary, not adversarial, is a transition point. Intercessors who learn the balance between the priestly and the prophetic are to be celebrated. As intercessors are integrated into the ministries of the church, and teamed for prayer support, you are at another transition point.

Intercessors can be free spirits. Thus, mobilizing them can be a challenge. You want intercessors who are led by the Spirit in prayer, certainly. You must also have intercessors who are willing to embrace the discipline of intercession in order to carry prayer assignments: prayer for the pastor and staff, church ministries, members and constituents, the neighbors around both them and the church, as well as the city, the state and nation; missions and missionaries; unreached people groups and geo-political nations.

Common Mistakes

<u>You cannot leave such a critical role as intercessory ministry to chance.</u> Every ministry requires someone who leads and stewards it – music, youth, children – and prayer does as well. <u>Don't make the mistake of assuming that intercessory prayer is completely intuitive. Intercessors need training</u>, especially for balance; and they need regular affirmation, as well. The most common mistake in our era is the marriage of intercession and spiritual warfare. That makes intercession a preoccupation with the darkness. While intercessors inevitably encounter spiritual warfare, resistance from very real demonic powers, their focus is not on the darkness, but the light – on the reconciliation of the lost to Christ. Intercessors must be taught the power of the uncomfortable middle, the goal of peacemaking by prayer, while the hornets swirl around them. The goal is not enemy engagement, it is 'Saving Private Ryan!'

Some scoff at the notion of training people to pray! The best musicians can benefit from vocal or instrumental training. The best preachers, anointed by God, can benefit from training – learning to interpret scripture soundly, to preach with tempered passion, to construct a logical and Biblically sound argument for the cause of Christ, and more. Because prayer as a ministry has not even been on our radar screen, we have ignored intercessors. In some places, the term intercession is strange and unfamiliar. Yet, intercessors are as naturally drawn to prayer as musicians are to music. Intercessors are graced to pray. We need to recover the prayer-fire of intercessors. Identify them and train them.

We should again sound a caution raised earlier. The heart of prayer is communion with God. Intercessors love to pray! Is that a problem? Yes! In the same way that preachers who love to preach can become imbalanced. More than 60% of American pastors read the Bible only in preparation for their sermons. They sometimes fail to value scripture for its devotional character – they see sermons in every inspiration point. In the same way, intercessors may fail to value prayer for the "sheer pleasure of God's presence." If they always move past communion to do the "work" of intercession – they not only run the risk of imbalance, but the danger of burnout.

Training Intercessors

Intercessors have to be pastored as well. An intercessor without a teachable spirit is a time bomb waiting to go off. Isolated to themselves, they will get out of balance. Without direction, they will lock into a single focus and style of prayer that lacks *breath* and vision. Finding those who have a passion for prayer is as simple as beginning a choir ministry. Make the announcement, "We are beginning a music ministry here at our church. Those interested in participating please show up Wednesday night." You'll get a mixed group of talented and would-be musicians. And they will need a director to sort through them, train them, divide them in sections - tenors and altos, sopranos and bass, keyboard and percussion. And quite frankly, to send some of them on their way.

When you call for intercessors and those interested in prayer, you'll get genuine intercessors. Some will be veterans. Some will be prayer novices. Some will be would-be intercessors. Someone will need to direct the process and sort them out. They will need to be trained and teamed. Section leaders will need to be identified – those who can assist with emergency prayer, lead healing teams, prayer chains, crisis prayer, and all the other various passions you will find among the intercessors.

The training elements might include:

- Prayer basics – Intercessors need to be encouraged to balance their prayer time. Relational prayer time (communion with God for the sheer delight of His presence) is foundational to people called to do the work of prayer.

- Prayer focus – Keep the focus on the lost, those who have not made a decision to follow Christ. Spiritual warfare sometimes becomes intense when you begin to pray consistently for unbelievers. The Evil One does not want to release those who are captive to sin. As the warfare intensifies, intercessors may shift their focus from prayer for the lost, to a preoccupation with the demonic. If they do, they will become the victims of a prayer diversion, unknowingly falling into the trap of the Evil One. He will do anything to redirect our prayer efforts away from the unsaved. Train intercessors to be vigilant in keeping their prayer focus on the lost! Their warfare is not primarily with the demonic, it is over souls.

- Prayer theology – <u>Bible-based praying</u> is the anchor for experiential, Spirit-led praying.

- Prayer <u>resources</u> – <u>How to pray</u> for the lost, for world missions, for the city, for other believers, for your pastor, for missionaries, etc.

- Listening prayer – <u>How to hear God</u>; journaling – recording the experiences of the night watches.

Many intercessors are intuitive, but not all know how to handle the burden they feel, the strange sense of desperation for someone they hardly know, or the drawing to a particular city in a far away nation. <u>They need coaching and training</u>. And all of us need to recognize, as the prayer movement expands, we are on new turf. We don't have or even need, neat answers for all God is calling us to experience.

Leadership Required!

The intercessory prayer process will not naturally unwrap. Someone will need to emerge who will serve as the leader of the army of intercessors. Only someone with a heart for prayer will inspire prayer and be respected by the intercessors. And only a leader will lead! Don't make the mistake of placing an intercessor without leadership and organizational skills at the head of your prayer ministry. And don't make the mistake of choosing a leader who has organizational skills, but is not a person of prayer, preferably an intercessor, at the head of your prayer ministry.

To reference our earlier analogy, not all singers can direct a choir. On the other hand, it would be rare to find a choir director who was not a singer. Look for a person of prayer, with a call to pray, who has leadership and organizational skills. Not all intercessors can direct a prayer meeting.

Teaming Intercessors

Team your intercessors for encouragement and confirmation. Many intercessors are loners! Teaming is not to create another intercessory prayer group. It is for the purpose of mobilization, distributing prayer needs and assignments, and harvesting insights out of the watch of these intercessors. Create a network of communication and encouragement for intercessors.

Do this in four different, virtual ways:

1. Establish *Prayer Teams.* These should number about three to five; or five to ten intercessors, depending on the size of the church, smaller to larger. Encourage youth intercessory teams. At least one intercessory team should be a youth team with a youth prayer leader. The teams may not necessarily meet to pray together. They are "partnered intercessors," teamed for prayer assignments and communication. Appoint a contact person, a lead intercessor, for each team.

2. If you have as many as five or ten teams, you may want to group them into *brigades.* Use your own terminology. With each team, you mobilize 3-5 *intercessors.* With each brigade, you mobilize three to five *teams.* And you should be able to do this with the click of an email or create group texting. Or yet, a closed facebook group.

   If you send all the prayer needs of the congregation to every intercessor, expecting them to pray for each one, the number, even in a small church, will be overwhelming. Too many requests will make the prayer mobilization effort ineffective. Too few will likewise send the wrong message. Teaming intercessors will allow you to rotate the mobilization of your prayer teams – sending one request to one, the second to another, and so on.

   An entire brigade could be mobilized for needs with the highest urgency. All prayer needs could also be posted to the church's website and viewed by all. And of course, if you have a prayer center, they would be featured there.

   Your prayer teams could also be assigned different prayer tasks. They could be deployed team-by-team, or brigade-by-brigade. A general call for intercessors will always bring the faithful core, but if that is your model, you may burn them out. This strategy allows you to spread out the intercessory load and involve more people.

3. Further *grouping of these intercessors might be by zip code*, precinct or by area of the city. This is a part of mobilizing the church *diaspora.* This would allow the intercessors to connect and give the gift of prayer to the city, zone-by-zone.

4. Another way to group them would be in terms of their *prayer support for the various ministries of the church.* Here are the priorities:

   ✓ First priority – prayer for the lost and the harvest field. This assure that your prayer effort is not internal. It is missional.

   ✓ Second priority - prayer support for the pastor and for every staff member - a PIT (Personal Intercessory Team) crew for every leader. One experiment indicated that when leaders were prayed for every day, for 15 minutes, 89% reported a discernible difference in their effectiveness.

   ✓ Prayer support for every church ministry (Example: Interface intercessors with the prayer-evangelism focus, family prayer efforts, prayer groups, the pastor and more) and every church event, mission trip, etc.

   ✓ Group intercessors in terms of their heart – their passion and burden for prayer (Youth, Gangs, Drugs, Addictions, Crime, Women's Issues, Men, Singles, Seniors, the City/County, UPGs, the Mayor/City-County Leaders, Schools, Fire/Police, Courts, Poverty, Children, Hunger, etc.) These are themes around which you might want to organize prayer groups.

Some of these intercessors may lead "prayer groups" during the week. Some intercessors may function as regular "prayer mission" teams praying at various places in the city for change and renewal.

You may want to develop a code system for your prayer requests.

   • Code BLUE – Urgent. Life or death. Here, the situation is not a matter of days, but of hours.

- Code RED – This is an emergency. It may be life-threatening. It is typically time-sensitive, and should be updated within 24-48 hours. This is developing crisis, and additional details might be needed, and they might change the status of the alert.

- Code ORANGE – This is a critical need. It may be a chronic need – the sickness or prognosis is severe, and may even be terminal. Surgery may be involved. Test outcomes may be awaited. Outcomes are uncertain.

- Code YELLOW – A concern, a sickness, an accident, a need, a typical prayer request.

- Code GREEN – Improvement. Stable, but continued prayer is requested.

- Code GRAY – Family in grief over a loss; family member committed to nursing care; dealing with dementia, etc., adolescent family concerns.

Debriefing Intercessors

The scriptures tell us to "watch and pray." The ancient word for prophet was *seer!* There is a connection between the prophetic and prayer. Don't let the word prophetic confuse you. This is not meant in a strictly charismatic sense. Rather, God reveals things to intercessors. For this reason, they need to be teamed (for confirmation), debriefed (for valuable input) and directed (for more effective watching).

A dialectic needs to form between intercessors and elders; prayer leaders and staff. Elders need the helpful eyes and ears of intercessors, and intercessors must learn to offer their report to the elders at the gate and leave it in their hands, trusting their authority.

Because intercessors have not been trained, they don't understand the parameters of their authority. They have nowhere to go with the burning heart given them in prayer, or the clear signal from the Holy Spirit about some issue in the Church. Some pastors complain that intercessors in their congregations get out of order. This is confusing to the intercessors, since no order for intercessory prayer ministry has been established. They have no outlet for their insights. No connections for confirmation. No direction and clarity for prayer focus. They have been left to themselves. And without a pastor, they get out of balance.

Interfacing With the Elders

Intercessors have to be taught that they are "watchers on the wall" – not the "elders at the gate." They are to submit their night-watch reports to the community of elders! And the elders/deacons/church council should take their prayer hunches seriously! This will be a new experience for both intercessors and church leaders. If intercessors know that their prayer investment is valued, they can more easily rest in the reality that it is not their calling to "wake up the church or the city!" The mobilization and leadership of the church is the calling of pastors and elders. Watchers on the wall who do not respect elders at the gate will never be security for the spiritual community. And elders, who have little regard for the warning sounds of the watchers, will not harvest the wisdom of intuitive and discerning pray-ers. For intercessors to feel passionately that a warning go forth, and to submit that message to the elders through prayer leadership channels requires maturity! What if the elders do not share the intuitive deduction of the intercessor? What if the intercessor has translated their intuitive insights into concrete conclusions, without awareness? Can the intercessor submit to the eldership? Can the eldership hear the heart implications of the intercessor and take that into consideration? Can they gently correct and simultaneously affirm? We can all become enamored by our own gifts and fail to see that they are not really our gifts at all, but gifts to the body!

Engaging Intercessors

Here are some ways intercessors can be used:

- *Sweep the Sanctuary* – every Saturday night. Do it in teams - VPTs! Stagger the teams so they have duty once a month or quarter.

- *Every classroom should have a PIT crew*. An intercessor should occasionally meet the teacher before the Sunday School or discipleship class begins. Or, as the Sunday School teacher comes into the classroom, the intercessor might be leaving. "I'm praying for you. I know you'll have a great day!"

- *Simultaneous intercessory prayer* should be offered during the worship service and preaching of the Word.

- *Prayer for the lost loved ones* of church members should be offered regularly – the names of the friends and family members called out in prayer at least once each week, until they come to Christ.

- *Every staff person should have a PIT crew* - an intercessory support team. The rule should be: ***An intercessor for every worker – and every worker an intercessor.***

- Every ministry in the church should have an intercessor or intercessory team assigned to it. Every ministry should be a prayed for ministry. The *Moravian Principle should be applied:* ***No one works unless someone prays!***

- *Prayer for the mission endeavors of the Church* and for the missionaries supported by the Church is the work of intercessors. Sending funds for missions is not enough. We are throwing money at the darkness. We must provide the investment of prayer energy as well.

- *Prayer should be offered by intercessors for every member family of the congregation* as often as a reasonable cycle of prayer will allow. In a mega-church, it may only be once or twice a year. In a smaller congregation, every member family can be covered in prayer weekly or perhaps, monthly.

- *Prayer should be offered for every business owned by church members.* Pray for the blessing and favor of God. Ask God to bless these business owners in order that the Kingdom might be blessed.

- *Adopt a local fire station or police station.* Do so especially if you have peace and safety officers in your congregation. Or if you have a fire or police station in the neighborhood of the church. Go a step further. Adopt police and fire personnel for personal prayer coverings.

- *Adopt a local School* – one near the church. Bless them. Pray for them. Ask how you can serve them.

- *Consider "prayer ambassador" teams* that are sent out to give the "gift of prayer" to the community. These teams of 3-5 people go in a priestly mode. They go to bless. They bring back needs – and allow the church to pray for specific needs in the city and neighborhood around the church. In such times, God shows himself alive to these people.

- *Pray for neighboring churches.* List their name in the bulletin. Have the congregation, or at least intercessors, send them a note of encouragement, "We at Second Church are praying for you!"

- *Pray for places where sin abounds.* For strongholds of evil in the city or even the neighborhood around the church to be broken. Pray light *into* the area, not merely the darkness out. Asking God to remove something only creates a vacuum (Matthew 12:43-45). Don't pray evil things *out* without praying holy things *in*.

- *Redeem the land.* God wants the "trees to clap their hands," (Isaiah 55:12) the "seas to roar with praise" (Psalm 96:11) – all the earth to acknowledge him. Look at the places that reflect disorder, darkness, depression, oppression – and send teams to pray in those gaps. Invite God's light. Pray that the land and buildings would be used for godly purposes. Ask that the owner and operator of the building would come to know God. Begin to pastor the community *"by prayer!"* (Ezekiel 22:22-30; Deuteronomy 32:43; Numbers 35:33)

- *Pray for the city.* Pray for city leaders and for community needs (1 Timothy 2:1-2). Have the intercessors take their prayer cues from the community newspaper. Nothing escapes God. Nothing is outside the concern of his kingdom. So many things have spiritual implications. Set the intercessors to praying for the city.

In mobilizing and engaging intercessors, in the examples above, we have already started the process of prayer evangelism. Intercession and prayer evangelism flow into and out of one another.

MILESTONE THIRTEEN
Prayer Evangelism

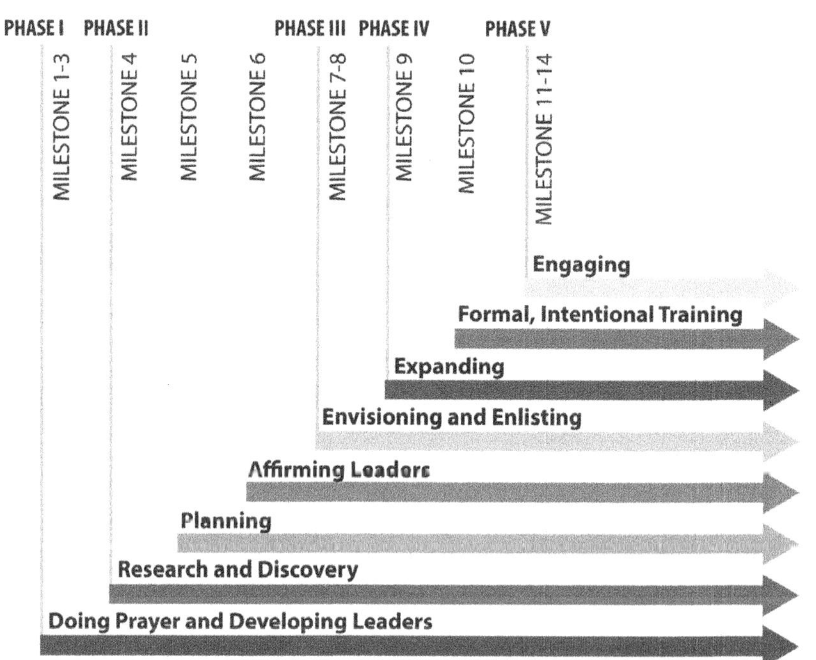

Proposition

Prayer is at its heart worship, and at its edge mission, and in between God meets our needs. Sadly, far too much of our prayer energy today is focused on our own needs. Not only do we undervalue prayer for the sheer pleasure

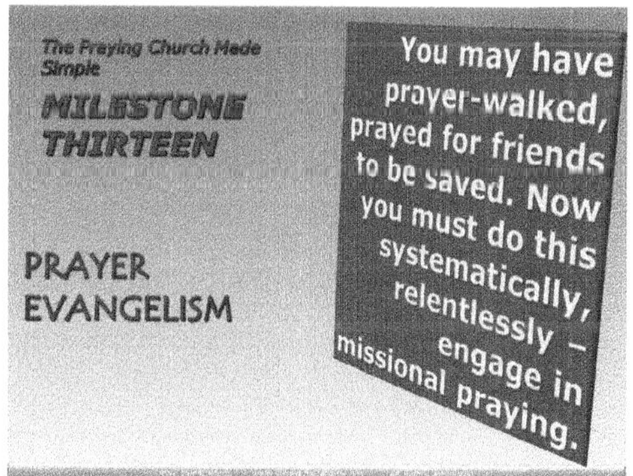

of being with God, we invest far too little prayer in mission. <u>The prayer ministry of the church is not complete unless it has a missional interface</u> and its intercessors, as well as families and the congregation, are engaged in prayer evangelism. God opens doors by prayer. Any missionary that finds a door of ministry unlocked will, on examination, discover the fingerprints of an intercessor on the doorknob.

Timing

Intercessory prayer is posited on the understanding of prayer as communion. <u>Establish worshipful prayer as communion with God, before you develop the prayer evangelism effort.</u>

Resources

The Praying Church Handbook – Volume IV is specifically focused on *Intercessory Prayer and Mission*. It is a collage of over 1400 pages, written and electronic, on topics related to intercession and mission. Another great practical tool is Steve Hawthorne's annual guide, *Seek God for the City!* In addition, Steve collaborated with the late Ralph Winter in the production of the great missions course, *Perspectives.*

Duration

Refer to your research/discovery, demographics and needs in your harvest field. The prayer evangelism effort is <u>perennial, relentless and ongoing.</u>

Focus

<u>Every church needs a mission field near</u> – around the church and its facility; <u>and a mission field afar</u> – a nation, an unreached people group, etc. <u>Every member needs to see themselves as a missionary to their neighbors, and inside their vocation network</u> (workplace).

There are five neighbors for whom each member should pray, care about, and when possible, share Christ: the (1) physical neighbors who live next door and beside whom

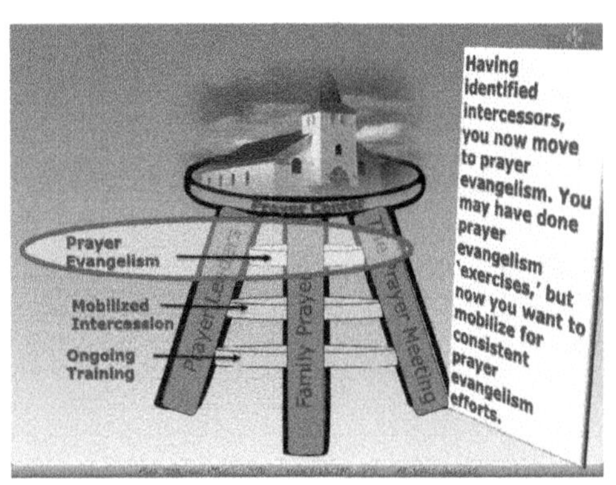

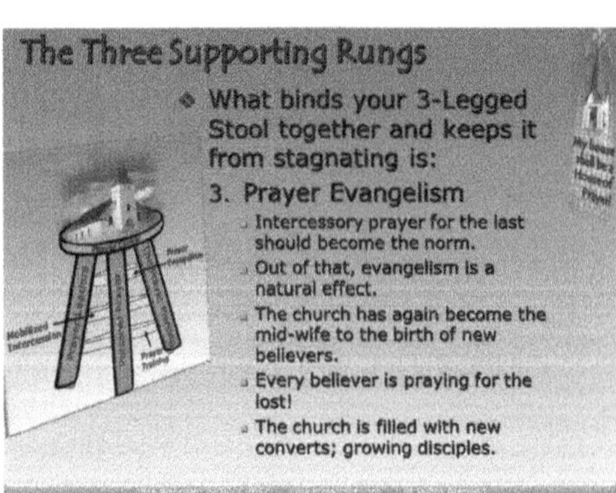

we (2) work; our (3) family and (4) family-like friends (including shopping and trade networks); and then, that special (5) 'Jericho Road' person who desperately needs a neighbor – a needy person whom God seems to put in our path.

Involvement Goals

Like intercession, some people are gifted for evangelism, but all Christians should be evangelists – sharing the good news. <u>The goal is every member an evangelist – a 'good news' advocate</u>. Teach the power of thankfulness as a 'good-news' tool as well as the power of blessing. Appoint Prayer Ambassadors. These are folks who relate as ambassadors of the Lord, and the church, to city leaders, business owners, influences. With their feet shod with the 'good news of peace' they build prayer bridges with community leaders, businesses in the same neighborhood as the church. They reach out – and give the gift prayer. Introduce relational evangelism. Plan systematic prayer walking in your mission field near – around the facility where you worship. Conduct prayer missions into the city. Don't do this randomly, do it systematically. Encourage every member of sign up to pray for their neighbors at www.pray4everyhome.com. Encourage them to prayer walk their neighborhood and their workplace.

Transition

The transition comes <u>when prayer walking and prayer missions are no longer a quaint exercise but a regular endeavor</u>, and stories begin to emerge reflecting the impact of your prayer evangelism efforts. Specifically, the number of souls saved begins to increase.

Common Mistakes

<u>You cannot see prayer evangelism as exotic</u>. You cannot do it randomly, on occasion, casually – you must own this as a priority. Prayer evangelism is not magic. Don't be unrealistic about results. You are often praying against closed doors, in a nation that has increasingly displaced Christianity, denied prayer in the name of Jesus, and

championed pluralism. <u>Be patient. Be persistent</u>. Prayer walk and conduct prayer missions, listen to the Spirit and collect hunches and impressions from intercessors, then narrow your focus, and do another wave of prayer evangelism.

MILESTONE FOURTEEN
Prayer Groups

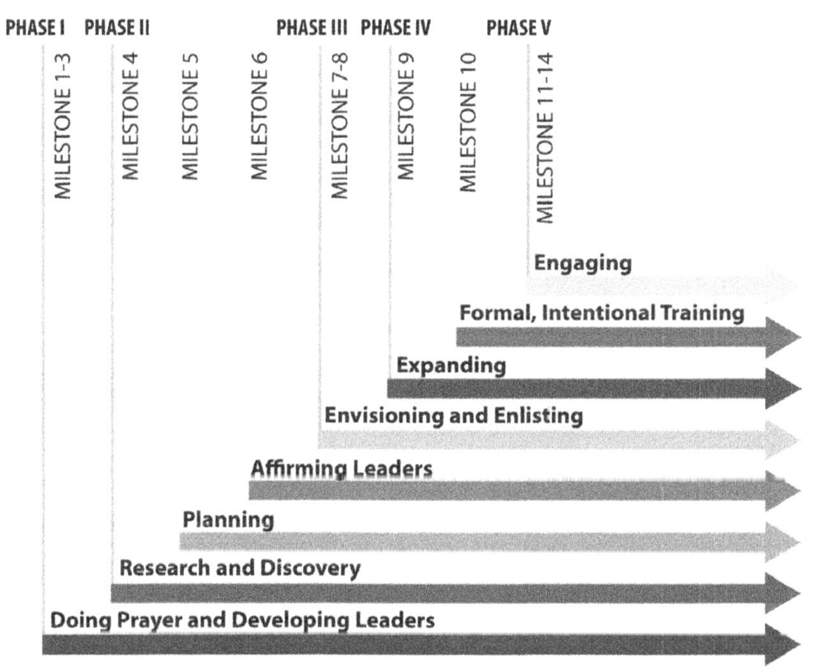

Proposition

<u>People learn to pray by praying – there is no other way</u>! The best way to learn to pray is with a small group of praying people. Small prayer groups are the best vehicle to accomplish this goal. <u>Form prayer groups, never</u>

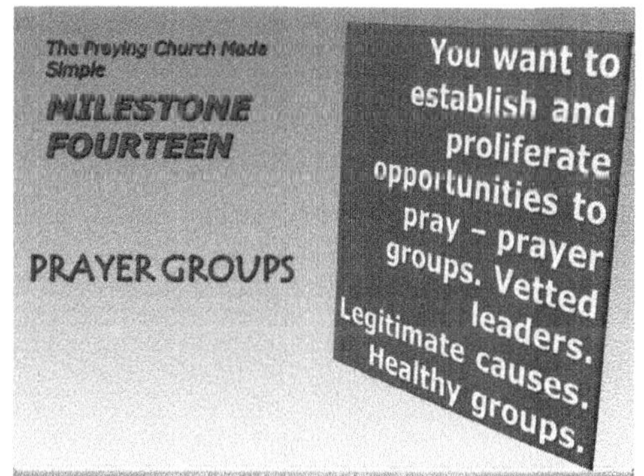

to exceed a dozen members. <u>Organize them around specific themes</u>. Appoint a mature leader. At times you may be approached by someone who wants to lead a prayer group. The themes might vary – Prayer for Lost Loved Ones, Mothers Praying for Daughters; Fathers Praying for Sons; Prayer for Unreached Peoples; Prayer for Revival and Awakening; Prayer for City Fathers; Prayer for the Nation and its Leaders; Singles Support and Prayer Group; Witnessing Teens Prayer Group; Prayer for Community Schools; Prayer Missionaries; Prayer for Nations; and more. The presenting reason for every prayer group attracts participants, but the underlying reason is that prayer groups are the places people learn to pray. The small intimate setting with trusting friends invites people to pray aloud. Praying aloud is liberating to prayer. Here, those learning to pray are affirmed by veterans. They are mentored, raised to peer status, and thrust into leadership in another small prayer group.

Timing

<u>The prayer groups</u> in your congregation should <u>revolve around a healthy all-church prayer gathering</u>. They should not be a substitute for the entire congregation gathered in prayer, led by the pastor. Healthy intercessors are necessary to lead them.

You want groups where people can meet to pray for a particular need and support one another in prayer. <u>For every 100 attenders, you want seven prayer group opportunities</u>. These groups are organized and bound together by a desire to pray for a particular need. For example, there might be a single mom's prayer support group, a prayer group for lost sons and daughters, a prayer group for unreached peoples, an addictions prayer group, a prayer group to pray for missionaries. There are so many other prayer focuses; and the point of interest binds the purpose of the group together; but most importantly, it creates the context to learn to pray. Limit the size of the groups to twelve. Keep them small and informal enough for the people to feel comfortable enough to continue to pray – we learn to pray by praying, and we pray best when we pray about the things we also deeply care about.

Caution: Don't attempt all these ideas at once!

Most small group specialists will say that single-purpose groups work best. With multiple purposes, one cause usually suffers. In some cases, multiple purpose groups might be necessary – prayer and support groups, prayer and study groups, prayer and action groups, etc. If you engage multiple purpose groups, create clear boundaries to protect both causes.

Resources

There are a number of prayer group helps available in *The Praying Church Resource Guide, Chapter 5.*

Duration

Prayer groups should be <u>a permanent feature of the congregation</u>. For every 12-15 members, you need a prayer group (7:100). These are <u>small, three-to-twelve in number</u>. Most will average five-to-seven folks. Encourage them to multiply regularly, typically, annually. You never want a prayer group competing in terms of attendance with the prayer time led weekly by the pastor – that is not healthy. It is an upside down arrangement usually indicating that style or personality have become more important than prayer. Prayer must never be about personality – it must be a gathering around Jesus.

<u>Once a year, ask each prayer group to renew its commitment to continue to pray for a specific cause or need. Introduce new prayer groups</u>. At least <u>20 percent of your groups should be new each</u> year (1:5). In order to help people transition in and out of groups, choose a month of the year in which you suspend your prayer groups, for example, December. When you begin your prayer group ministry again, do so with new leaders and fresh themes. Don't break up groups intentionally, unless they are unhealthy. Do encourage them to multiply.

Focus

Prayer groups <u>are a means of connecting prayer needs in the congregation and missional needs in the community with regular people who intercede</u>.

Involvement Goals

A good goal is <u>a third-to-half your congregation in prayer groups</u> that meet weekly and not less than monthly. This is where you disciple people to pray.

Transition

When prayer groups are abundant, diverse in focus, and <u>reports emerge of God-moments</u> among the faithful, you will find faith and fervency rising.

Common Mistakes

<u>Fearing prayer groups</u> as divisive is a common reason to resist starting such groups. At the bottom of this concern is the absence of prayer group leadership training, and not setting clear parameters. Prayer groups can, and sometimes do, become church plants. If that is a part of your strategy, plan for such eventualities; if not, set clear guidelines from the start. <u>Vet your prayer group leaders.</u>

The Prayer Celebration

Think about prayer groups in these four ways:

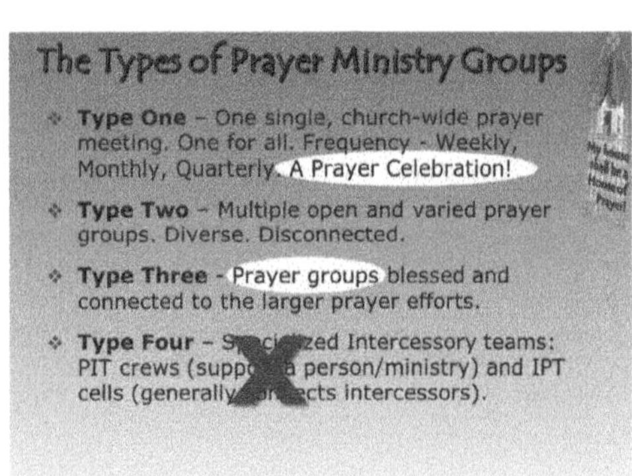

- **Type One** – The single, church-wide, typically pastor-led prayer meeting. One for all. Frequency - Weekly, Monthly, Quarterly. ***A Prayer Celebration!*** It is *homogeneous*. This is MILESTONE ONE.

- <u>***Type Two***</u> – *Multiple open and varied prayer groups. Diverse. Disconnected.* ***Ad-hoc Prayer Groups.*** These are typical. They are described here, because they are typical, but they are not recommended. They lack focus. They are too informal. They sometimes gossip more than they pray. Such groups cause pastors to forbid authorizing prayer groups.

- **Type Three** – ***Intentional Prayer Groups***, sanctioned by the prayer ministry, of 3-12 people, blessed and connected to the larger prayer efforts. It is *heterogeneous*.

- **Type Four** – ***Specialized Intercessory teams***: PIT crews (supports a person) and VPTs (generally connects intercessors).

TYPE TWO is a type of prayer group ***you do not want to encourage*** – but these will persist without training. If you create a culture of prayer, prayer groups will be spawned spontaneously. Some will be healthy and respectful. Others may be unhealthy and independent. If you attempt to tightly control and orchestrate all prayer, rather than humbly stewarding it, you may end up fighting the Holy Spirit. Remember, He, not us, not man, is in charge of the Church!

Yet, why would a prayer group leader 'not' want to be connected, in an official and sanctioned way, with the church prayer ministry and its leadership team? If prayer group leadership training were available, what reason would someone have for 'not' wanting to take advantage of that training? In rare cases, you might have someone who does not 'need' the training. Allow for exceptions, but don't make exceptions the rule. The purpose is trained and sound leaders of healthy prayer groups. Keep the goal in mind, the vision of a praying church and the strategic objection of prayer mobilization, the tactic of prayer groups – not the regiment of training or the rules that help you accomplish the objective.

TYPE THREE are ***the prayer groups you want to encourage***, to keep healthy, to track and encourage others to join and start. <u>They are led by people who have some training, even experiential training, and are connected to the church prayer ministry.</u>

TYPE FOUR – are your PIT crews supporting various church leaders and ministries and your VPTs, a means by which you configure your communication with your intercessors.

The Homogeneous

The place many people will connect with the prayer ministry is the Church-wide prayer meeting. From there, you want to encourage them to join or start a small prayer group.

The HOMOGENEOUS Prayer Meeting – the <u>whole Church</u> seeking the face of God together *in one place, at a fixed time,* for an extended period or season, as an

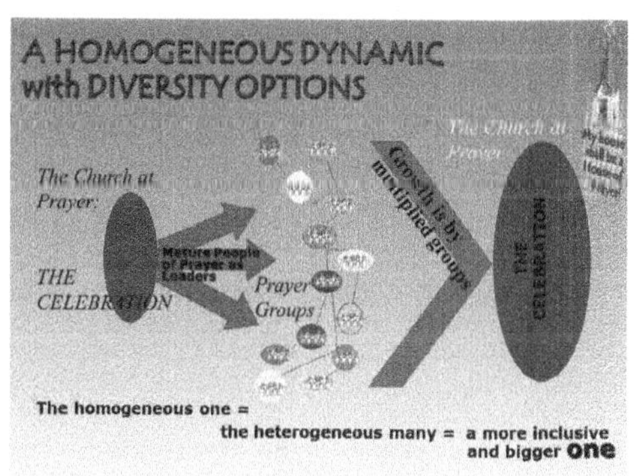

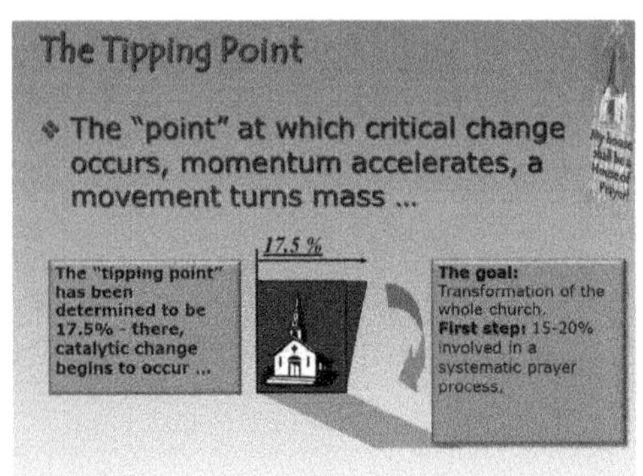

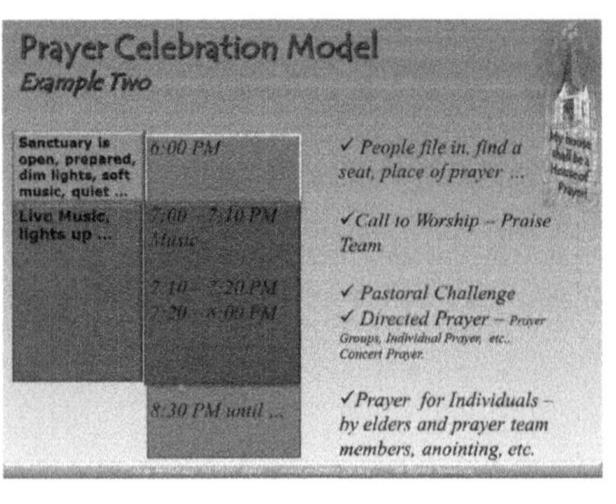

expression of dependence on God, of unity and love, for the sake of the spiritual transformation of their lives and *the whole Church* - every age-group, department, ethnic representation, gender, status, rank and position.

The threshold goal for the 'all-church' prayer meeting may not sound bold enough – but it is only 20 percent of the Sunday morning attendance as a baseline. The 'tipping' point is the 'point' at which critical change occurs, momentum accelerates, and a movement impacts the larger mass.

The 'tipping point' has been determined to be a mere 17.5 percent. At that point, the bubble-up effect on the entire congregation is felt. The goal, of course, is the transformation of the entire church into a house of prayer – a praying people. But the first stage is 15-20% consistently involved in a systematic and passionate prayer process.

Critical Mass is a chemical term referencing that point when certain *elements, added together, act and react with one another* so as to combine and thereby *create an unstoppable transformation*, so much so, that *what is produced is* not merely the sum total of the ingredients, but *something that is substantively different, the elements* being *altered* from their original form, *creating something new.* Build slowly and deliberately. Small and tight. With depth and vitality of commitment.

The church-wide prayer celebration is typically, pastor-led! It is a "prayer meeting" – not a teaching or praise and worship meeting. The focus of these gatherings is transformation. And they usually take the shape of a guided prayer experience.

MODEL ONE

Schedule

6:00 PM	Doors Open
	Music Softly Plays
7:00 PM	Call to Worship – Praise Team
7:10 PM	Pastoral Challenge
7:20 PM	Directed Prayer
	Spontaneous Prayer Circles
	Concert Prayer
	Moments of Personal Prayer

9:00 PM   Dismissal
Afterglow Prayer for Individuals
          Prayer Teams

Open your doors for prayer and encourage a reverent atmosphere. Discourage talking and visiting. Offer soft music – even if it is taped. Some may come to the altar. Others may sit. The point is the preparation of hearts for the prayer gathering.

If necessary, offer a gentle call to quiet during this hour of preparation. At 7:00 p.m., seamlessly, the music should go live without an abrupt beginning. A simple unbroken transition into live worship is preferred. After a few minutes of warming hearts in praise and worship, the pastor or prayer leader should move to the microphone and continue the praise – again, a seamless transition.

Once the music stops, the pastor, already at the podium may call for special prayer and anoint a mission team. He may offer some special prayer focus. The best practice is to call attention to a passage of Scripture and use its principles as markers for prayer. Occasionally, he will offer direction – move to groups, reach out and connect with a person near you, "Pray this with me!" Leading prayer meetings is both a skill and a spiritual art form. Some things you can learn, the major portion demands sensitivity to the Holy Spirit.

One of the consistent characteristics of your prayer meeting should be passion, with discipline Bible-based prayer with missional eyes. In this gathering, people pray aloud, sometimes tearfully, but typically in their place. The room is often packed with little room to navigate. At 8:30 p.m., the pastor will urge them to catch a ride on the subway and get home at a reasonable hour. Quite remarkable.

MODEL TWO - Small Church

Example Schedule One

5:00 PM   Optional Prayer Class
6:00 PM   Optional Prayer Class
          Sanctuary Open
          Soaking Prayer Time
          Soft Music – Quiet Prayer

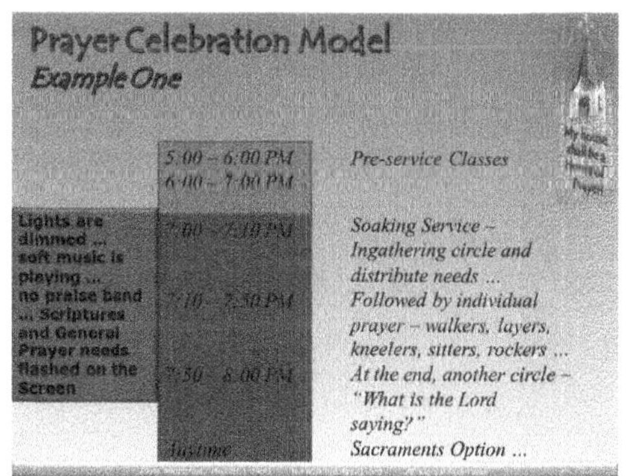

7:00 PM   Ingathering Circle
          Scripture
          Distribution of Prayer Needs
7:10 PM   Individual Prayer/Group Prayer
7:50 PM   Circle Re-gathered: "What is the Lord saying?"

During this entire hour, the communion table is open for individuals to come forward and receive the cup and the bread. (Caution: This privatizes communion. There is a theological argument for corporate communion.)

Example Schedule Two

7:00 PM   Call to Worship
7:15 PM   Bible-principled praying
7:45 PM   Pastoral Prayer over 'Prayer Box'
                  (Containing Prayer Requests)
          Prayers of Agreement
          A Season of Praise - Praise Music
          Specific Prayers by Intercessors/Everyone at Microphone; Concert of Prayer model (planned, one-at-a-time prayer)
          Concert Prayer (All pray aloud together)
          Spirit-led Prayer
          Prayer for Special Needs
          Close with Praise

This model is much more dynamic, more fluid than the first model. It is also designed for use by a smaller church. Further, it allows for greater participation by 'intercessors.'

The prayer training as a pre-service option is a great idea. Once the group activities are over, usually around 8:30 p.m., the majority of attenders feel free to leave.

The model of soaking prayer is unique. During this time, individuals are encouraged to take a need, a prayer burden and pray over it. Some walk. Some lay before the Lord. Some sit. Each prays. Music may softly play, but it is not dominate, and typically not live. Musicians also need time to pray.

During this hour, the communion table is open to anyone and everyone. Families sometimes come. At other times, individuals come and kneel around the table – or take the elements to the altar and wait with them before the Lord. In a liturgical church, a pastor will need to serve the elements. The liturgical model reminds us that all of us need to be served.

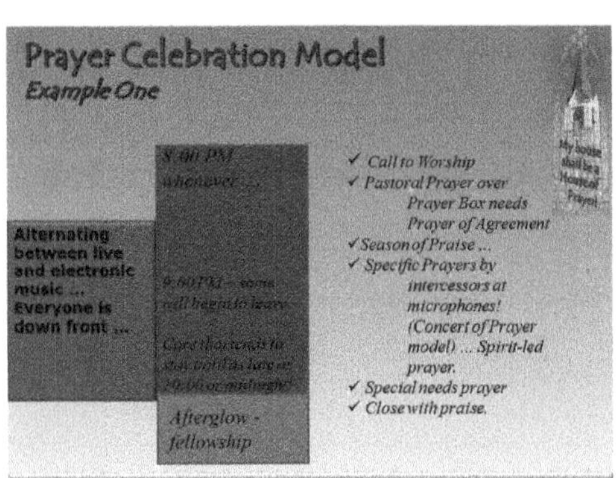

After an hour or so, the leader calls those in attendance together. His question to intercessors is, "What is God saying?" The answers may determine the direction of the next session of prayer. The group may enter into additional prayer or a season of worship – as determined by the leader.

At some point, the pastor or prayer leader takes all the needs and offers them to the Lord in prayer. Worship often follows, although, the experience is very fluid and dynamic. In addition, intercessors may come to a microphone and pray, as the congregation agrees in prayer.

The evening is concluded by an offering of personal prayer for those present with needs. After the corporate session, individuals slip away. Others may tarry.

PURPOSEFUL MODEL

Remember, the goal of a corporate prayer meeting is not merely prayer activity. In large part, this is where we learn to pray. You want intentional experiences in prayer that reveal balance and teach people prayer practices for their personal prayer lives. It you model it in the prayer meeting, they are likely to emulate it personally. If you ignore some aspect of prayer there, they are likely to conclude that it is not important, a non-essential.

In Paul's prayer theology, he sets forth four broad categories for prayer – thanksgiving, worship, supplication (petition) and intercession (1 Tim. 2:1). This is a proposition for a balanced prayer life. I recommend using these elements to construct a healthy, well-balanced corporate prayer experience.

Schedule

    6:00 PM   Sanctuary Open
              Soft Music – Quiet Prayer
    7:00 PM   Worship - Reflective
    7:10 or 7:15 PM
              Word Engagement – Praying the Scripture.
              Some passage is introduced and used as a
              prayer guide; some aspect of God is a point
              of reflection, etc.
    7:30 PM   World Engagement – Pray for the lost,
              for nations, for unreached peoples,
              for the city, etc.
    7:45 PM   Wound Engagement – Prayer for Personal

          Needs, Prayer Requests,
          Sickness, etc.

8:00 PM   Praise and Thanksgiving

8:15 PM   Dismissal (small spontaneous groups)

BOTTOM LINE

Keep Pauline prayer theology in mind – prayer as worship, the privilege of petition, the duty of intercession, all wrapped in thanksgiving. Begin with praise and worship until there is a sense of God's Presence. Move to Scripture – and let some passage guide the prayer time for the first movement of prayer. Dance through transformational, communal themes – the welcoming and honoring of God and His Presence, purity and repentance, perspective recalibration out of scripture (Seeing God, ourselves, our world through the lens of scripture, is a helpful model out of Isaiah 6.) Ask, 'What is God saying in this passage and how does it relate to prayer, to me, here and now? How do I pray this? How do I live this?', love and holiness. Good prayer is at the crossroads of faith and God's love and holiness. Move to intercession – pray for nations, for the lost. Save time for prayer requests. End with thanksgiving.

Prayer Groups

A Homogeneous Dynamic with Diversity Options

The the church gathered as one is the homogeneous prayer group. Prayer groups represent the heterogeneous:

HETEROGENEOUS – *the <u>Whole Church</u> seeking the face of God regularly and consistently <u>in many places, at varied times</u>, for brief but significant periods, as an expression of dependence on God, unity and love, for the sake of the spiritual transformation of their lives, <u>with a focus on a specific sector of the church and/or a specific region of the city, some need or condition</u> - multiple class & kind gatherings. Specific and need or focus defined gatherings.*

Here the Prayer Celebration, the 'homogeneous' one, is translated into the heterogeneous many, leading to a more inclusive and bigger 'one'.

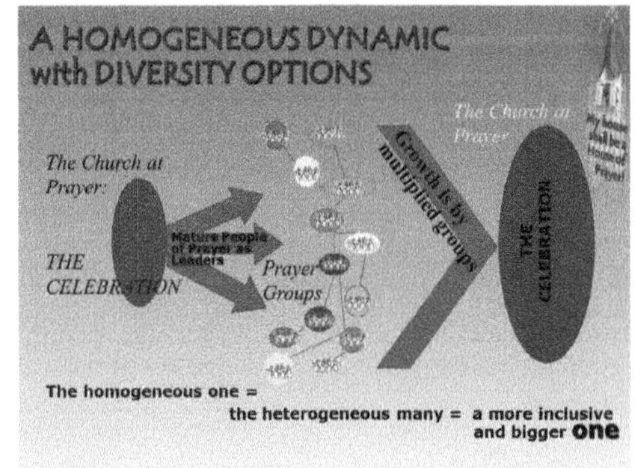

Unlike the weekly church-wide gathering, these prayer groups meet at diverse times, perhaps at diverse places. Their focuses vary. They utilize different styles. Mature people of prayer lead these prayer groups. Here, individuals become comfortable with one another – comfortable enough to pray aloud, to pray freely, to test their sensitivity to the Spirit. This is where people grow in prayer, and ultimately the spring of the congregation's spiritual energy. There is accountability here, mentoring in prayer. Here, people catch prayer-fire and share prayer burdens. They bond. And love always fuels prayer.

As prayer groups multiply and grow in passion, the church prayer movement deepens and expands. New leaders are affirmed. The prayer groups should eventually incorporate twice as many as attend the corporate prayer gathering, and yet, these two should track together. Corporate prayer times, led by the pastor, should feed into the prayer groups, and the force of the prayer groups should be felt in the prayer celebration, leading to a larger prayer celebration.

<u>Prayer groups disconnected from the Prayer Celebration are not healthy for the congregation.</u>

The Prayer Celebration with Prayer Groups – Why Both Are Important

The Prayer Celebration is generally 'whole-church' in its focus. It sees the larger mission. It may, from time to time, focus on specific needs, and special missional components, but it will not be able to steadily focus on any one matter.

However, the prayer groups regularly focus on specific needs and ministries. The Prayer Celebration is 'whole church' in its focus – a shotgun, but the prayer groups are more precisely focused – a rifle. They meet to pray exclusively for the youth, or children, or a list of lost people, or the mayor and city leaders. Their passion is causes within in the whole. You need both a Prayer Celebration and these specific cause prayer groups.

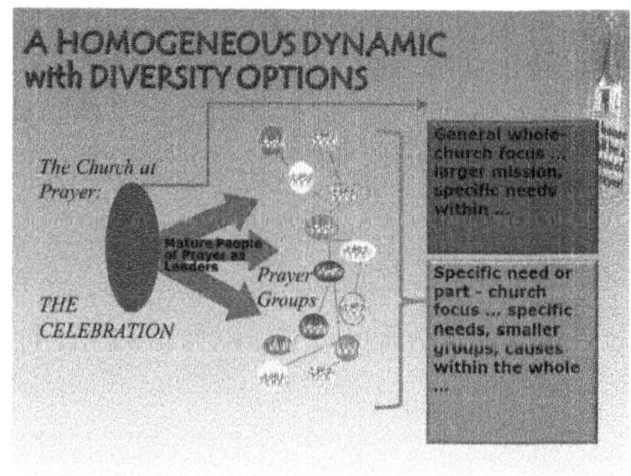

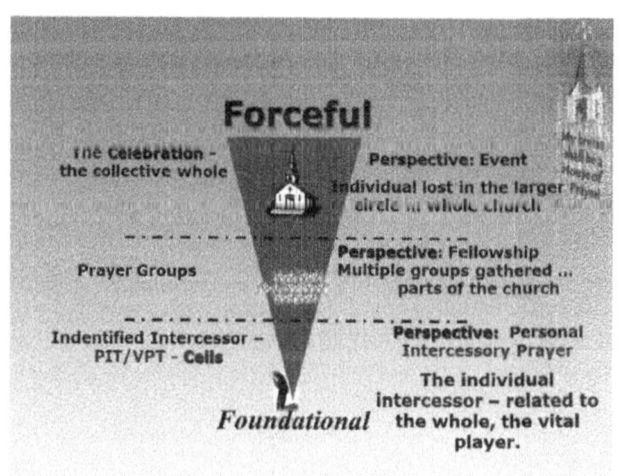

The Foundational and the Forceful

Intercessors are the foundation for prayer ministry. You will make little progress without them. They will pray – when no one else is praying.

Getting intercessors into teams makes them a part of a whole. It connects them to the larger church prayer movement, and pulls them into something bigger than themselves. So often, intercessors pray alone, and do not have adequate networks. Connecting them, makes the prayer all the more forceful.

With connected intercessors, praying personally with focus, agreeing together in prayer, teaming for impact and information, the force of such synergy bubbles up into the Celebration. At the Celebration, the individual is lost in the larger whole church prayer effort. But not at the individual intercessory level.

Between these two are the prayer groups – multiple groups gathered for prayer. Parts of the church, bound together with common concerns and a shared burden in prayer.

The individual intercessor – praying alone, at home, but not disconnected. Members in prayer groups, gathering regularly, to pray for things that are dear to their heart. And the whole church coming together for prayer. You need all three levels of prayer. The personal is foundation. The corporate is forceful.

Kingdom Math

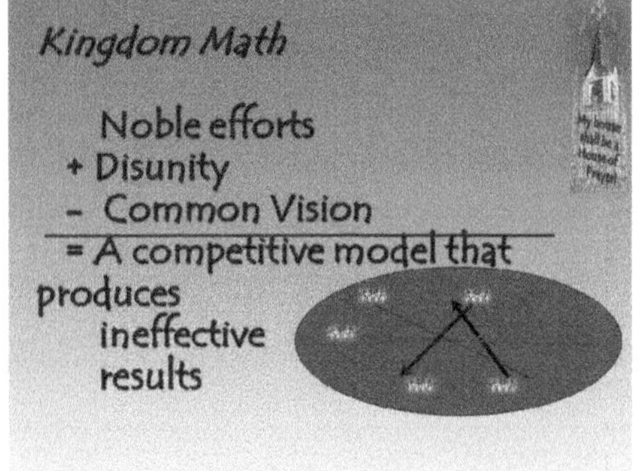

If the prayer groups are not connected to the whole – you have division of vision and mission. The passion for a piece of the ministry needs to see its place in the whole. The result is noble efforts that lack a common vision, competitive prayer groups, and ineffective results.

Even though the prayer groups have a specific focus, they also need to share the burden for the whole. If they disconnect, they are ineffective. Connected to the larger vision, they share a unified vision for city impact by their congregation. That larger vision defines direction and clarifies purpose in the prayer effort. The whole prayer effort is moving together.

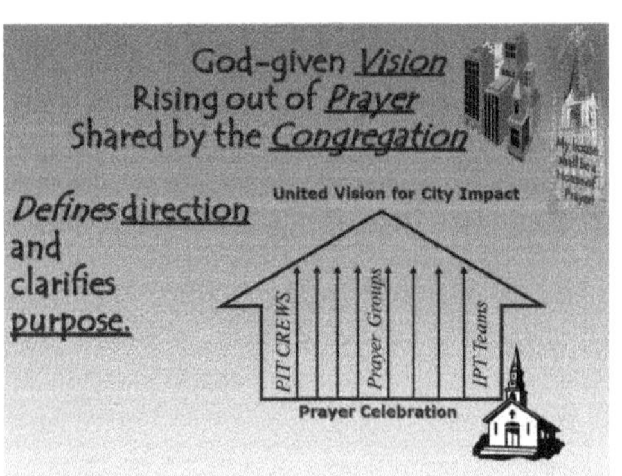

Prayer Celebration and Prayer Groups

The goal of the Prayer Celebration is to spawn a movement of prayer, characterized by at-home-daily prayer, and a proliferation of opportunities for prayer in small groups that are more personal in nature and more focused in mission. Those who attend the prayer celebration invite others to join them in prayer about this or that.

People who do not attend the Prayer Celebration are invited to participate in prayer groups. The goal is twice as many in various prayer groups as attend the Prayer Celebration.

The two – the Prayer Celebration and Prayer Groups – move together. Both provide opportunities to join the church prayer movement. The goal is long-term, covenantal relationships of godly, missional people who know that 'without Him,' they 'can do nothing!'

Some people, of course, pass through a prayer group. Some groups may function as 'open groups' that do not require members to make a commitment to attend. They are usually less effective, for a number of reasons. And yet, the commitment to attend a prayer group is best if the obligation is that of heart.

Healthy and Unhealthy Prayer Groups

Many leaders want an open group – anyone should be able to come to pray! However, with an open group where there is not a covenant to pray together, for a specific purpose, a number of obstacles surface.

Among them is a lack of relational commitment. The aberrant openness, the coming and going, results in a lack of relational definition in the group. This is simply a failure to steward one another. Remember, the key to healthy prayer groups is the creation of space to learn to pray, to pray passionately, to grow in prayer, to develop one another. Open groups fail in this mission.

The lack of covenant and deeper personal connectedness sabotages the effectiveness of the group. In an attempt to be kind, open to all, not exclusive, it fails its own members.

The openness, the unpredictability of who might be

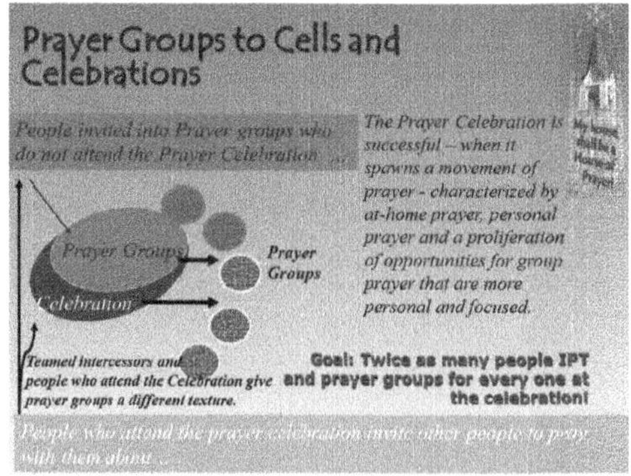

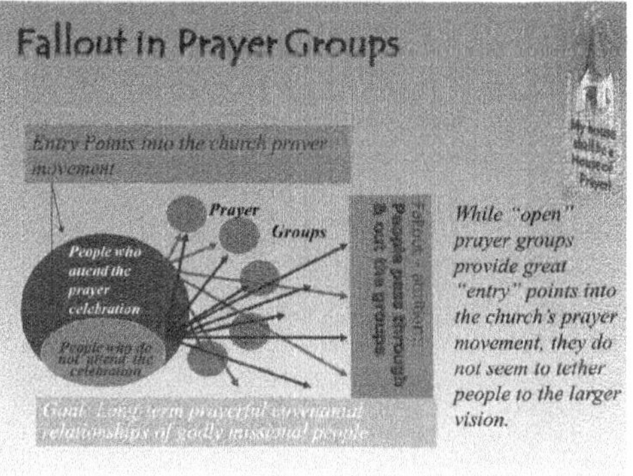

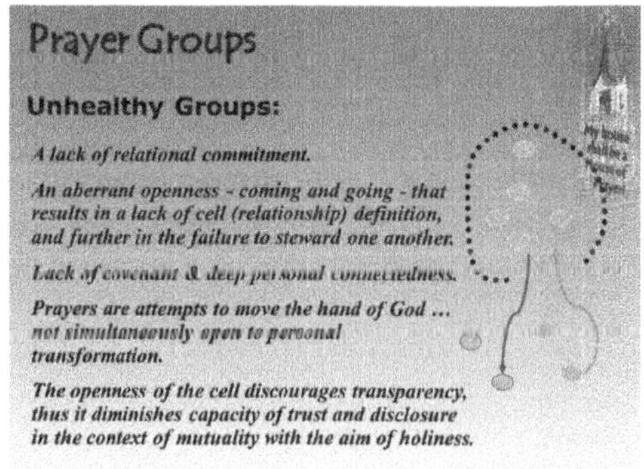

present, discourages liberty and transparency, and diminishes capacity of trust and disclosure in the context of mutuality with the aim of holiness, apart from passionate praying for the organizing missional cause of the group.

Prayer Group DNA

Whatever DNA you create in the host group will be transmitted to subsequent groups created out of the original. And without relational connectedness, new members simply pass through new groups. Relationally shallow groups, open with no commitment, results in shallow bonds in new groups.

In every prayer group, there is a core of people, typically two or three, whose relationship with one another and their passion for God, their concern about the organizing theme of the prayer group, sets the atmosphere for the whole group. When others in the group catch this dynamic, form similar bonds, a healthy pattern of interaction, then you have the core for a second prayer group.

This "relational core" of two-or-three people of prayer is the heart of the prayer group. In a sense – they *are* the prayer group. Their natural bond creates a *"we be family"* atmosphere. Their passion for prayer infects the whole group. There is a non-toxic, non-competitive atmosphere. Differences enrich, but do not debilitate. Among this core, there is transparency and openness. In this triad, this relational core, there is unconditional love and trust. These empowering relationships foster an - "I believe in you" attitude among other members as well. There is also a commitment to excellence, "You must become the best you can be in God." Informal accountability develops, driven by relational authority.

The "Triad" and the Prayer Group Core

Without triads or relational cores, prayer groups are open prayer meetings where commitment is random and relationships are, more often than not, too superficial. The "relational core" gives shape to the intended relational commitment to walk together in prayer. They provide

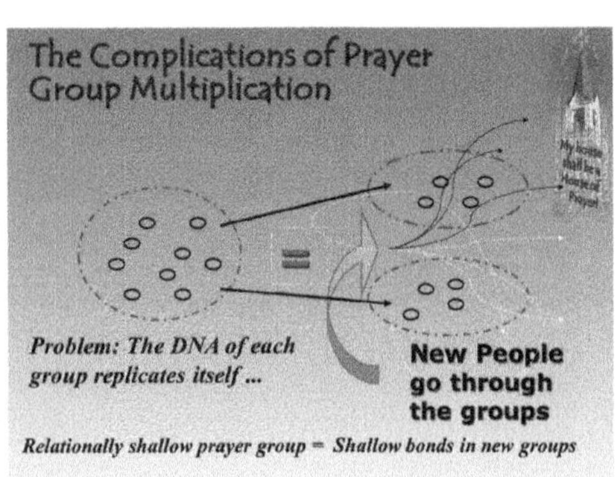

Problem: The DNA of each group replicates itself ...

Relationally shallow prayer group = Shallow bonds in new groups

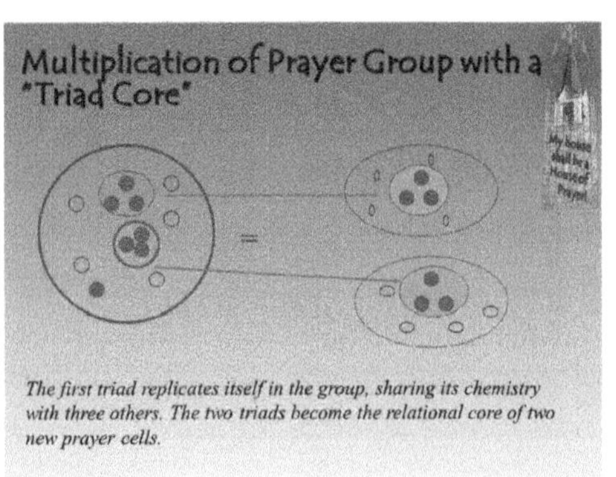

The first triad replicates itself in the group, sharing its chemistry with three others. The two triads become the relational core of two new prayer cells.

a stable center and model the prayer-based, relational covenant between people.

Replicating DNA

The "relational cores" – triads/threes should not be contrived. They spontaneously form. They are natural. Despite the deeper bond among them, the group they create is inclusive. It is organically developed, not a matter of organization and tight uniform structure. It cannot be tightly orchestrated or controlled. It must be developmental, relational, and that requires TIME!

For groups to be successful, you must replicate the relational core of a healthy prayer group in another. The first 'triad' must pass along its DNA into another triad – and typically, this happens almost unconsciously. The relational core (the triad of two or three committed prayer group members) is not necessarily distinguished from the other members of the group in some formal way. They wear no insignias or sit in any special seats. Their authority is relational. They command respect by their demeanor, their balance, and their passion for God.

One way to jump start the prayer group process is to look, not for a prayer group leader, singularly, but for triads, for small teams for people who know one another, love and trust one another, share a concern for a similar focus, and invite others to join them in a prayer group effort. All the while, they work to identify another triad in the group that might give birth to another prayer group at the appropriate time. The triads give birth to new prayer groups. And the prayer groups combine to enhance the prayer celebration.

Replicating the Core (Triads)

One adaptation of the Prayer Group are prayer triads. In this model, the triad is the prayer group. At certain points, the triad opens itself to a fourth man who is invited to observe, to participate, and then to launch another triad by finding two others. He becomes the first man in the new triad.

Another variation is to invite another group of three

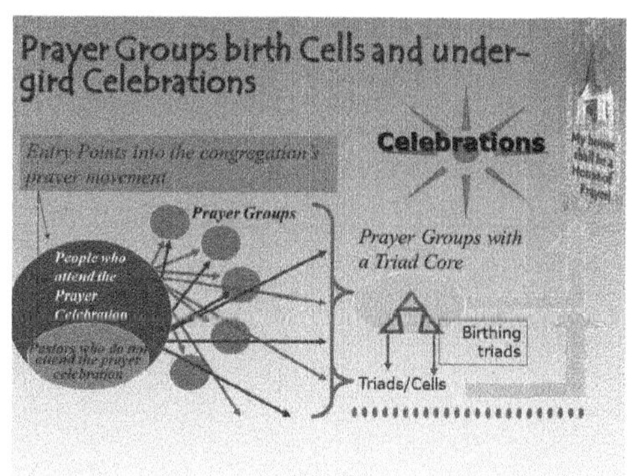

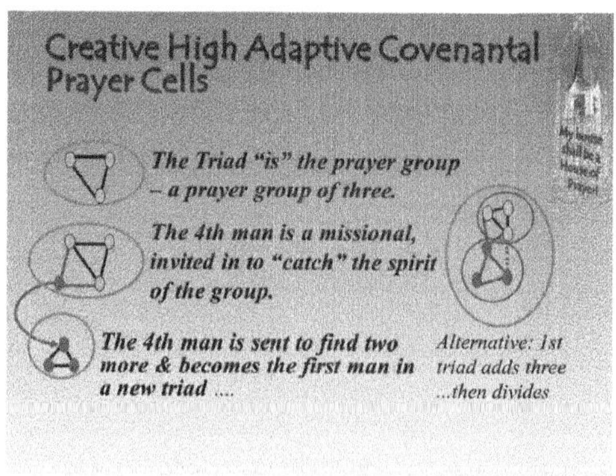

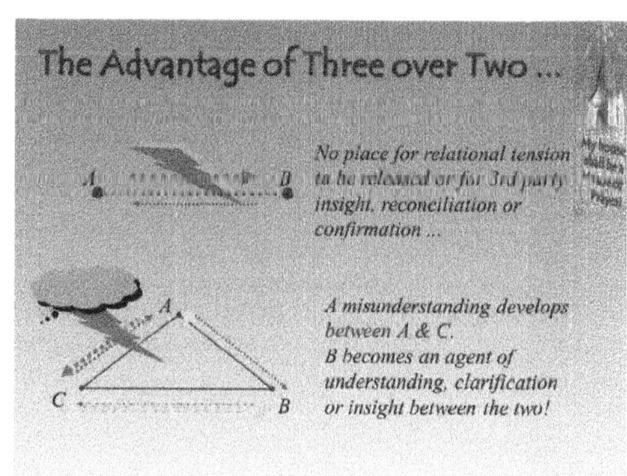

men. For a short season, the six pray together. And then they form a new triad. The two triads might be the original three – and the three additional men. Or it might be a complete reconfiguration of the six into two new triads.

The advantage of a triad is that relationships are more intense and more personal. Scheduling is more convenient, adaptive, and flexible – only three are involved. Relationships grow deeper, not wider. Accountability is easier, more intense. A tighter circle increases trust and the potential for higher levels of vulnerability.

Prayer Group Dynamics

Why sets of three, and not two? When two people pray together, the relationship is two dimensional. If tension develops between the two, there is no place for relational tension to be released. There is no third party to offer unseen insight, to broker reconciliation or to conciliate the conflict. There is no outlet for the tension.

In a triad, if a misunderstanding develops between 'A' (Al) and 'C' (Charlie). 'B' (Boyd) becomes an agent of understanding, of clarification or insight between the two!

Let's say, in a triad, 'Al' attempts to minister to 'Boyd' and Boyd rejects his attempts at correction or is cool to his comfort. Communication between them is strained, stalled. 'Al' is baffled. 'Boyd' pulls away. He doesn't return calls from 'Al.' Their strained relationship threatens the health, perhaps even the survival of the group. In a triad, if 'Al' attempts to share a concern with 'Boyd' who at first rejects 'Al,' draws back from the relationship, 'Charlie,' with love and gentleness is in a position to urge 'Boyd' to listen for the truth in the counsel of 'Al,' to not react. He may also coach 'Al' to use different language. To make sure his message of truth doesn't eclipse the fact of his love. 'Charlie' has the opportunity to temper the words of 'Al,' without speaking for him. He may be working with both 'Al' and 'Boyd'. All three grow in the process. Appreciation for each other in the triad deepens.

Incredibly, the movement from two people praying together to three advances the dynamics from a two dimensional model to a twelve dimensional model (See the diagram).

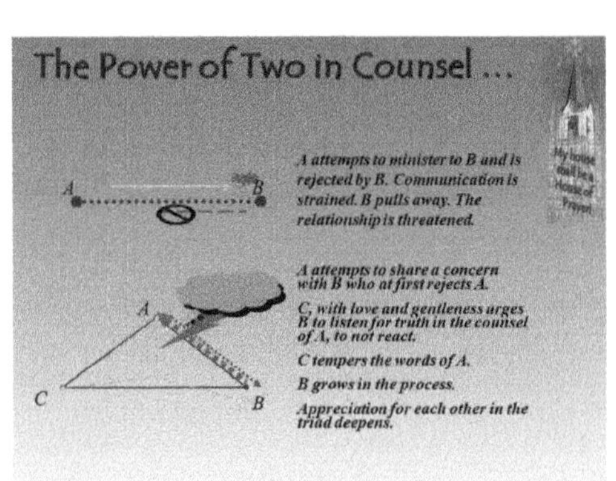

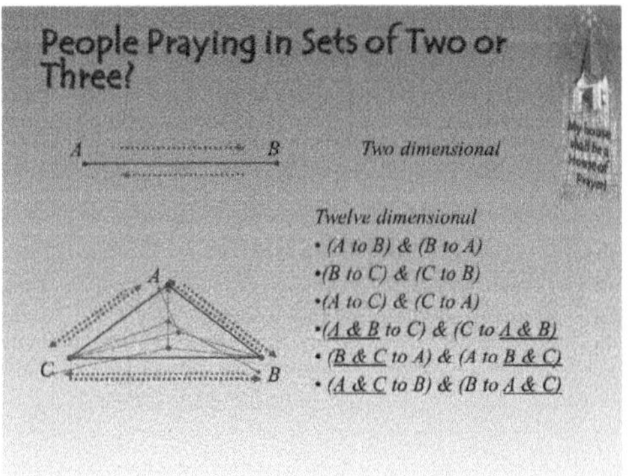

People Praying in Covenant

THE ACTIVITY: A relational-transformational prayer focus with DNA replication and prayer-group multiplication, proliferation of prayer as a goal.

THE PARTICIPANTS: People of prayer; all the people.

THE BREADTH: Every Christian in the congregation.

THE FREQUENCY: Weekly, typically.

THE DIRECT RESULT: Unity and spiritual growth, love and mutual support, mission. Changed lives. Insight and impact in the area of focus.

THE INDIRECT DYNAMIC: Relational accountability and care-driven confrontation. "Iron sharpens iron!" People learn to pray. Passion increases. Missional connections deepen.

THE DIVERSITY: topically, geographically, age and gender, status and stylistically varied, diverse prayer options.

THE GOAL: Critical mass through multiple prayer groups resulting in congregational renewal.

The Prayer Group Covenant

1. Our covenant is first to seek the face of God; and then His hand upon the organizing focus of the prayer group.

   ✓ To seek His face is to have an Isaiah 6 moment.

   ✓ It is to see the sovereign God above the unstable kingdoms of our present world...

   ✓ It is to see an enthroned and holy God...

   ✓ It is to hear the seraphim crying, "Holy, holy, holy!"

   Two aspects emerge - his absolute authority and his absolute holiness...

   ✓ His **_sovereignty_** calls for our subordination - a servant heart.

   ✓ His **_holiness_** calls for our repentance - a quest for purity.

   The result is <u>a servant community</u> committed to <u>holiness and character</u>.

2. We fulfill our covenant to God and one another,

Prayer Group Rules ...

- Pray, don't talk.
- Keep prayers brief.
- "Camp out" on a single issue.
- Protect Unity.
- Start with Communion, Cleansing ...
  - Allow for quiet times ... worship.
- Keep a balance – in terms of prayer styles.

Prayer Group Rules

- Inconsistent Personal Prayer Time
  - Don't substitute group prayer time for personal prayer time!
  - Don't ask "the prayer group" time to do for you, what only "personal quiet time" can do ...
  - Without a foundation of *personal* prayer, the *group* lacks authority in prayer! The group cannot be more than its members!

as we walk together as a community of servants committed to holiness. ***We will pray and worship together to the end that we remain a holy people of God called to impact our community and our world***.

3. Our covenant is to <u>humility</u> of heart - a servant spirit. <u>We will serve</u> ***one another. We will care for one another.***

4. Our covenant is to <u>unity</u> of the spirit - the evidence of his love is that we love one another. ***We will demonstrate our unity by praying together weekly and in other supportive ways.***

5. Our covenant is to focus our prayer effort – on <u>some common issue</u>. ***We will seek God's hand, we will pray in unity and agreement about this issue, this need.***

6. Our covenant is to worship, walk and work together to the end that as "lively stones fitted together." We see as our goal ***transformation in the lives of our group members and of some sector of culture. We want to be a holy and unified people who become vehicles for a sovereign touching down of God's glory in our congregation and in our city. We will not stop until that goal is a reality.***

7. Our covenant is ***to nurture a climate of holy hunger inviting a sustainable renewal that touches the entire congregation and our city.***

8. Our covenant is ***to complete our prayer term commitment, and then multiply as a group, replicating our DNA in another "relational core" (triad) and another prayer group.***

9. Our covenant is ***to see a missional church, contextualizing and incarnating the gospel in every sector of the city until everyone is being prayed for – and all have "seen" the message of Christ demonstrated by a loving life.***

10. Our covenant is ***to hold the harvest.*** By recruiting converts to prayer groups!

Persevering and Maturing

Phase VI

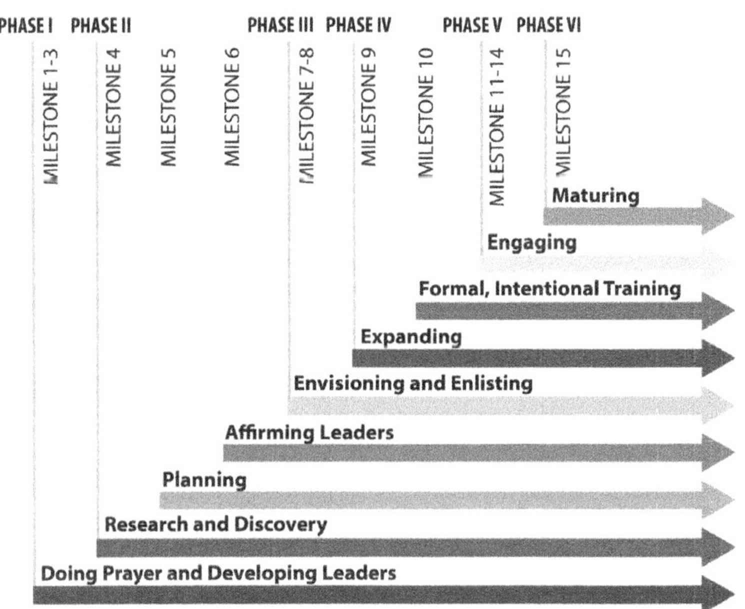

Congregation

The desire is for a culture of prayer. The threshold is the integration of prayer into every aspect of congregational life, not prayer as activity, but prayer as natural and reflexive. Here you have embraced a discipline of prayer that is natural, out of a rhythm of daily, weekly, monthly, quarterly, and annual prayer emphases, designed to measure the pulse of prayer in congregational life. The worship event should now include prayerful pauses, deliberate and intentional moments of congregational prayer engagement. An emphasis on holiness should persistently point to vibrant, healthy lives. An emphasis on intercession should focus on prayer evangelism and mission. A

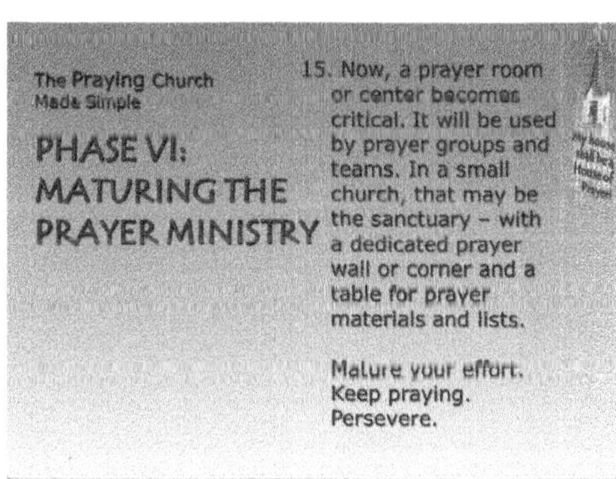

sense of God's love in prayer should nurture lives and create a congregational prayer bond. Worship should be at the heart of prayer. Bearing one another's needs in prayer should be a component. You have developed a prayer room/center, depending on the size of the congregation; and organized prayer groups make use of the prayer room or sanctuary weekly. Intercessors use the prayer room. You have a method, Facebook or otherwise, for emergency prayer needs.

Leaders

If you have persisted to this phase, leaders who pray remain and those who resisted dependence on prayer have probably found another home. Keep insisting; a praying church demands praying leaders. Allow for prayer retreats in the schedule of the staff. Pray together as a leadership team. Make sure the elders and deacons are doing likewise. Insist that every pastor and ministry has a prayer team. Press the importance of pastoral staff and elders and deacons praying with spouses – it is the best insurance against divorce. Model prayer. Let it be the first response to both problems and possibilities.

People

By now, a significant number in the your congregation should have prayer fever. They have learned to live, not from Sunday to Sunday, but daily, from their time with God, over an open Bible. Your prayer service is healthy. You have identified intercessors. A significant number of your people, by survey, are engaging in family devotions. You have prayer evangelists and prayer missionaries focused on the needs of the community and the lost. The people are praying. A number of congregational prayer members have a prayer closet at home.

MILESTONE FIFTEEN
The Prayer Room

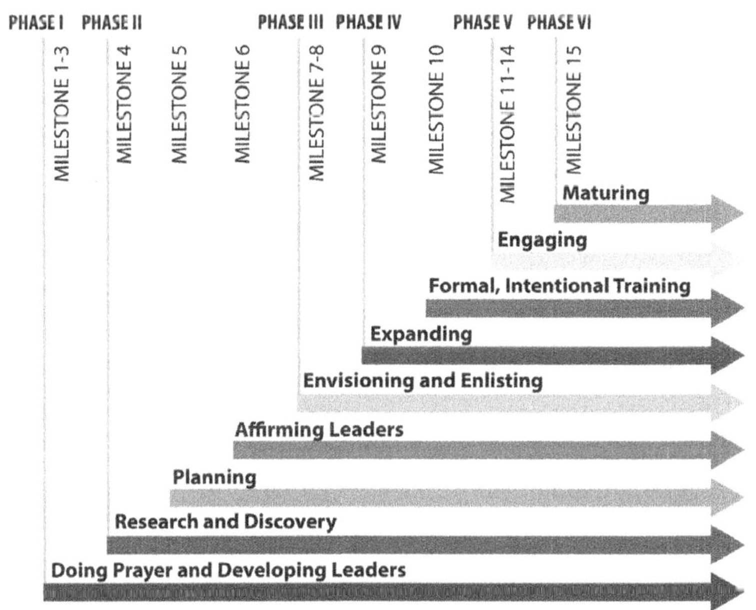

Proposition

Everything needs a place. Depending on your size, create a prayer center (larger congregations) or a prayer room (smaller congregations). Create a prayer counter for information and a way to connect with the on-going prayer effort. Create a focal point for prayer in the sanctuary itself – a prayer corner, a wall, a prayer display, a cross decorated with the names of lost loved ones and prayer

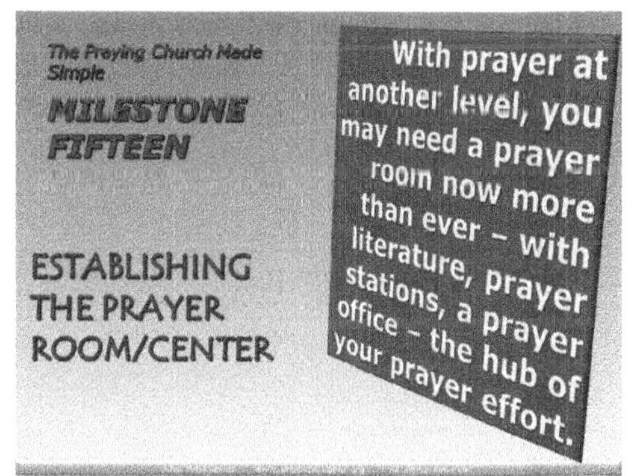

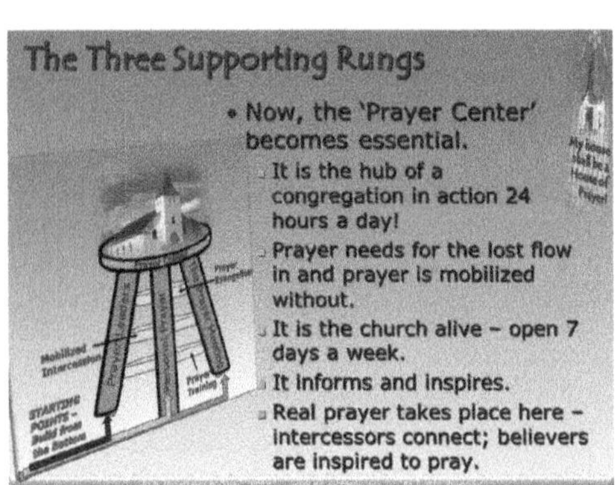

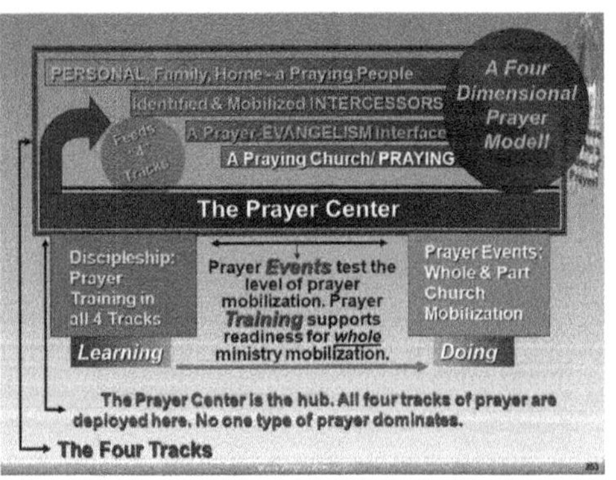

needs, an altar laden with pictures of friends and families with needs, especially those who need God. Where, in your facility, are people regularly, visibly engaged in the call to pray? Where can intercessors retreat to for prayer? Where can those in simultaneous intercessory exercises go for prayer? Is there a place where prayer groups can meet not only on Sunday, but during the week? Is the sanctuary dedicated as a prayer room seven days a week? Open and accessible? Made palatable to prayer – lights and worshipful music, or, is it a strange idea that people might come to the church to pray during the week?

Objectives

- Get the Prayer Room/Center functional.

- Create prayer displays. (The Prayer Room is more than a room – it must have information that informs and inspires prayer).

- If used correctly, the Prayer Room/Center can serve as a "prayer hub" for the church-wide prayer ministry – with a focus on the city and the mission field beyond.

- Identify an intercessory team or prayer group for the day who will come to the church, use the room, the sanctuary, and fill the church with the sound of prayer.

- Use the *7-circles of care and concern,* and identify a leader or organize a prayer group around each of those circles of concern.

- Encourage your prayer council leaders to consider leading a "prayer group" using the prayer room/center.

- Increase the number of intercessors and intercessory teams.

- Sweep the sanctuary in prayer each week using one of the intercessory prayer teams.

Timing

Early in your effort, you are <u>repurposing the sanctuary as a place of prayer</u>. Your first act was the establishment of a church-wide prayer meeting – typically, held in the sanctuary. You may have also begun to lace into the Sunday morning service special prayer moments. At some point, you will need to determine if you want to establish a prayer room, and how that will be used. Prayer Centers typically demand a congregation of a thousand or more.

Resources

In the book, *Transforming Your Church into a House of Prayer – Revised Edition,* there is a section on the prayer room and the prayer center.

Duration

<u>Ongoing</u>.

Focus

The Prayer Room/Center can be <u>the physical place where all of your prayer efforts converge</u>, and from which they flow. Information should be in the room. Displays should reveal the on-going, diverse nature of your prayer effort. The physical space feeds the four-dimensions – personal and family prayer; the church as a house of prayer, intercession, and prayer evangelism.

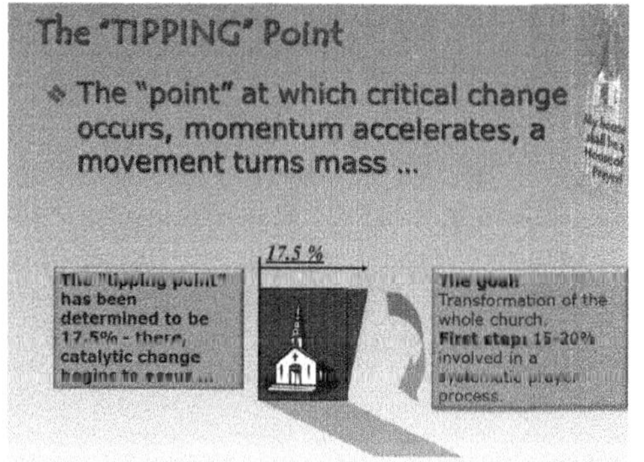

Involvement Goals

The Prayer Room might be <u>the place where various prayer groups meet during the week for prayer</u>. Intercessors might be scheduled to come and spend time in the prayer room during the week, as well. Your ultimate involvement goal is the entire congregation a house of prayer; and, your people, a praying people. That does not mean that all will use your prayer room. Determine a threshold for regular at-church prayer during the week, hopefully, daily.

Transition

As your leadership team becomes a planning team, they will often need a space – for meetings, maps, and prayer and strategy sessions. That need will only increase. Once you identify intercessors and launch prayer groups, <u>the need for a place to meet and pray will intensify</u>.

Common Mistakes

Corporate prayer is critical. Private personal prayer cannot satisfy the need to gather in prayer. And the most obvious place to do this is the place the same people gather for worship. <u>Make the church about prayer – seven days a week</u>. Don't underestimate the power of praying together.

An excerpt from Transforming Your Church into a House of Prayer:

The Models

There are three distinct models for prayer that are appearing across the nation and around the world – the ***prayer room model***; the ***prayer center model***; and the ***Davidic house of prayer model***.

Let's distinguish between these three models. First, the *prayer room* is a kind of prayer retreat. Second, the *prayer center* becomes the nerve center of the church. It both trains and mobilizes prayer. Third, the Davidic house of prayer is characterized by combining the *"harp and the bowl,"* or *"worship and intercession."*

One of the primary purposes of both the prayer center and the Davidic House of Prayer is "to invite God" regularly to come into our midst – as individuals, families, a church, a city, state, and nation. He comes where he is invited.

The prayer center speaks to:

- Our ***hearts***...developing a relationship with God, loving Him.
- Our ***homes***...do I live in my home so that it is marked by the presence of Christ?
- Our church as ***house of prayer***...reclaiming the sanctuary for Him!
- Our city as a ***harvest*** field of unreached people!
- Our ***hope***...the reality that we are pilgrim people.
- Here are the *personal*, the *corporate* and the *kingdom* elements of prayer.

Three Intensive Local Church Room Types

As your prayer movement develops, you will need to choose a congregational prayer model. Each church must find its own place on the continuum. Each model requires various levels of staffing and planning. Let's distinguish three models one from the other:

- The "Harp and Bowl"
- The Prayer Room
- The Prayer Center

The Harp and Bowl model was introduced in Kansas City as a collaborative 24/7 prayer process to be an expression of city-wide prayer partnership of the churches of that city. It is the most widely known house of prayer in the world.[1] In some cities, this model is being introduced as a "house of prayer for the city" – apart from any particular congregation, hopefully supported by many, if not most.

The Differences

The Harp and Bowl is ongoing, worshipful, corporate prayer! The prayer room, by contrast, is typically private. It is a place for personal prayer, intercession for others and edification for self. It may be used by individuals or small groups, or by intercessors.

The Prayer Center is bigger in size and broader in focus than either the Harp-and-Bowl model or the Prayer Room. It is missional in focus. It will be used by individuals and small groups. It harnesses the ministry of intercession. It is about mission. Prayer for the lost and needs of the city is a key focus of the prayer center. The "prayer center" and the "prayer room" are often confused as one. They represent significantly different approaches. Let's take a closer look at each of these three models.

Harp and Bowl

The Harp-and-Bowl model emphasizes 24/7 prayer

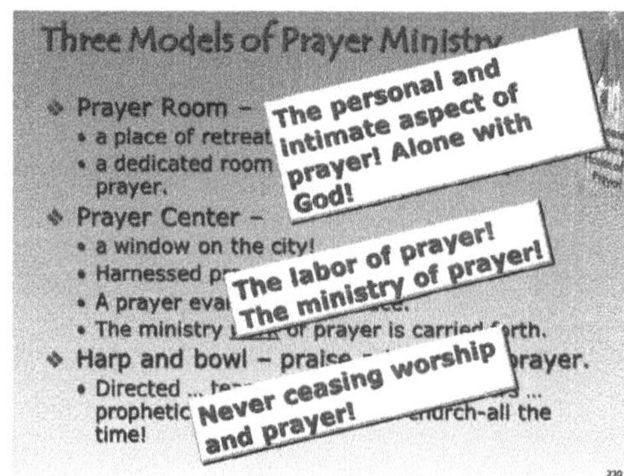

---

1   The ministry is under the direction of Mike Bickle. Their website is www.propheticroundtable.org/Harp-Bowl/Network.htm. You will find there information on the model as well as a listing of other sites.

and worship – 24 hours a day, 7 days a week. This follows the model of the Tabernacle of David – a constant stream of worship, prayer, and praise, offered to God from Mt. Zion that was never ceasing (2 Samuel 6:17-18; 1 Chronicles 6:32). This bold vision longs for the day when in some part of the city, there will never be a time when someone or some group is not in prayer and communion with God in behalf of the city and the purposes of God. For most churches, this is an impossibility. For the "Church of the City" this could easily be a reality given unified support.

The phrase "harp and bowl" is from the Revelation (5:8) where we get a glimpse of heavenly worship. The harp is a symbol of praise and worship. The bowl is filled with incense, a symbol of prayer. So here are the images of worship and prayer – mingled together. This has led to a relatively new emphasis in prayer, which insists that joyful praise and worship be connected with intercession.

In the Harp and Bowl model, the prayerful incense of praise mixed with worship is offered to God. This connection of prayer with praise may be unique to some intercessors. Yet, in the Old Testament, *feasting* was more often connected with prayer and worship than was *fasting*. There, the high and holy days of prayer and worship were "Feast Days!" The exception was the Day of Atonement. The Sabbath was also a weekly *day of prayer*. And it was associated with *rest*, with peace.

What are the characteristics:

- In the Harp and Bowl model, the focus is vertical. The worship and prayer experience is directed to God. It is offered to Him as a gift – from worshippers who represent the Church, or even the city.

- The worship is interspersed with prayer and praise. It is by nature more corporate than private. Worship teams lead the experience. They often do this in two-hour shifts.

- Music in the vertical dimension is critical here - it is more than background and atmosphere for prayer. It is more than Christian entertainment. In a typical worship service, the activity of worship, and the music of worship, is more horizontal

– the choir and musicians sing with a focus on the audience; even the preacher preaches with a focus on the participants. In the house of prayer model, the activity of prayer and praise is vertical. God is the audience. Others listen in – as music is offered to God, as prayers are prayed to Him, as praise is offered through Biblical and fresh prophetic psalms. It is almost unimportant how many people are present in the room – since God is the audience. Participants sometimes join in the singing and praying. Others may be prostrate before God in worship and prayer. Some stand. Some sit. Some kneel.

- Psalmists and prophets flow together. Intercessors and worshippers become one.

- As the incense of praise and prayer ascends to God, heaven reaps the harvest of the sweet incense. And the descending dew of the Holy Spirit often results in the prophetic – insights are gained, revelations given, admonitions come and do new psalms of praise, words of encouragement or warning.

- The goal of the harp and bowl model is to offer constant praise and worship to God – a never ceasing stream of worship.

- Here, the church is open for worship 24 hours a day. Worship leaders and participants slip in and out – but the prayer and worship continues.

Prayer Room

The prayer room is a physical place dedicated to use for prayer by believers. It may be small or large. Typically it is a smaller space – 200-300 square feet, more or less, the typical size of a large Sunday School classroom.

- The emphasis in the prayer room is on prayer, more often private than corporate.

- Literature may be present to enrich the prayer experience, but the use of that literature is optional.

- Prayer stations may be established – in the form of thematic banners, or information on people in need of prayer, issues for prayer, missions, etc. Because of the size of the room, these may be wall displays. (Available from AlivePublications.com).

- People slip into the prayer room, typically unscheduled. They pray according to their own heart, following the direction of the Spirit. They leave when they have satisfied the prayer-call on their heart. Small groups may use the room in the course of week for prayer meetings.

- The room may become a place for prayer counseling and prayer ministry to one in need.

- The room is often used before and after corporate worship experiences for prayer.

- It may or may not be staffed, most often it is not.

- It provides a retreat, a place to find quiet.

- Music is optional. If it is used at all, it is in form of a CD player with worship tapes. This can become a problem. Some "pray-ers" are used to bringing their own music as an accompaniment to prayer (this was a custom of the prophets and kings – I Samuel 10:5; 18:10; I Chron. 25:1f; Lk. 7:32; I Cor. 14:7). Remember, one person's music is another's distraction.

Prayer Center

While the prayer room is a bit of a "retreat" for personal or small group prayer, the prayer center is *a noisy window* on the needs of the church, the city, and the world.

THE PLACE

- Physically, the prayer center is a much larger place than a prayer room. It is recommended that a prayer center be at least 1,000 square feet, twice that if possible. Ten times that amount may be needed in a larger church. A city prayer impact center will require significant space.

- While the prayer room may have a desk for sign-in and sign-out registering people coming and going from the room, the prayer center has an office! It may be small and should be secluded to avoid distractions – but it is often very busy!

  ✓ Here prayer requests are harvested and distributed.

  ✓ Here prayer needs around the city and the world are collected and formatted for prayer.

✓ Here prayer assignments are suggested to prayer workers.

✓ Here alerts are prepared and flashed on the screens for prayer participants.

✓ Here, the music and video are controlled for the prayer center (in the prayer room, people often bring their own music, if not their own CD player. In the prayer center, the atmosphere is more protected).

- The prayer center should have carpet – at least in certain areas to invite kneeling or even lying prostrate before the Lord. Cushions can provide aid in kneeling, inviting humility before the Lord.

- Lighting should be designed for incremental levels and adjusted as appropriate! Lower levels of light are recommended, though varying levels are desired. More light should be available on the information displays and perhaps at the altar, and on reflective symbols – such as crosses. The point is to create a meditative atmosphere.

- Every center should have cubicle capacity – small sound-proof spaces for individuals to have a "prayer room" experience. This gives the prayer center a *retreat* capacity. This is an important balance, since the prayer center insists on being connected with the problems of culture around it. It exists to pray about those conditions.

- While the prayer room may have prayer stations and prayer support materials, the prayer center is not a true center without such materials.

- The prayer center should be interfaced with a prayer counseling station for phone and internet interactive prayer.

- It is intentionally missional. It programs the prayer focus to be missional. It assigns missional praying to its volunteers. It stewards its obligation to the Great Commission. The prayer room, by contrast, has no such consistent and intentional missional prayer program.

THE PURPOSE
- The prayer room exists so that believers can have a place for prayer. But the prayer center is not only for believers, it is also for unbelievers.

- The prayer center has a stream of information coming in to it – about needs, the lost, the world, the harvest; and it has a stream of people called to prayerful ministry flowing out of it to touch their community, nation and world.

- The heart of the prayer center is the constant exposure to the pain of the world and its response to that pain in prayer – in the context of "the rest" of God.

- The prayer center is staffed by believers, but it is open to unbelievers in need of prayer. It should be the place to which hurting people can come in times of need for prayer ministry from others. It should be a place that could receive prayer requests and needs from people in the church, the city and the world.

- While the prayer room is a retreat for personal and small group prayer; the center is a "window." Using technology, it is positioned electronically as a nerve center for happenings in the church, the city and world.

- The prayer center should have a media interface – a place where prayer requests are constantly harvested and prayers are sown in the heavens in response to those prayer requests. World news and events are flashed on monitors and intercessors/ people of prayer respond. Needs are rolled on screens, listed on video monitors – needs of people, church ministries, city-social-spiritual concerns, the world.

- As the function of the prayer center engages the needs of the congregation and city, it interacts with that congregation and city – notes of support are sent out; cards and letters are mailed; prayer mission teams may be deployed – systematically or spontaneously.

THE PERSONNEL

- The prayer center demands *staff* – trained staff both to assist others in prayer; and to do the work of prayer. They pray with both believers and unbelievers who come to the prayer center for prayer. They respond to email and phone calls for prayer.

- The prayer center director oversees the operation of the center which is open – hopefully 7 days a week. The ideal center is open 24 hours a day. But that is not always possible. Start by opening the center and having staff present during the "high use" hours – Mornings: 6:30 – 9:30 a.m.; Evenings: 3:30 – 7:30 p.m. For 24 hour impact, without the personnel to have the center open, use an ongoing prayer chain. Each day, have a different person serve as the "Day Watch-leader" and coordinate prayer for that day so the whole burden does not fall on the center director. The Watch-leaders might take responsibility for setting up and keeping current at least one of the prayer station displays and for leading a prayer group around the theme of that display.

- Prayer Center volunteers serve the center in 2-4 hour shifts. They are trained. They are present to pray for people who drop into the center. They are there to do the "work of prayer – to fulfill assignments in prayer!" They are present to harvest needs which come in by phone or email and post them for prayer, direct them on to the intercessors.

THE STYLE AND EMPHASIS

- Unlike the house of prayer model, the focus of the prayer center is not on worship/praise and prayer *at a corporate level*, but on *the corporate work of prayer* to support the ministries of the church and pray in the harvest.

- In the prayer room people come and go as they fulfill the call of the Holy Spirit for prayer. While the prayer center provides the opportunity for people to do the same, it also frames an agenda for prayer. And it harnesses the energy of prayer to do the work of prayer. Thus, some individuals come to the prayer center to take their shift as watchmen on the wall, to own responsibility for prayer support to various church ministries, city needs, and world concerns.

- The prayer center works vigorously to balance these areas:

  ✓ transformational prayer (personal growth through prayer)

  ✓ transactional prayer (doing business with God;

and the business of prayer – supporting every ministry effort of the church with prayer)

✓ intercessory prayer (watching before God; hearing from God – the prophetic and seer dimension of prayer)

✓ prayer that encourages the development of harvest eyes (This is a critical component without which the prayer room or prayer center takes on a too narrow and narcissistic gaze.)

- The prayer center harnesses prayer for the *7-circles-of-care-and-concern*:

  ✓ Ministry to God – for the sheer pleasure of His presence.

  ✓ Personal Renewal - through prayer; and with that prayer that our corporate worship will be especially laden with a heavy sense of God's presence.

  ✓ Family Prayer – and support for family needs by prayer.

  ✓ Church Ministries and Missions – under-girded by prayer. This is prayer to invite the power of God into the life of the congregation to the end that we fulfill our mission.

  ✓ City Prayer – praying for the pain of city around us; calling down the blessing and favor of God on the neighborhoods we live in. This is a concerted effort to bear the burdens of the hurting.

  ✓ The Nation – prayer for government leaders, the needs of the nation, moral/spiritual issues, current events, for great awakening.

  ✓ The World – for mission endeavors, for the 10/40 window. For the missionaries of the Church.

A crisis or casual approach to prayer ministry is not adequate (Level One). Further, a prayer ministry must not be our goal (Level Two). We want a "praying church!" There are various levels of intensity here.

1. All should launch *an aggressive, balanced prayer process* that seeks to engage the whole church in prayer. This is more than a prayer ministry. And yet, this church may not be able to set aside a room dedicated only to the purpose of prayer.

2. In some cases, a church may add to the aggressive,

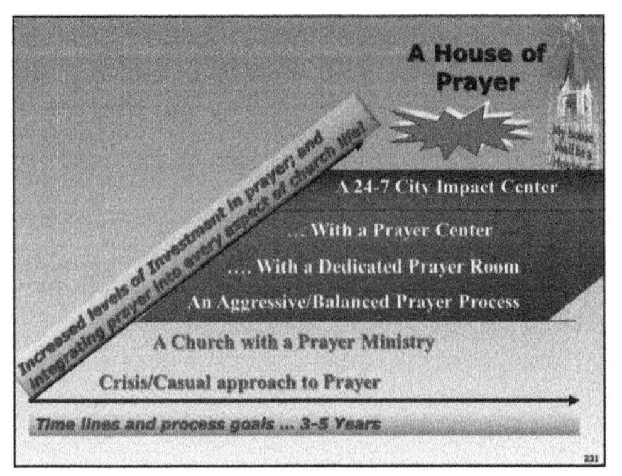

balanced prayer process, _a dedicated prayer room_ – a place set aside as a kind of retreat for personal prayer and small prayer groups to gather. All during the week, people will check in and make use of this prayer room. Intercessors might gather before or even during services to support worship activities in prayer.

3. A few churches will be able to move beyond a prayer room, which is a kind of personal retreat, to _a prayer center_ where prayer is constantly organized and mobilized for both people and ministries. It makes the church a prayed for church! At the prayer center, prayer support for every ministry is mobilized. Prayer training is offered. Prayer stations (physical displays) inspire prayer. People drop by to pray and for prayer. Needs are emailed or called in to the phone center. Intercessors do the work of prayer – praying over church events, praying into needs from around the world, supporting ministries and missionaries in prayer! The community is bathed in prayer.

4. A very small number of churches will be able to move beyond a prayer center to _a 24/7 prayer impact center_. In such an arrangement, the church is constantly open for ministry and service 24 hours a day, seven days a week. The doors never close. And prayer never stops. Teams are deployed from the church to respond to crises around the city – all hours of the day and night. Wherever there is a need, the church is responding! Wherever there is pain, the church is on-site offering the love of God!

The transformation of the church into a house of prayer for the nations is no small process. Plan on a three to five year transition. At first, the response will be glowing! Everyone will declare that they want to learn to pray, and they want the church to be a praying church. But when the newness of that idea wears away, sheer determination will be needed by a devout group of intercessory leaders to pursue the process. It is not merely activities that are being added. You are changing both the culture of the church and the daily disciplines of its members. Quite an undertaking!

Forever

Phase VII

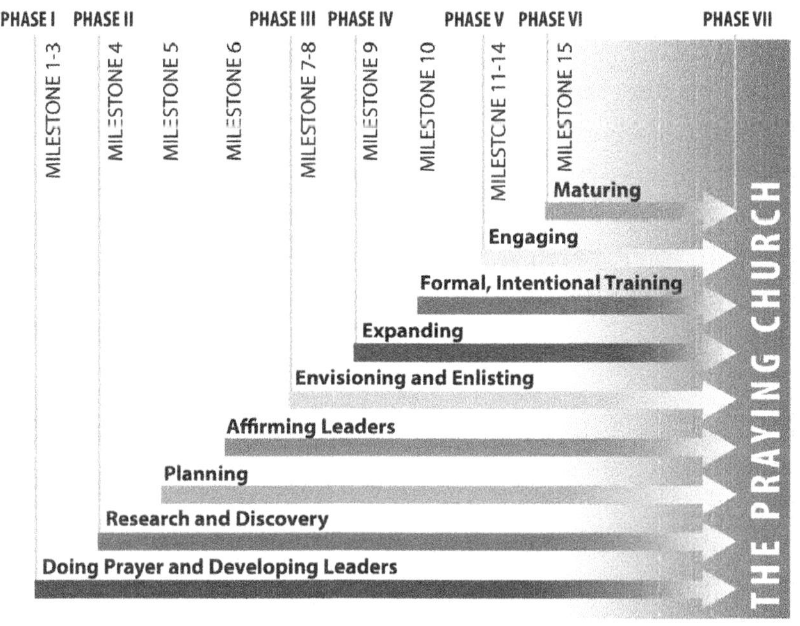

Congregation

Your goal is a 'house of prayer for the nations.' The journey will be the most challenging mission of your ministry. And once you reach the top of the mountain, be careful that you do not tumble backward. Maintaining the church as a house of prayer may be more difficult than its transformation. You must persist in a culture of prayer. Maintaining the rhythm of daily, weekly, monthly, quarterly and annual prayer emphases, is critical. Don't give up on prayer!

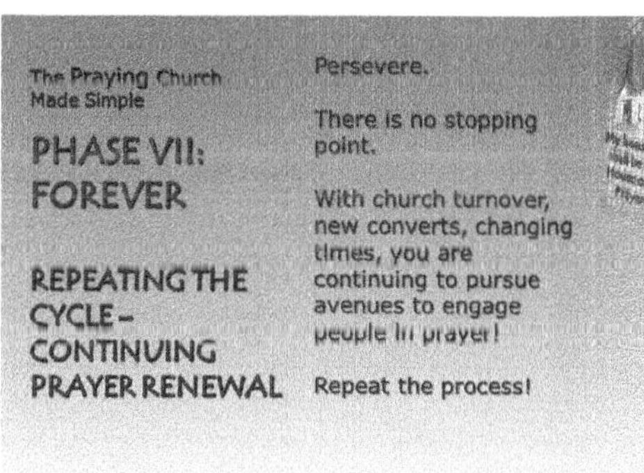

Leaders

In the busyness of ministry, even prayer ministry, sacrificing personal time with God for ministry in his behalf is seductive. Leaders must lead from God's Presence. There is no other way. To do so, they must be vigilant in the maintenance of their own daily prayer habit. Model prayer. Keep insisting – we are all following God, and to follow Him, we must know Him and spend time with Him daily.

People

As the number of people who have learned to live out of their daily time with God increases, not a few will be deployed by the Holy Spirit into ministry. As a church waits on the Lord, and the Holy Spirit ministers, he will repeatedly send forth laborers (Acts 13:1-2). New people need to be recruited to the prayer ministry leadership effort.

You have become a house of prayer and a place of mission for the nations.

STAGES

VISIONING STAGES

- **Phase I –** You are <u>casting vision for the church as a house of prayer</u>, primarily, <u>with a small group of learning-leaders</u>. Incidentally, simply by having a congregational prayer meeting, you are casting vision for the church as a house of prayer. And you are encouraging daily, personal prayer.

- **Phase II –** Now, to enlarge your leadership team in order to accomplish your research, you want <u>to cast vision for a discovery process</u>. You will probably do this <u>quietly</u>, <u>at your prayer gathering, and among your learning-leaders</u>, who will recruit others to this effort. As you translate research into an informed plan for prayer engagement, you must consider, 'How do we share this data?' – that's vision casting. At the end of this phase, your learning team becomes your leadership team – and someone from among them needs to be able to vision cast in a compelling manner.

- **Phase III –** **_This IS your vision phase_**. You have compelling data – about how much and for what you are praying; the history of prayer in the congregation; the needs around you; models of other congregations – it is time to share some of that data, and lay out a plan for congregational engagement in prayer over the next year. These represent the introduction of prayer opportunities, prayer activities – but not the launch of your actual prayer process. In this phase, you will conduct a congregation-wide envisioning evening. You recruit team

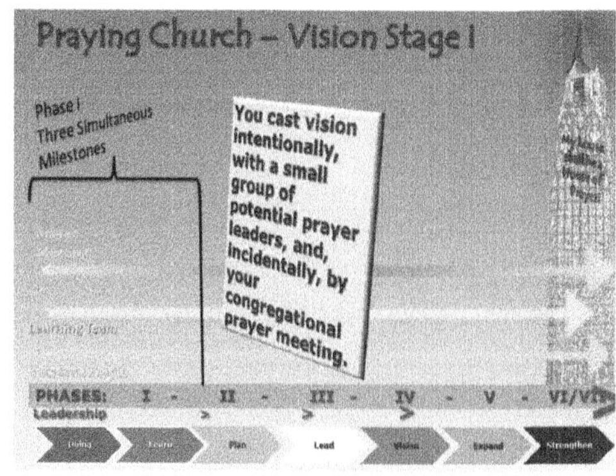

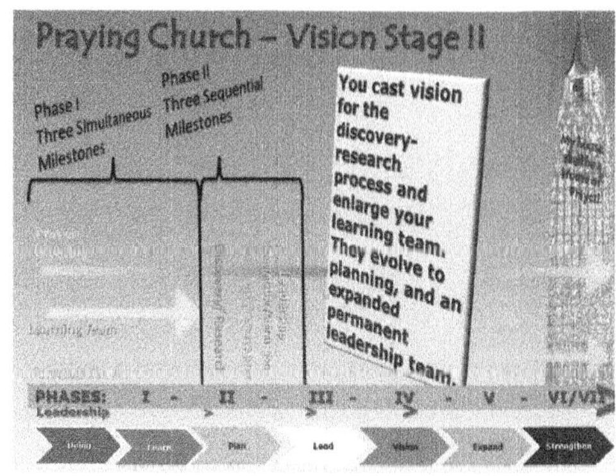

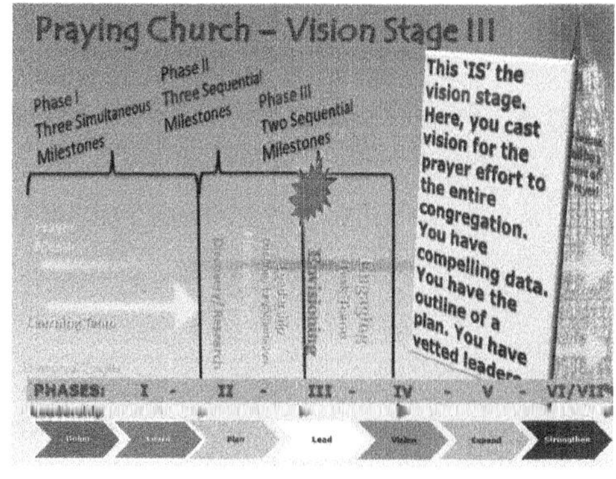

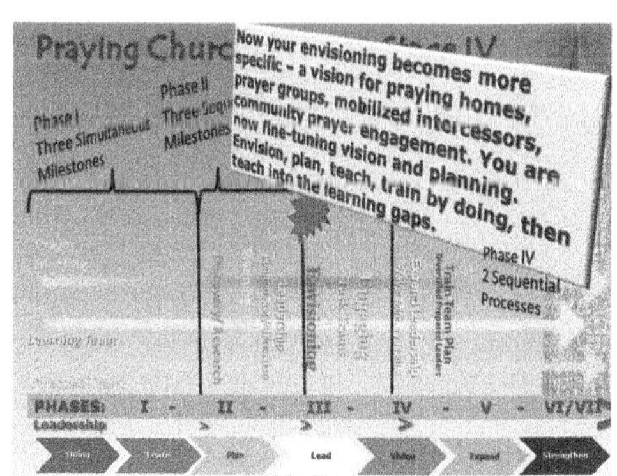

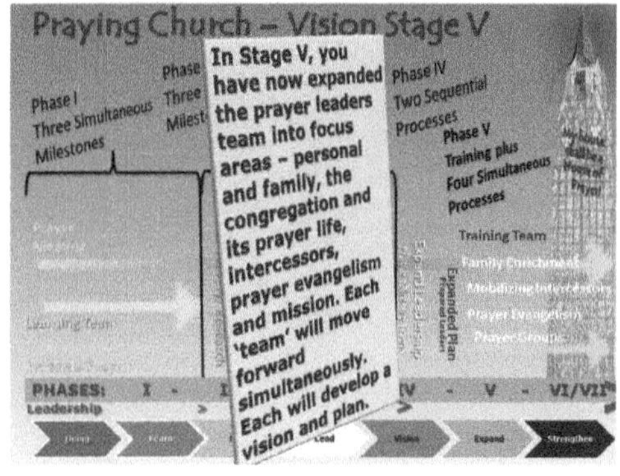

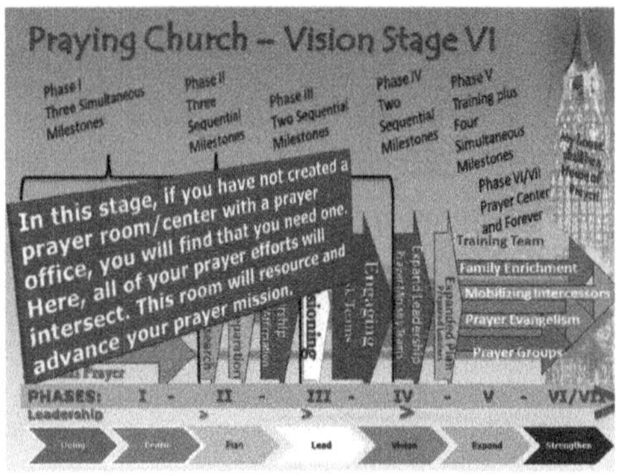

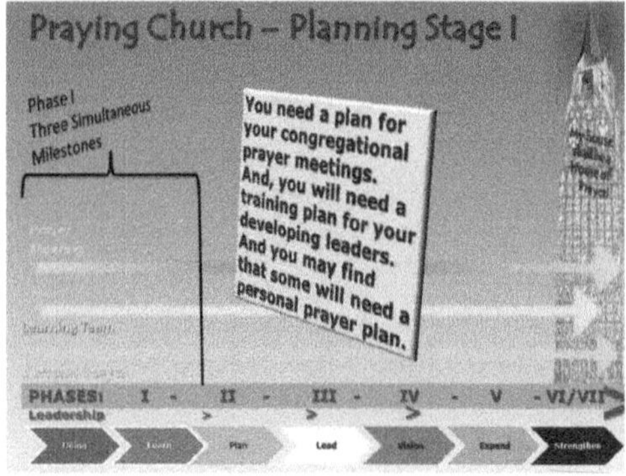

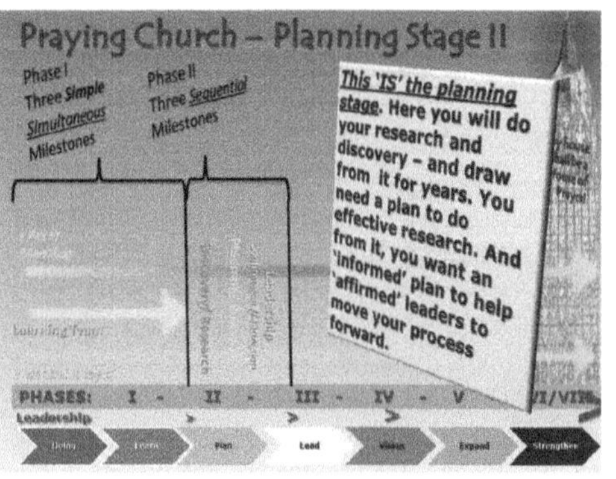

members to help plan and promote the various prayer activities projected for the year.

- **Phase IV** – Strategic Task Teams to lead each focus area in the prayer effort. Each of these teams, working in these various dimensions, will set forth a vision, a plan and a teaching-training process for the next 2-3 years, for example, of praying homes, etc.

- **Phase V** – Now you cast vision and develop plans for a prayer process in the four dimensions – praying homes, a praying congregation, intercessory prayer, and prayer evangelism-mission.

- **Phase VI** – Your prayer room/center, if planned and maintained correctly, will carry forth your prayer vision. People will walk into the prayer room, or view the prayer ministry wall or corner, and grasp the breadth of your prayer ministry vision.

- **Phase VII** – Cast a fresh vision, and renew the process.

PLANNING STAGES

- **Phase I** – You will need <u>a plan for your congregational prayer meetings</u>. You will need a <u>plan for the meetings with your learner-leaders</u>. See Phase II, 'Resources' for suggestions. Most of your people will need <u>a devotional plan to succeed in daily prayer</u>; that might include a simple Bible reading guide.

- **Phase II** – ***This IS the planning stage***. Here you do your <u>research and discovery</u> – looking in, back, out, around, and up. You need <u>a plan for this research</u>; otherwise, it will only be opinions. Here, <u>from the research, you will develop an INFORMED PLAN</u>, and you will affirm leaders to move that plan forward. They need a plan of action, clear instructions about their role and authority.

- **Phase III** – You need <u>a plan for your envisioning evening</u>. What data from your discovery-research process will you share? What vision will you cast for the year of congregational engagement? What prayer opportunities will you offer? How will they appear on the calendar? You will want to create engagement teams to help you promote and lead these various prayer experiences during the year. In many cases, these people will emerge as a part of your expanded prayer leadership team, each taking on some dimension of the prayer effort.

- **Phase IV –** Out of the response from prayer activities, you want to set forward <u>a prayer teaching-training-engagement process</u>. This has to be more than mere activities on your prayer calendar. Your various prayer activities in Phase III, gave you a measure of hunger and interest. They may inform your plan for teaching and training, letting your know the base line, for example, of interest in couple's prayer, or prayer evangelism, etc.

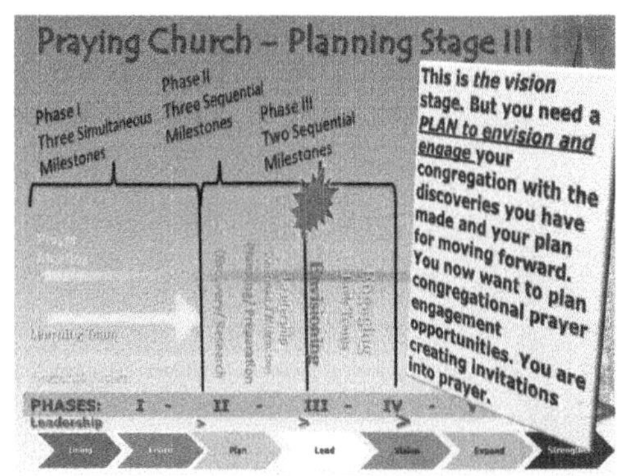

- **Phase V –** Now, your newly formed leadership teams, specific to each of the four dimensions will begin to execute their plan for (1) family prayer; (2) the recruitment and training, organizing and deploying of intercessors; (3) prayer evangelism and mission; (4) the proliferation of prayer throughout congregational life. They will work simultaneously toward creating a culture of prayer in your homes and your congregation.

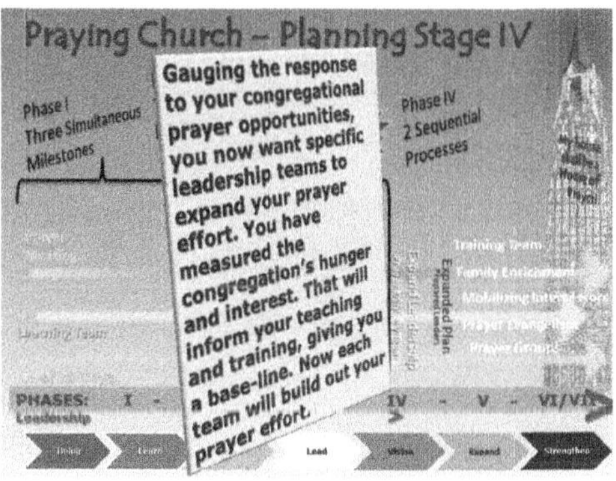

- **Phase VI –** Now <u>you need a place</u> for all these various prayer processes, these people of prayer to connect. <u>You need a prayer center</u>. That is not merely a room. It should be <u>tastefully planned</u>, for function and inspiration, balanced in all four dimensions of emphasis. And you need a plan for its use.

- **Phase VII -** Chances are, this process has taken you longer than you anticipated. Five to seven years have passed since you entered the process, maybe a decade. By most measurements, half your present congregation or more were not members when you started the process. They entered at some stage along the way. It's time to go back to Bethel. Visit the vision again. Relaunch the process.

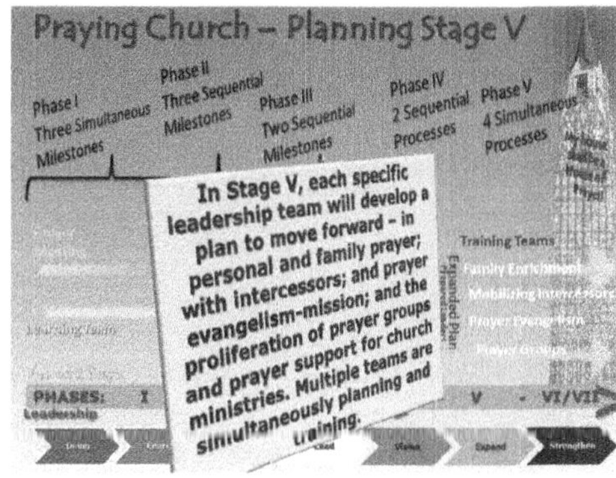

LEADERSHIP STAGES

- **Phase I –** You began with a group of <u>learning leaders</u>. **This IS the leadership phase.** It is quiet and off the radar screen, but the small core group you are developing will be at the center of any

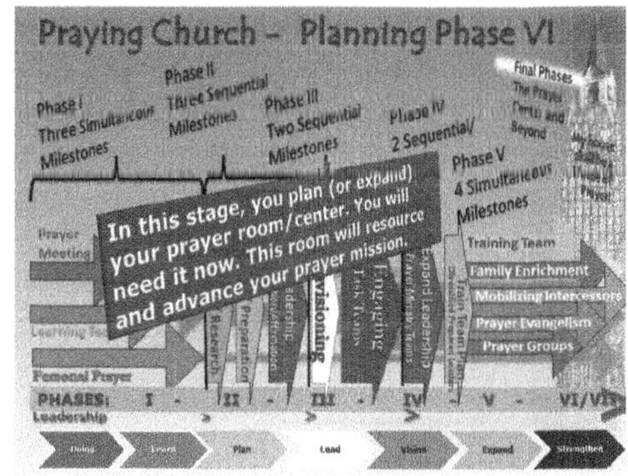

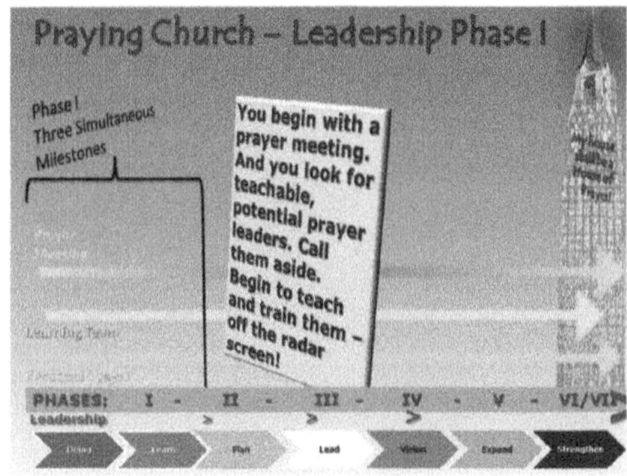

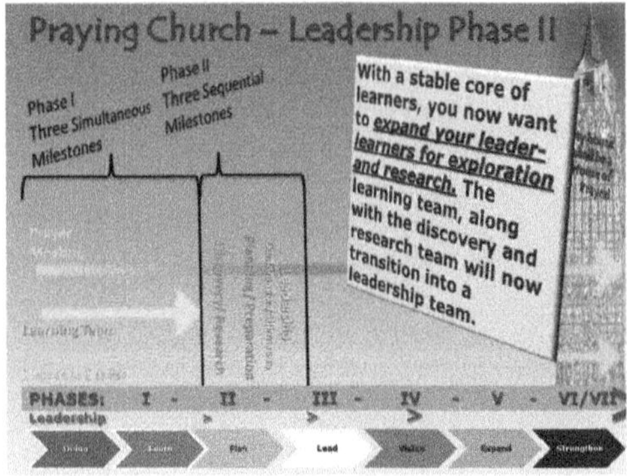

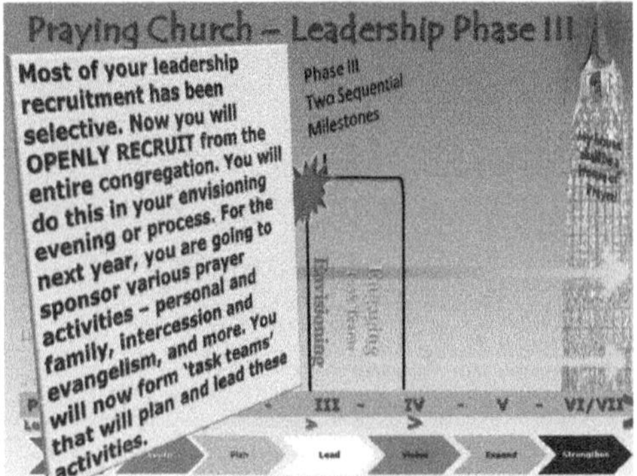

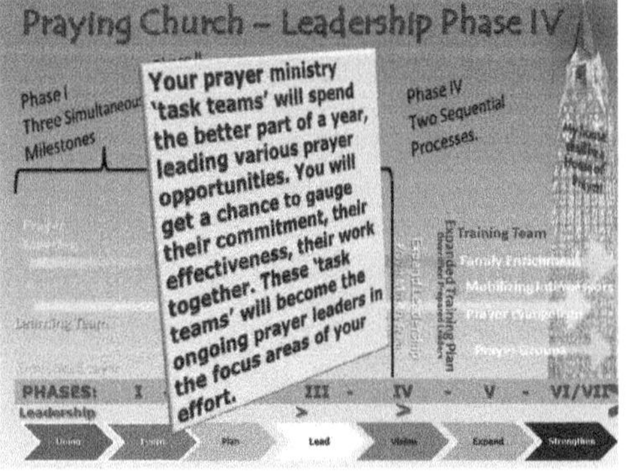

successful congregational prayer effort.

- **Phase II –** In the research and discovery process, you will <u>expand the leadership circle</u>. Quietly recruit additional participants at your prayer meeting or through your existing learner-leaders, and perhaps, from your elders-deacons and staff. In Phase I, you *formed* leaders. In Phase II, in research and discovery, you *informed* them with prayer ideas and models. Discovery and research will give way to planning. You will conduct a planning retreat – and at this retreat, you will unwrap your data and forge a plan for moving forward. Now, <u>you need another expansion of your leadership team</u>. Now you need to *confirm* and *affirm* leaders. At the very least, you need key leaders exposed and informed about your intent to transform the church into a house of prayer. <u>The last step in Phase II is this *empowerment* of a core, prayer leadership team (SPLT)</u>.

- **Phase III -** Now <u>you will again recruit leaders</u>, this time, more openly – <u>from the entire congregation</u>. In an envisioning evening, you will cast vision for the church to become a house of prayer, bringing prayer to the center of all you do. As you share some of the data and dreams, you will find some folks drawn to one aspect of your prayer plan more than others. They will become Strategic Task Team <u>leaders to help with the prayer activities that you planned for congregational engagement</u>. And then, to provide permanent leadership.

- **Phase IV –** You spent a year, perhaps, doing various introductory, congregational prayer activities. Now you will launch for example, for family prayer or intercessors, etc. You want to teach and train each of the four dimensions to come alive with prayer. Those who worked on the various prayer activity initiatives or bubbled to the surface, for example, around prayer evangelism activities, may become STT members to move that dimension of prayer forward. You have a primary prayer coordinator. Around that person, you have a core leadership team (SPLT). Each of them may serve as the leader of a specific prayer process – ministry or prayer pastor over one of the four dimensions or various aspects of prayer (STT) or as a liaison. As in the beginning, you need research (data), an informed plan, leaders, envisioning and engagement specific to each track.

- **Phase V** - Now you want to move forward, simultaneously, in the various aspects of prayer – not merely advocating prayer resources and activities, but discipling in prayer. That requires a broader leadership team.

- **Phase VI** – <u>Prayer leaders collaborate (SPLT, STT-implementers, intercessors, prayer council) to establish a prayer office</u>, a prayer room/center.

- **Phase VII** – It's time to begin again. Envision fresh leaders. Raise up a new generation.

Your leadership team should begin with folks humble enough to learn about prayer. That team, with others, explores the 'harvest force' (the church) and the 'harvest field.' The exploration team becomes a planning team, and finally, a leadership team. In full maturity, you will have multiple teams focused on the various aspects of prayer.

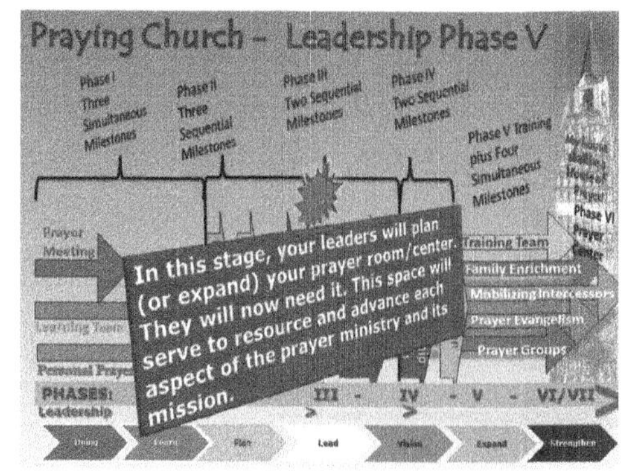

DEFINITIONS

24/7: Prayer, 24 hours a day, seven days a week. This can be seasonal or permanent. A church of a thousand or more is usually required to sustain this level of prayer intensity.

Architect: A member of the Prayer Leadership Planning Team or a consultant/coach who helps with critical, strategic thinking in the design of your prayer process.

Church-wide Prayer Meeting: The call to the entire congregation to gather for prayer, typically, under the pastor's leadership to seek not only the 'hand' of God, but also the 'face' of God. This is not a leadership or intercessory prayer gathering, but an every member prayer gathering with a focus on standing before God and hearing God as a congregation. Scripture-based prayer is encouraged, moving to missional prayer, without forgetting prayer requests and personal needs. This is Milestone One in the process. Call the entire church to gather to pray.

Core Leaders: This is essentially the same as your Strategic Prayer Leadership Team. These 3-5 leaders are the driving force of your prayer ministry effort. Up until Milestone Six, all your 'leaders' should be 'learners.' They assist with discovery-research and in developing a congregational prayer ministry plan. That assures vetted 'core' leaders who agree with the mission and vision, the values and strategic process. At Milestone Six, you affirm them and other leaders around them.

Church-wide Enlistment: A further stage in the growth of your prayer effort. It occurs late in Phase III, at Milestone Eight. Prior to this point, you should be selective in recruiting prayer learner-leaders and those who assist with research and planning. With a vetted, stable core of leaders, you are ready to invite members from the congregation, not merely to pray together – you have been doing that – but to assist in leading some aspect of the prayer effort.

Discovery Process: This is Phase II, Milestone Four. This is the research phase. This phase will take at least three months of intensive involvement. You will need to expand your leadership team during this process, bringing around your SLT a group to help with the discovery/research process. You will need survey instruments to measure prayer and prayer interest in the congregation. You will be well served to pay for a mission profile of your community (Contact PROJECT PRAY for more information, 855-842-5483). You need hard data on your harvest field and your harvest force.

Envisioning Evening: This is a tool for church-wide enlistment. On this evening, or a series of evenings, you will invite the congregation to a prayer vision event. You will attract those interested in involvement in your prayer process. You will share the vision and mission for prayer, data from your discovery/research process, and ideas for moving forward. You will recruit volunteers to specific focus areas and from them form implementation/event planning teams.

Ethos: Refers to the 'culture' of the church, not the tangibles or new tools, not to ministry techniques and practical ideas, but to the environment in which they are implemented – the levels of grace and love, kindness and forgiveness, the 'spirit' of the teams. Prayer *praxis* is not adequate; we must change the culture of our churches and leadership teams.

Focus Areas: Focus areas are the micro areas of prayer. They are tied, to an extent, to the four dimensions and the Seven Markers of a Praying Church. Each focus area – personal and family prayer; intercessory prayer; prayer evangelism; marketplace prayer; the prayer room/center, and even specializations like children, youth/teen prayer, singles, seniors, etc. – will need a leadership team.

Implementation Team: Essentially the same as 'task teams' who are either leading a 'focus area' and developing a plan for that specific area or planning and leading an event, whether it is a learning or doing event. Implementers begin their work in Phase III, at Milestone Eight, as you begin to unwrap prayer events and opportunities in the congregation, testing interest on different fronts. The 'permanent' leadership teams are formed in Phase IV at Milestone Nine.

Intercessors: All believers are charged with the ministry of intercessor, tied to reconciliation. Intercession does not appear to be a spiritual gift, but there are often in a congregation, a small group, who are hard-core intercessors. They usually comprise five-percent of the congregation, no more than ten-percent. Identifying them, teaming and directing them, debriefing and affirming them, can often spark a spirit of intercession in the whole of the church. Intercessors are identified and organized in Phase V, at Milestone Twelve.

Intercessory Prayer Meeting: This is a gathering of intercessors to intercede. It is not the church wide gathering. It is transactional, missional prayer. It often tends to be more intense than the church wide prayer meeting.

Learning Team/Learning Leader Team: In the early going, you build a leadership team by building a learning team. Insist that in the area of prayer, everyone is a learner. Humility is critical to unity. Your initial team will remain a learning team through the first year, meeting to pray and review learning materials. They will evolve into a discovery/research team, then a planning team, and finally, their leadership will be affirmed.

Milestones: Measures of progress in the journey to make a church a house of prayer for the nations. There are fifteen Milestones, unwrapped in seven Phases, typically over a 5-year period in a congregation. Some of the milestones are unwrapped simultaneously, others, sequentially. These are the basis of the book, *Milestones – Markers on the Journey Toward Becoming a House of Prayer,* by PROJECT PRAY. An overview is found in the book, *Transforming Your Church into a House of Prayer – Revised Edition;* and, the first three milestones are the subject of the book, *The Praying Church Made Simple.*

Micro Teams: These teams lead pieces of the larger prayer ministry. They are also referred to as implementers or task teams. They may be responsible for one project or they may become permanent.

Mission: A prayer mission statement is a concise declaration who, what is being done, and for what purpose, with what outcome in view. The mission statement declares what you are called to do, that is, what you 'should do,' where you are going. It is a declaration of organizational direction.

Multiple Leadership Teams: At the heart of your effort is your SPLT, and your Core Leaders, but around them, perhaps with members of the SPLT leading different aspects of prayer, serving as captains of task teams, are multiple leadership teams. These micro teams carry the burden for some specific aspect of the prayer effort.

Phases: The process of transforming your church into a house of prayer is a multi-year journey. We have divided that journey into Milestones, measures of your progress, and grouped those into phases. In some phases, your milestone efforts are sequential, one following another. In other cases, they are simultaneous.

- Phase I – Learning About and Doing Prayer – The Launch (3 *Simultaneous* Milestones)
- Phase II – Discovery (3 *Sequential* Milestones)
- Phase III – Going Public: Feeding the Prayer Fire and Finding Leaders (2 *Sequential* Milestones)
- Phase IV – Expanding Leadership Teams and Long Term Planning (2 *Sequential* Milestones)
- Phase V – Engaging the Four Dimensions (4 *Simultaneous* Milestones)
- Phase VI – Maturing the Praying Church (1 Milestone)
- Phase VII – Forever – Repeat the Cycle with new leaders!

Prayer Council/Prayer Ministries Council: Your Prayer Council is every prayer ministry leader in your congregation.

Prayer Implementation Plan/Strategy: Out of your research and discovery, and using this resources, perhaps with others recommended, such as *The Praying Church Made Simple* and *Milestones – Markers on the Journey Toward Becoming a House of Prayer*, you want to project a multi-year implementation strategy, a big picture plan. Of course, it will be revised, perhaps, numerous times, but this is your blueprint for moving forward.

Prayer Force: The sum total of your prayer efforts, the full force of people and prayer activities in your congregation. It is leaders and planners, strategists and implementers, specialized intercessors and all others.

Prayer Leader Continuing Education (PLCE): The PROJECT PRAY PLCE is a quarterly gathering of prayer learner-leaders from 3-12 congregations for a two-and-a-half hour gathering that involves teaching, the introduction of tools, and time for each congregational prayer team to 'talk-it-over and take-it-home.' It is a 15 session, 43 month program that is designed to encourage congregational prayer teams in the early stages of their journey to make their church a house of prayer.

Prayer Ministry Surveys: Every church needs to measure the depth of and commitment to prayer by its members and leaders, as well as prayer theology and assumptions. A number of instruments have been created to assist in that assessment process. Contact PROJECT PRAY (855-842-5483) for more information. These instruments can be used throughout your journey, but they are particularly helpful in the Discovery phase.

Research and Discovery: In Phase II, at Milestone Four, you enter discovery-research. Here you conduct research on the levels of prayer inside the church. You look back at the history of the congregation. You look for models of prayer. You look around for prayer needs in the community. This is when a demographic harvest field assessment is helpful. This information is critical for your planning.

Strategic Leadership Team/Strategic Prayer Leadership Team (SLT/SPLT): We often refer to this team as the SLT. However, you may have a congregational SLT, and therefore, you may need to add the qualifier 'prayer' – SPLT. This group of critical leaders steward the prayer process. In a small church, what we have called your 'core' leaders may constitute the SPLT. A larger church might demand a larger leadership team. At the heart of that SPLT might be a loosely defined team of two or three leaders, that are the very 'core,' the heart of your prayer effort. The SPLT might also be leaders of micro-teams, implementation teams, that carry on the specific areas of your prayer effort.

Strategic Planning Team (SPT): This team is typically a very small group of strategic thinkers – three-to-five. It may be the pastor, the prayer leader/coordinator and a strategic planner, an idea architect, who knows how to strategically, and sequentially, lay out a multi-year plan that integrates learning and doing, building out the four dimensions and Seven Markers of a Praying Church.

Strategy/Tactics: Strategy is the 'big picture *plan.*' Tactics are the short-term *steps* of that big-picture process – the parts. Strategy is the architectural plan; it guides the contractor. Tactics are subset plans, at times that are a collection of small steps, at others, a single step. This is the stuff of sub-contractors. Tactics push the one domino over – the one program, the one event; strategy lines up the dominoes in order that one program and event leads to another, and that the energy of the one event is carried over into another. Tactics focus on a single endeavor; but strategy aligns and harnesses the various endeavors, noting: this (training) is being done to prepare for that (event/exercise), and that (event) sets up what follows. One failure in the chain and the process is endangered. The architect (SPT) builds in back-up plans.

Task Teams: Task Teams are essentially the same as 'implementation teams' who are either leading a 'focus area' and developing a plan for that specific area or planning and leading an event, whether it is a learning or doing event. Implementers begin their work in Phase III, at Milestone Eight, as you begin to unwrap prayer events and opportunities in the congregation, testing interest on different fronts. The 'permanent' leadership teams are formed in Phase IV at Milestone Nine.

The Four Dimensions: The core of the philosophy of prayer ministry in all of the works of PROJECT PRAY. They are at the heart of the Seven Markers of a Praying Church. The four dimensions are actually two pairs in the prayer process. The first pair is praying homes and a praying church; at-home and at-church prayer. The second pair is intercessory mobilization turned outward in prayer evangelism.

The 'Ragged' Notebook: As you begin your journey, you want to collect, in one place, all the prayer efforts that exist in your congregation. This will include those who lead groups, advocate for prayer causes, etc. It should include formal and informal prayer groups and opportunities. It might include such things as, how many 'Our Daily Bread' resources are distributed by the congregation. Are seniors praying – when, where, how many? Do your teens participate in SYATP (See You At The Pole), a September, public school prayer gathering held in late September annually. This will be invaluable in your planning effort.

The Seven Markers of a Praying Church: Includes the four dimensions – praying homes and a praying church, defined by homes with a family altar and a church with a pastor-led prayer meeting; and identified, teamed, directed intercessors with a definitive prayer evangelism-mission focus – and with those, a pastor-led prayer leadership team, on-going teaching and training, and a prayer room/center.

Values: Values are not the things that you *call* important, but what you are actually *doing!* By doing, you demonstrate the value of the idea. Do you value prayer? Hammer out *idealized* values – what you *should* be doing and how you *should* behave – and chart your course toward transformation as you compare those with what you are actually doing.

Vision: Vision sees; mission feels; strategy draws a map; tactics are the steps to the end goal. Vision dreams of what the church will look like when it is a house of prayer for the nations.